BEFORE WE GO

BROCKENHURST MEMORIES
OF
PEACE AND WAR

c. 1914-1945

To David and Valery

Very best wishes and luck from

Richard (Taylor)
Rosemary

August 1995

An anthology
compiled and edited by

Richard Taylor, MBE

Illustrations by
Rosemary Taylor

Mr. R.E.S. Taylor,
17 Moorlands Close,
Brockenhurst,
Hampshire SO42 7QS

ISBN 0 9526028 0 6

To my wife Rosemary
with love and gratitude

BEFORE WE GO is an Anthology consisting of memories of men and women all of whom live, or have lived, in the Brockenhurst area. It is not a history.

While strenuous efforts have been made to ensure historical accuracy, the Editor cannot guarantee it. Recollecting precisely, events well over half a century old, is often hard; although perhaps less difficult than remembering what happened yesterday!

Produced by MRM Associates Ltd, Unit 4, Weldale St.,
Reading, Berkshire RG1 7BX

CONTENTS

ACKNOWLEDGEMENTS

This anthology has been produced by a team of volunteers, all of whom have given much time and enthusiastic support for a project which we believed to be worthwhile. Without their help 'Before We Go' would not have been produced.

Particular gratitude is owed to the following:

Geraldine Roberts, assisted by her husband Daniel, has acted as General Secretary, collecting and organising material and providing wise counsel.

Bé Cooper has been responsible for inspiring, collecting and collating most of the material provided by the post war Residents of Brockenhurst. She has also given enormous help in organising the production of the book.

Ann Curtis has undertaken most of the typing and has prepared most of the text for the printers. Her skill and quiet efficiency have been indispensable.

Denis Outlaw has been one of our principal interviewers and, with the help of his wife, Rosemary, provided much of the material for the local section. Sheena Archdale has also done invaluable work as an interviewer.

Keith and Shirley Crampton have helped greatly with editing and collating material. They have provided additional secretarial help, as has Wendy Cheeseman who has also assisted with fund raising.

Douglas Ferry has made a masterly précis of reports from the *Lymington Times* between 1938 and 1945.

Geoffrey Hawkes has given editorial assistance and written the introductory paragraphs for Brockenhurst at War.

Richard Power has provided the background information for the ANZAC graves and also for the Second World War casualties named on the Village War Memorial.

David Lee, Archivist at the Wessex Film and Sound Archives, has given valuable advice and provided tapes and copies of the interviews.

I would also like to acknowledge the help of the Friends of Brockenhurst. Ever since I mooted the idea of the anthology, the Friends of Brockenhurst Society has provided enthusiastic support and financial help. Particular thanks are due to the President, Major General John Woollett, who has provided constant encouragement as well as written contributions, which I have been pleased to include. The Vice Chairman, Tony Johnson (and indeed his parents) has given important information about Brockenhurst and its past. Tony has generously allowed the use of photographs of old Brockenhurst from his fine collection. Andrew Parrish, the Treasurer, has given practical help and has persuaded many that the book was worth supporting.

I am immensely grateful to all those in Brockenhurst, who have taken the time and trouble to share their memories of over fifty years ago for the benefit of us all, and for future generations.

Finally, my special thanks must go to Rosemary, my wife, who has not only provided fine illustrations, but, as always, constant support for yet another ambitious venture.

Richard Taylor

LIST OF SUBSCRIBERS

Donations towards helping to meet the considerable cost of producing 'Before We Go' have been generously provided by the following:

Joe and Sheena Archdale
Mr JE Bloomfield
Mrs Hilary Blurton
Jack and Mollie Brindley
Brockenhurst Parish Council
Ted Brown
Mrs Susan Burgess
Mrs J Chisman
Mrs CM Clark
Mr and Mrs A Cleveland
Bé Cooper
Ian and Bridget Corrie Hill
Keith and Shirley Crampton
Miss VA Croxford
Ann and Ron Curtis
Mrs E Doran

Dr Douglas Ferry
The Friends of Brockenhurst
Bill and Evelyn Greer
Joyce and Vernon Marchant
Lt Col RM Power
Ken and Betty Scott
Denis and Rosemary Outlaw
Andrew and Sarah Parrish
HA (Frank) Rashleigh
Mrs VH Ridley-Martin
Daniel and Geraldine Roberts
Rosemary Taylor
Captain JKM Tod
Captain Joe Williams
Mr and Mrs PD Whitmore
Major General JC Woollett CBE, MC

I am very grateful to them and equally, to the many Brockenhurst people who have not only shared their memories but given practical help and encouragement. Without all the above the dream would not have become reality.

My immediate financial concern is to cover expenses. If we make a profit, then it will be donated to the recently established Oakhaven Hospice in Lymington.

Richard Taylor

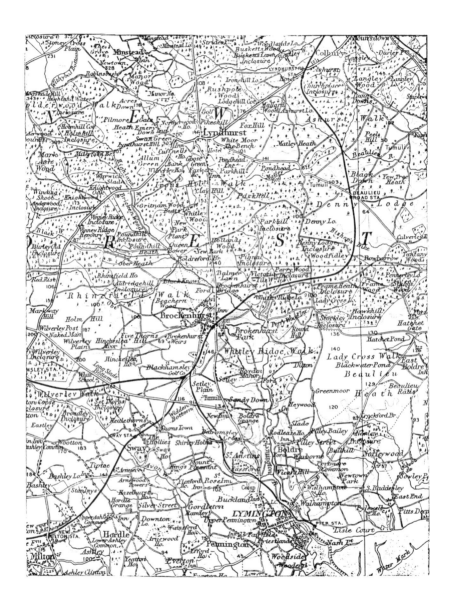

MAP OF BROCKENHURST

INTRODUCTION

Inspiration for this anthology came from Liam, an eighteen year old 'A' level History student. He was studying British History with me and, as a special subject, Nazi Germany. He was enthusiastic – so enthusiastic that to every lesson he brought a different German medal for me to hold; for his last lesson he wore his Panzer greatcoat. Yet although he abhorred the Nazis and wanted to know more about their rise to power, when he realised that incredibly I was alive then, his thirst for knowledge became almost insatiable. Why didn't I tell others of his age what it felt like? Actually I couldn't because I was only eleven when war broke out, but I might find men and women who did know what it felt like. With well over a hundred people, all at one time Brockenhurst residents, willing to relate their experiences, this anthology has emerged.

It is, I believe, important that younger generations born after 1945 should learn what it felt like, not necessarily through combat, but just to be alive at a critical period in our history.

It's also helpful to remind ourselves what would have happened had the Nazis won. The deaths of millions of innocent people in concentration camps was only one aspect of the monstrous evil of Hitler's regime and its allies.

All wars are terrible, but as a student and teacher of history I do not know of any other war which was more clearly a battle between good and evil. Nevertheless I could still deplore, for example, pugnacious clergy seemingly praising war: my sympathies were with men like Dr. Bell, the Bishop of Chichester, who because of his pacifist sympathies was accused of being a traitor. However the fact that he was allowed to express his views illustrates one sort of freedom which Britain was trying to defend.

So 'Before We Go' is certainly not, as a few have suggested, a glorification of war. Like almost everyone else I detest war. Indeed, although I am not a pacifist, I recognise the moral courage shown by many conscientious objectors in both World Wars.

Others have argued that we should look forward not backward "Let's forget the bloody war". With respect, as politicians are apt to say we should do both. I was brought up in the war years when we were sometimes encouraged to hate or ridicule our enemies. 'Don't Let's Be Beastly To The Germans' was the opening line of a popular mocking song by Noel Coward. Now I have to come to believe that by far the most important benefit of the emerging European Union has been to make another European War almost inconceivable. Attitudes have changed partly through our learning lessons from the past.

This anthology which is meant more for dipping into rather than for total immersion is an attempt to record for posterity the memories and attitudes of a number of Brockenhurst residents. We are only just in time. Indeed a few contributors have died since we embarked on this enterprise. I am particularly glad that their recollections along with others are now preserved on tape by The Wessex Film and Sound Archive Office in Winchester.

Another reason for this anthology is to reveal the strong community which Brockenhurst used to be and, in some ways, still is. Recently I was listening to 'Desert Island Discs' when Jack Ashley, the former MP (now Lord Ashley), who was on the brink of a brilliant political career, described graphically the shock of suddenly becoming totally deaf. His deafness lasted for decades. He also described the death of his father when he was only five years old and how his mother took in washing and scrubbed floors while raising her family in their Widnes house where there was no running water, no indoor toilet and a shortage of all but essential food. Yet, he said: "I had a very happy childhood because in Widnes there was a marvellous sense of community." For Widnes you can read Brockenhurst. The strength of the pre-war community spirit here cannot be overstated. In Brockenhurst in the 1920's and 1930's there was indeed great poverty, hardship and often job insecurity, and yet these handicaps were often the spur to show ever greater concern for neighbours. What people have told us about their early years has often been amusing and generally inspiring.

Why do the old (it's all right I am one of them!) feel that despite greater prosperity they are worse off in other respects? Not just because of nostalgia – 'Fings Ain't What They Used To Be' – but because communal ties are weaker. The grandmother used to play a crucial role in keeping the family together, but nowadays many families are scattered and Granny is 'somewhere else'. The great increase in the size of Brockenhurst since the war has also affected the community. Since 1939 the village population has risen considerably (*see Appendix*). There has been a great influx, some would say invasion, of people who could buy expensive houses built on beautiful farm land, like those along the Rhinefield Road. The Rhinefield Mob is the name sometimes given to them – or us – for I am one of them.

This book, by including memories of those bred in Brockenhurst as well as post-war residents, attempts to show that we have had many

8

common experiences.

Those of us who have moved around a great deal can learn much from those with Brockenhurst roots who have stayed put. Perhaps they too can learn something from us. This anthology might encourage greater mutual understanding. I hope so.

Brockenhurst   Richard Taylor
May 1995

PART I

BROCKENHURST
IN
PEACE AND WAR

1910-1938

Diary of National and International Events

1910	Edward VII died. George V became King. Asquith (Liberal) was Prime Minister.
1912-13	Balkan Wars. Serbs, in particular, victorious.
1914 June 28	Austrian Archduke Ferdinand shot by young Serb in Sarajevo, part of Austrian Empire. Austria declared war on Serbia. All great powers mobilised.
August 3	Germans invaded Belgium.
4	Britain declared war on Germany. Beginning of First World War.
1915 May	Australian, New Zealand, British troops landed at Gallipoli. A costly failure. Italy joined Allies.
1916 April	Sinn Fein Rebellion in Dublin. Kitchener lost on torpedoed cruiser – 'national disaster'. French suffered huge losses at Verdun.
July 1	Battle of the Somme. First day heaviest losses in history of British Army – 60,000 casualties. Sir Douglas Haig, Commander-in-Chief.
November	Now half a million casualties. (The total of British casualties in these five months on this one front almost half those of the British and Commonwealth forces on all fronts during the whole of the Second World War – 1¼ million). Submarine (U-boat) menace – 423 ships sunk.
December	Asquith forced to resign. Lloyd George became PM of Coalition.
1917 February	First Russian Revolution – Provisional Government.
April	U.S.A. joined Allies.
November	Bolsheviks in power. Many Allied reverses in West. Mutinies in French Army. Passchendaele – heavy British losses.

1918 March	German offensive. Failed after early successes.
November 11	Armistice Day – 'War to end War' over. Reform Act – Men over 21, Women over 30 allowed to vote.
1919	Treaty of Versailles. League of Nations created – influenced by President Wilson.
1922	Mussolini 'March on Rome' – took over Italian Government. Lloyd George resigned. Conservatives withdrew from Coalition (hence 1922 Committee). Baldwin became PM. Irish Free State created. Northern Ireland opted to stay in UK.
1924	First Labour minority Government under Ramsey MacDonald. Lasted nine months. Baldwin returned.
1926	General Strike. Food convoys escorted by troops. Unions defeated.
1929-31	Second Labour Government. Worst economic crises world had ever known. Labour split on cuts.
1931-35	MacDonald's National Government.
1933	Hitler became Chancellor, then Führer of Germany.
1935	Italians invaded Abyssinia to found Empire. MacDonald retired. Baldwin returned as PM.
1936	Germans occupied Rhineland. Breach of Versailles treaty. War more likely. George VI (1936-52) succeeded Edward VIII who abdicated. Rearmament had begun. Spanish Civil War 1936-9.
1938	Irish Free State became Eire. Britain handed over 'Royal Navy' Irish ports to Eire – great handicap in Second World War.

CHAPTER 1

BETWEEN THE WARS
1918-1938

*"What is our task? To make Britain a fit
country for heroes to live in."*

The Prime Minister, Lloyd George
speaking at Wolverhampton.
November 24, 1918

MAJOR GENERAL JOHN WOOLLETT, *President of the Friends of
Brockenhurst, gives a short insight into life in England during the years
leading up to the Second World War.*

An account of war-time memories would be incomplete without an
understanding of Britain before the war. In the late 1930's, anyone
over the age of twenty would have had some memories of the Great
War (1914–18), and most people over forty would have taken part in
some capacity. The casualties had been very heavy and many people
had lost relatives, but coupled with the sadness there was a general
feeling of pride, and of the importance of the world role of the Empire
in preserving peace and security.

Living conditions were very different. There was electricity and gas
in most large towns, but central heating was rare. In London, coal
fires were normal and suffocating fogs were common in winter. In the
country, wood fires and oil lamps provided heating and light, even
in prosperous households. Car ownership was growing, but only
about one household in ten had one. Travel was by tram or train,
though air travel was just beginning. Holidays for the great majority
were taken in the UK, by the sea, but quite a lot of people hardly ever
left their home areas.

Britain was a much safer place for people and property than it is
now. Houses in the country were almost never locked, and many
people in towns did not bother to lock their doors either. We lived in

14

WATERSPLASH, 1905.

London, and, as a child, I could move freely about and so could my girl cousins. When I was sent to visit my grandparents in Kent, my mother, who was a war widow and working in London, would put me on a train, give the guard a small tip, and tell him to see that I got off at Sittingbourne, where my grandfather would send in a pony and trap to collect me.

Both men and women dressed much more formally, according to their occupation – dark suits, bowler hats and umbrellas were correct for men working in London offices, and sailor suits for children were worn by many. Evening dress was widely worn for dances and similar functions. The main source of entertainment was the cinema and every small town had at least one. There were theatres in large towns, and the music hall was popular in London and the big cities, and not expensive. There was no television, and the main source of the news was the newspapers, though radio – known as 'wireless' – was growing in ownership and popularity.

As the threat of war grew, after the invasion of Czechoslovakia in 1938, the danger from enemy air attack was causing increasing concern. In the Great War there had been a number of Zeppelin raids on London. I remember as a child being picked up from my bed by my mother during an air raid warning, and seeing through the window a Zeppelin coming down in flames some miles away. Now that aircraft were far more effective, plans were prepared to evacuate women and children from London and other target cities, into the country. With war imminent in August 1939 these plans were put into effect, and trains left for the west and north loaded with evacuees who were then billeted in country villages. In spite of the inconvenience and clash of cultures most settled down well, though during the 'phoney war' period, before the German attack through the Lowlands and France in May 1940, many returned to the towns.

BROCKENHURST BETWEEN THE WARS – RICHARD TAYLOR

The First World War had a considerable impact on Brockenhurst. There cannot be many English villages with a population of well under 2,000 (see Appendix) which cared for literally thousands of wounded soldiers. Why?

The main reason was probably its closeness to Southampton and Portsmouth, both easily accessible by train. If (and many didn't) the wounded men recovered, they could be returned rapidly to the trenches.

Another attraction which Brockenhurst held for the War Office was the abundance of large houses which could be converted rapidly into Military Hospitals. The Balmer Lawn Hotel was one of the most important. It was used as a Field Hospital. The convalescents were transported from Brockenhurst station on luggage trolleys: a few local residents still remember seeing badly wounded soldiers wheeled up to the Balmer Lawn, sometimes in very bad weather.

Many of the soldiers came from different parts of the British Empire – now like 'The Great War' an obsolete phrase but not then. It has been moving to learn of the tremendous support which Great Britain, the Mother Country, received from the Dominions and Colonies. Most came from New Zealand and India, but there were also many Canadians and Australians. In the First World War many of the Indians came from Meerut: ironically the place at which the Indian Mutiny had first broken out in 1857. Meerut Road, which runs past the Cloud Hotel and Butts Lawn is a permanent reminder of the substantial Indian presence.

JO CHISMAN, *then a young girl, remembers them well:*

Most of the Indians who came were wounded. I remember King George V and Queen Mary coming here. I was held up by my father so that I could see them arrive at the Forest Park Hospital (converted from the Forest Park Hotel) where many of the Indians were. To me, the Indians seemed so funny because they had their shirts hanging out. Lots of people were frightened of them, but Mr Martin, the chemist, was very fond of them. I remember him with a turban, standing in Brookley Road with his own children, surrounded by his Indian friends.

*

16

NOVEMBER 1919. VISIT TO BROCKENHURST OF KING GEORGE V AND
QUEEN MARY.

The New Zealanders, again mostly wounded soldiers, came in even
greater numbers to Brockenhurst. They were nursed at 'Tin Town',
a large 'temporary' hospital consisting mostly of tin huts in the fields
near St Nicholas Church (*see Appendix*). The father of Clive Cargill
was a New Zealander, who had been through the Dardanelles
Campaign as well as Egypt. He came to Brockenhurst in 1916 and
worked at Tin Town until the end of the war. Although he returned
to New Zealand for two years, he had married a Brockenhurst girl,
and she was missing her home village, so they returned here and,
indeed, Clive was born on the boat on the return voyage. This was
fortunate for Brockenhurst and particularly the Golf Club where Clive
was, for 28 years, a very successful 'pro.'

Not only servicemen, but Canadian lumberjacks came to help the
war effort, felling and logging in the New Forest. One of these
Canadians, after his lumber-jacking, eventually returned here to
marry his Brockenhurst sweetheart. So we can thank him not only for
his forestry, but for being at least partially responsible for his son,
Stan Schisan, for many years a barber at Brockenhurst and still a
lively raconteur.

All who were children in that earlier war remember being told of
the appalling slaughter and seeing the long black-edged newspaper
columns of Killed, Wounded and Missing. Not surprising,

17

DECEMBER 1914. INDIANS IN BROCKENHURST.

considering over one million Britons alone were killed.

Yet, despite the enormity of the slaughter and suffering, many young men had volunteered before 1916, when conscription was at last introduced.

The father of the late LES JOHNSON was in the 15th Lancers. He was killed in the last month of the war. Les told me how, in 1915, his father and three other men, Collins, Perkins and Short were working in St Saviour's Churchyard:

Roy Short came up to the other three and said, "Kitchener needs us!" Within hours all four had volunteered. As quick as that! Immediately after the end of the war the other three used to call in on our family regularly to see how many we were and whether we needed anything. Roy Short had been badly shocked and so had a job looking after the churchyards. It was only just before he died that he told me that the four men, on the day they volunteered, had promised if anyone did not come back, the others would look after the families of the one who was killed. They kept their promise didn't they?

*

At 11 am on 11 November, 1918 an armistice came into effect and the thunder of the guns died away.

The Brockenhurst social hierarchy was largely unshaken. There were the big houses with their autocratic but benevolent families. The

18

Morants, who were by far the biggest landowners provided many amenities, including the Morant Hall, Brockenhurst Club Football ground, tennis courts with their famous tournaments, and much else. The Walker-Munros of Rhinefield House, who had built St Saviour's Church, provided employment for a very large number of villagers. So did many other wealthy families serve the village very well. Everyone whom we interviewed contradicted the now prevalent view that Life Downstairs was made miserable by the Gentry Upstairs. Not at all they said. We were well looked after – not often well paid, but looked after. They also appreciated the jobs and care provided by the owners of the large shops, like Mr Purkess and Mr Chalk, the fishmonger.

However, there was also a darker side to this cheerful picture. Despite the tremendous assistance given by the British Legion, I do not believe that the governments did enough to help the ex-soldiers, particularly those who had suffered terrible injuries. Many remember one popular Brockenhurst ex-soldier who had had half his jaw blown off; another who was shell-shocked and unable to hold down a steady job for the rest of his life.

Lloyd George's electioneering dream of creating a land fit for heroes to live in, proved to be no more than empty words. By 1921 there were two million men unemployed. Unemployment affected all parts of Britain including Brockenhurst. The struggle for jobs became intense and persistent.

GEORGE JOHNSON *remembers, in 1933, sitting on a bench at the Golf Club, where he was caddying, and saying to his friend, Leslie Myles, son of Nurse Myles:*

I've had enough of trying to find work. I'm going to join the Lancers. Will you come with me? Leslie did, and we were both posted to India.

*

Yet to the hardship and depression there was a silver lining. It was provided by the exceptional concern which Brockenhurst people showed for each other. The greater the deprivation the more the practical help: whether anonymous gifts of food and vegetables, helping to deliver a neighbour's baby or caring for the sick and wounded. "We all knew each other and we all helped each other," said many.

Another notable quality of Forest people was acceptance – "You just got on with it." Whether this attitude was strengthened by the churches is difficult to assess. What is evident is the significant part played by the local churches in the lives of many.

BETTY MARDON, *born in 1915, describes her early life and involvement with St Nicholas:*

19

I didn't like my christened name, so I've always been called Betty. My mother, one of eleven children, was born in Greatham House. Her father, my grandfather, built many Brockenhurst houses. My father, Mr Prosser, was stationmaster at Brockenhurst and eventually Bournemouth Central. I lived in Partridge Road and went to a private school of some thirty boys and girls, called Glenholm, near the Baptist Chapel. When I was eleven I went to the County School and stayed until sixteen. My father ran lots of things including the church choir, as well as playing the organ. When the vicar, Mr Haslam, went to Switzerland shortly before he died, my father did about everything at St Nicholas Church except take the services. I went to church usually three times on Sunday, the 10 am service at St Saviour's, 11.15 Matins at St Nicholas, and then Evensong. Sometimes there were afternoon services, when, if I was very unlucky, I'd have to play the organ. I knew three hymns! We were all friends in the choir and they'd deliberately sing too fast or too slow! In the 1930's I remember Mrs Walker-Munro of Rhinefield House, sending over fifteen employees (maids and gardeners) by carriage to Morning Service at St Saviours. It was through the church choir that I was to meet my future husband, Tom.

*

Even in the late 1930's jobs were still hard to get. As our interviews show many changed jobs frequently either to get a better wage or because prospects were brighter. Forestry obviously could and did provide a good career, but it was physically very tough.

An even more important employer of very large numbers was the railway: in those days The Southern Railway. I still remember the excitement of travelling from Waterloo to Sway and seeing the first advertising board declaring: "You are now entering the Strong Country." The fact that, aged twelve, I disliked Strong's beer was irrelevant. *Ed.*

JIM LAWFORD's *memory of his childhood, search for work and life on the railways, reveals much:*

I was born in 1920 in Partridge Road, my father working as a porter-guard on the railway. When I was five he had an accident and lost a leg; the railway tried to pay him off with a lump sum but the Unions fought hard and successfully, making them give him a job for the rest of his working life. They gave him several jobs that he could manage; eventually they forced him to this little signal box at Woodfidley.

I was seven years old when he went there. It being so isolated and around a mile and quarter from the road, we couldn't get to school. My sister went to Portsmouth, staying with my auntie and so to school there, my two elder brothers were either in work or looking for it. Us two younger ones missed schooling for two years, having been at the Village School from five until the accident my father had. Mother taught us the best she could. She asked the Council if the bus taking children from the Beaulieu area to Brockenhurst Grammar School could pick us up at Lady Cross. They said the bus was full. She then suggested that the bus being empty on its return journey to Beaulieu could collect us and take us to Beaulieu School. We would only be quarter of an hour late at school, but they wouldn't allow this either. Eventually Mother got permission from the railway to walk along the railway track to Beaulieu Road Station, then we went by train to Brockenhurst. We reckon Mother walked about 5,000 miles, to and from the station every day delivering and collecting us. When about twelve we got a bike to share between us, my young brother being about the same size as myself, and taking it in turn to either sit on the back or pedal.

In the summer we often used to walk the whole way there and back, coming home with friends such as Pat Hawker who walked on to Dilton leaving us at Lady Cross. Also John Reeves who lived at Whitley, the journey being four miles each way.

My first job when I left school at fourteen was with Baker and Spencer at 5/- per week, washing cars with a hose, cleaning the wire-wheels with paraffin. This job only lasted three months because one day I stepped back, breaking a large sheet of asbestos being used for repairs. Mr Baker said, "Get your cards"; I was sacked with just a minute's notice.

I then went to work for Mr Purkess for 10/- a week as an errand boy. I remember there was a staff of 26, 4 vans and 500 bread customers, one van doing nothing else but deliver fancy cakes to the whole area.

The village in those days had many large houses in the grounds of which were cottages where their staff, such as the cooks and gardeners, lived. The village seemed divided between the rich and the working class. I can remember the people from Hincheslea arriving by horse and trap. Mr Purkess would go out bowing and help the lady down from the carriage and then carry out her groceries for her. In those days when someone new moved into the village, the very first day, even before they had unloaded their furniture, someone from one of the grocers either Purkess or the International would be there ready to get their order.

The village then had 4/5 grocers, 2 bootmakers, 2 butchers, 2 greengrocers and one chemist.

When I was fifteen, jobs being scarce and no apprenticeships going, my father said that there is a job down on the railway and you are taking it. I wasn't very pleased or happy for the first few months, the job being junior porter-lamp boy at 16/- per week. One of my jobs was looking after the signal lanterns, one of which was a double-aspect

21

signal having two lanterns. This was very tall. I had to bring the lanterns down, fill them with paraffin, light them, turning them up high because once you had climbed the high ladder there was no way you could relight them up there if the wind blew them out.

By 1939 the nation and Brockenhurst were preparing for war. There was none of the old blare of trumpets, beating of drums and patriotic fervour which had once sent volunteers in droves to enlist: adults were aware that the struggle of 1914–18 had brought almost unimaginable suffering and slaughter. This time they knew that the task ahead would be arduous and bloody. But they also knew that they could not stand idly by and watch Hitlerian evil spread unhindered across Europe. Brockenhurst men and women, like everyone else in Britain, wanted to play their part in defending not only their country but European civilisation. Little did they know that one year later their country would stand alone against Nazi barbarism.

THE OLD DAYS

Extracts from a talk by ARCHIE CLEVELAND *to the Village Hall AGM on January 25, 1995. For many years he was Elected Verderer, Member of the Parish Council and Undertaker.*

Until Hitler spoiled it, Brockenhurst was a self-contained village. There used to be lots of shops and large houses which had been in the same family ownership for over a century. Now there are three: New Park Farm, Hayter's Garage and Purkess. There were eight large farms.

The Morant family, the largest landowners, employed 62 outside men. They worked on the farm, brickworks or the tilery making clay tiles, bricks and chimney pots at Roydon Manor.

The Walker-Munros who owned Rhinefield House and Ober Farm (their Home Farm) employed over thirty outside men.

Other places of employment were the local shops, the famous toy factory employing 6 people, and after 1936, Wellworthy's factory producing piston rings. As there was no Council refuse collection, rubbish was taken, often by independent collectors, to Hollands Wood, and North Weirs (near the seat still there).

Lighting was by gas or oil lamps. There was no main drainage until 1925, and none in South Weirs, where I live, until 1966.

There were hunting stables at the Rose and Crown.

Gypsies were scattered throughout the New Forest until 1927 when the Forestry Commission put them in camp sites like New Park Farm.

Very few people had cars. Even some wealthy people only had

horse drawn traps. Dr Freeland of Broadlands Road used to visit his patients in a dog-cart pulled by a horse shod with rubber shoes. Sometimes you wouldn't hear him coming until you felt a horse-whip around your back!

The Railway Inn (now the Snake Catcher) had a large herd of cows which twice daily were taken across the level crossing on the main A337 to fields in Mill Lane. Imagine that now!

Asked by the Editor whether The Old Days were really as good as was claimed, Archie replied – *You* said it . . . They were different. There wasn't a lot of money, but it was a happy village. We never starved in a land of plenty. We grew our own food – there were 16 acres of allotments. Now there are only two. (Corrected to three by Jack Hull, much respected Clerk to the Parish Council.)

What is more we made our own entertainment. We had our own football, cricket and tennis clubs, our race course at the back of the Balmer Lawn and our own very good dance band.

CHAPTER 2

BROCKENHURST BRED

This Chapter and Chapter 6 contain recollections from those born or raised in Brockenhurst. Most were recorded on tapes which are now preserved in the Wessex Film and Sound Archives at the new County Record Office in Winchester.

We had an overwhelming response to our request for interviews, so overwhelming that pressure on space and finances has, very sadly, made it impossible to include, either in the Brockenhurst Bred or War Service chapters, everyone to whom we spoke. However, the insight which we gained into Brockenhurst half a century ago has been of immense value in helping us to give what we hope is a reasonably balanced view.

We are deeply grateful to all who agreed to be interviewed and 'remembered' – for the benefit of us all. It was a privilege to be allowed to hear so many interesting and varied experiences.

A list of those who have helped is on page 286.

HARRY BURT
I was born in Brockenhurst in 1925 and have lived here in South Weirs since I was eleven. Mum was born in Wiltshire and Dad was born in this place. My grandmother used to take in washing and grandfather worked up at Rhinefield House a few years. Father was the youngest one in the family. He used to go round with a hand cart, pick up the washing, bring it home. Grandmother would do it and he would take it back. I think he got half-a-crown a week for that but I am not sure. I think it was three women came from Sway and used to help and she used to pay them 1/6d a day and food.

Then my grandfather worked up at Rhinefield House when I think they built it. He worked up there for £1 a week, a golden sovereign. He had to get there for six o'clock in the morning, get home at five at night and then he and Father had to go to Sway, pick up a few dozen eggs, butter and one thing and another and come home by train. Then on Saturdays he used to go to Lymington with horse and cart and sell the eggs and butter. What money my grandmother earned at the wash tub kept them in food. The one pound a week he earned was put in a tin. Grandfather and Grandmother used to rear

HARRY BURT OUTSIDE HIS HOLDING.
(BY KIND PERMISSION OF THE NEW FOREST NINTH CENTENARY TRUST.)

calves, brought them up to heifer, got them in calf then took them by horse and cart to Ringwood, the calf up in the cart and the cow walked. Sold them and bought some more.

Father started at what they call hire carting, had a horse and cart and we used to go around when I was a boy. When I was about eight I was always with my father on the cart. When I went to school and when I left school I always used to go with him. We used to go rubbish carting around Brockenhurst, tip it where the caravan site is in Hollands Wood way up until the Council put a lorry in: go all round the shops Saturdays with a big cart with sides on. They used to pay sixpence for a small bin – an ordinary bin – and a shilling for a big one. Then we used to do lighting wood – wood ready for lighting fires, a bag of lighting wood cost three shillings and sixpence for a big coal bag. We used to take bags of logs all around the village and loads of logs to the big houses. Put about twenty ton in at a time in the summer for them for the winter. We always had plenty of work. We had a big heap of cord wood in the yard down there where them sheds are, we used to have that for extra in the winter if the weather was bad. There were big houses in Brockenhurst: all pulled down now and the houses – three or four – built on them. There was good gentry lived here, had horses, we used to get the manure from them for the allotments out there. We used to tip it up in a big heap and let it rot down and re-sell it again. We had brooms and spars, these came by lorry. Father used to go to Redlynch and Lover to people by the name of Newman. He used to buy the brooms off them up near Lover Church. He used to go twice a year I think getting birch brooms and heath brooms and old Tommy Street when he had the shop, he used to have a place down the Lyndhurst Road, he would have so many dozen of these brooms. Father used to make enough money out of what he had, to pay for his day's work.

We did Forestry Commission work up in the Rhinefield with horse and cart, on contract, not like it is now with tractors and that. There was a nursery there. There is still a fence round it today.

We had three horses, Father had one, perhaps he would do logs and that around the village, perhaps clear ashes from houses and schools. I used to go to the forest with one horse and cart working for the Forestry Commission. When the war was on I saw taters grow up there.

For the whole of the wartime I worked for the Forestry. I never passed for the Army. I went up for a medical, I used to suffer a lot from carbuncles and boils and all that, I had 'em for years big as eggs on the back of my neck. They were terrible, the pain, why they were I don't know, so I never passed.

I worked for Father all the time and we were a partnership up to when he became 65. He used to still help with logs and that, he lived here with Mother and me. We had allotments out there and we were practically self-supporting in vegetables.

When the war was on we used to put four loads of logs a week into the Forest Park Hotel to keep the boilers a-going. They used to keep pigs and that around there. My father used to take 'em in a cart up to Holtoms, the butchers. They used to have what they called a cattle cart and then my father would take them up to Southampton, can't remember the name – proper big important people – oh dear! It's a long time ago. There was always work for horse and cart, we would pull gravel from Setley to Lyndhurst and that. Also there was stuff from Morant Estate to be pulled, you had to do it by so much a tender. You had to see Captain Sutton, he ran the estate, then see Bob Harpenden, he was in charge of all the hire carting and that.

Old Sutton was never no good to the working class, he was always for these jumped-up people. There ain't no gentry, not in Brockenhurst nowadays. We had monied people, you know, when you look at Brockenhurst years ago.

As for us we have always had forest ponies. I got ponies now but no cow, got nineteen ponies. They go into the yard and have a feed of hay twice a day. In about a month's time depending on the weather there will be enough grass out there to keep them. We have always done a lot of showing of ponies, won a lot of championships. One of my mares went to Wembley to support the New Forest Breeding Society.

I don't do none of that now. Come the bad weather the ponies come knocking at the door. They will come in until the end of the month, depending on the weather, maybe a bit longer. When grass grows a little bit they get fed up with hay, they will widdle off onto the grass and stay there until say October.

The Forest has gone all to pieces, it's getting boggy – we are losing our grazing on it, there's a lot of ferns. The Nature Conservancy won't let them do any burning or any sensible thing, it's really going to ruin. One of these days someone will say we have gone wrong and it will take a lot of money to put it right. Trouble today in the Forest is we haven't got the people that runs it properly, they all go away to these colleges and learn this and that, then they come out here and gets a job. They upsets the commoners straightaway because they don't know what they are talking about. Years ago the fathers and sons worked all the way through. In the burning season we would go with horse and cart and two 40-gallon drums to where the gangs were burning. We used to burn a hundred acres in a day and that is true. We used to burn more in a day than they burn in 12 months now. We used to do what they call cover burning, which was to burn round the edges of the covers. The keepers used to get around and see what needed doing, now they've got vans and all that and they don't see what wants doing. You can't see nothing in a motor car. The only way you see anything is by walking.

(Harry Burt lived in The Thatched Cottage: one of the rare New Forest cottages with cob walls and a ladder up to the first floor. He died on August 1, 1994 – Ed.)

FRANK BURTON

I was born in 1930 at Rose Cottage, Waters Green, one of three terraced cottages. My father worked for Jack Sprackland, the undertaker and builder.

I went to the Village School and couldn't wait to leave. But looking back, I enjoyed it. The Headmaster, Mr Stretton, used to say: "Go down and smell the corridor". That meant the cane in his office. He did it once to me. It was my first day in a new class. I couldn't understand the sums or something. God, it was painful! I remember going home and having supper. My hand was so swollen I couldn't hold my fork and dropped it. I daren't tell my parents because I'd have got another belting. But my father saw my swollen hand and went to see Mr Stretton. He said to him: "It's a teacher's right to cane children. But if you do that again I'll show you a parent's right".

My father (who had fought in the trenches in the First World War) was in the Home Guard. During one guard duty when one of the men, Tom Sayer, said: "I've lost my gaiters". Everyone spent half an hour looking for them only to discover that his trouser legs had come out and his gaiters were on his legs!

CLIVE CARGILL

I came to England and Brockenhurst when I was about a fortnight old. My birth certificate was recorded on a form issued by the General Register of Shipping and some of the details are as follows – Ship's name – RMS 'Ionic'. Date – 3rd August, 1920. Time – 3.05. Lat. 30° – 20N. Long. 74° – 57W. Father's occupation – Carpenter.

As a youngster we had plenty to do. We always had ponies. When we got home from the Village School there was always a couple of ponies to take out for exercise and a few animals around the place. We helped get the chaff for the animals and feed them. We had to clean all the boots ready for school next day. My sister would help in the house with my mother. We weren't working all the time. Fortunately where we lived we could always get out to play football, cricket on the green or knock a golf ball up and down. In other words we found and made our own amusement. Nowadays it seems to me youngsters need it all laid on for them.

My father had a pony and trap. This was the only transport we had. To get to Lymington, Southampton or Lyndhurst, you either went by bus or on the train or you could cycle. Our Sunday afternoon treat was to get in the trap and go through the forest.

As a boy I can remember I was smearing mud all over the notices near the Splash which said 'NO CYCLING', when I was given a clout across the backside which made me fall down and sit in the water. It was PC Scholls who said, "Tell your parents how and why you have wet pants or if you don't, I will." I never did it again. When I told my father why I had wet trousers he stopped me riding my bicycle for three months or something – that's the punishment I got. He was always the same once he gave a judgement, he never relented.

When I left school I went to an uncle who was a golf professional and I did my apprenticeship with him. Back in those days of 1935 all club making was done in the professional's workshop, so I learned how to do it.

I joined the RAF in 1939 so had an early demob. I went back to the University Course at Cambridge as assistant professional. Then I came to Brockenhurst.

Captain Sutton, who controlled the whole of the Morant estate including the golf course, saw me passing his office. "Hey, young Cargill! I want to see you. There are fifty applications for a vacancy at Brokenhurst Manor. If you want it you can have it." He knew I was a golf professional. So I put in an application and that was that. I was golf professional there from 1948 until I retired in 1985.

DAVID CHAMBERLAIN

I was born in 1929 in Sway in a mud-walled cottage and we came to Brockenhurst when I was two. My grandfather was a Master Builder and when they were building the Rhinefield House, he would walk there from Lymington every day. Later Father and Mother met when they were both in service there. The house had a huge cellar and Mrs Walker-Munro didn't like a particular wine. Father said to us, whenever we walked past the Rhinefield House, "I buried a lorry load of red wine in there", but would never tell us where it was. The Walker-Munros used to go up to Scotland where they had an estate. All the vegetables had to be taken up from her kitchen garden at Rhinefield. They were very good to the village. There was always a wonderful Christmas party for the staff. One year she knitted them all cardigans, everybody, all to one size of thickness of wool and knitted in the thickest needles. There was a man called Eddy Gulliver, a Brockenhurst character. He had a terrible stutter yet he sang in the choir with a beautiful voice. He put this jumper on and the sleeves reached the ground. Every one had to wear the jumpers at the Christmas party! All the employees were given coal from the Walker-Munro's own coal mines, enough for the winter. It was of very high quality – shining almost like glass.

Sometimes on the way to school by bike, we would go up to Aldridge Hill and set out lines in the river – dodge the Keeper who was quite a character. Then on the way home we would cycle round to see whether we had caught any trout – inevitably it was eels! The Keeper would go wild if he caught us. We were scared stiff of him, like you would be of a policeman in those days.

The ladies from Careys Manor had Careys cottages built and if you look in the back gardens of Careys cottages you will find, I think, an apple and pear or plum tree planted in each garden so the workers would have fresh fruit.

The British Legion was the hub of the village social life. They held late night dinner dances. Also a whist drive and dance. All the local workers would go. You played so many hands of whist and there was a dance afterwards. There was a little dance floor and at the other end a snooker room and a bar. The British Legion was never the same after the bomb dropped on it.

MARGARET CLARK

(Editor's note: Mr and Mrs Clark worked for my uncle, aunt and mother, very successfully brought up a large family and became friends particularly of my aunt, who moved to Brockenhurst. Mr Clark was not only an excellent gardener, but a talented maker of over 100 nest boxes, which were sited in the Hazelhurst grounds.)

My earliest memory was when I was two and a half years old. My father who was in the 1st Hampshire Regiment had been posted to Londonderry. He had served eleven years in India before he married my mother. Permission to marry had to be given by the Commanding Officer and it was only granted when he left India.

In Londonderry, aged two and a half, I wandered into the children's playing area in the barracks and got lost! I had been going on a swing and remember soldiers coming to find me in the early morning. They had all been looking for me.

In 1912 my father came out of the army after 21 years' service. When the First World War started he pestered the army to let him do something. Eventually they let him guard German POW's at Netley. He got friendly with some of them and one of them gave him a Meerschaum pipe.

In the First World War Winchester was a garrison town. I remember all sorts of troops at Morn Hill quite near our house in Andover Road. Canadians, South Africans, New Zealanders and others. I remember lots of horse drawn carriages in Winchester. Those horses must have suffered agony at the Front. I went to Hyde School, Winchester, a mixed church school. It was very good. In 1915 the Billeting Officer requested (ordered!) us to take soldiers in our house. He could only billet soldiers if there was a man in the home! We had a bombardier. He taught me to crochet. When he left he gave me his bone crochet hook. I kept it till after I was married and then one of my children accidentally broke it. My father used to knit his own socks and he taught me to knit on four needles. My mother didn't learn how to knit until she was 74.

In November 1918 we were told that an armistice was going to be signed. There were no lessons that day. All of us school children went marching round Winchester with our flags. The maroons went off at St Giles Hill and the cathedral bells rang.

At Danemark school where I went at 12, history and geography were my favourite subjects. I loved Henty's books, Clive of India. I wonder if Henty ever knew how much good he was doing. I also loved poetry. Longfellow, I liked especially 'Evangeline'. I hated algebra. But I learnt ever such a lot. My mother didn't approve of all my reading. She thought I could be doing more useful things.

At 14½ when I left school I went out to service with Brigadier and

FIRST WORLD WAR WOUNDED NEW ZEALAND SOLDIERS AT TIN TOWN.

Mrs Scudamore as a house parlour maid. I didn't know a thing, as my mother would never let my sister, brother or me do anything in the house.

I stayed there until I was 17 when I went to work for the Vicar's mother in Sway Road, Brockenhurst. She was a . . . Do switch that machine off!

After about a year I went to work for Colonel and Mrs Ward at Switchell's in Sway. It's now a nursing home. I went there as a house maid, then I became house parlour maid and later cook. Although we'd had a few cookery classes at school, no-one else had taught me. *But* I had Mrs Beaton!

RUBY COOKE
My parents came to live in Brockenhurst in 1910. My father was a carpenter on the Morant estate. We lived in a cottage at Palmer's Water. There was a fresh well there and we filled two baths daily for cooking and drinking. We used river water for washing. The boys collected fire wood for the field stove and later for the open grate with baker's oven. I started at the Village School at five and a half. We brought a packed lunch to school The girls' playground was quite separate from the boys'. In 1914 my sister went to Brown's Bootshop (now the Chinese take-away). They sold ready-made boots and shoes

31

there. She promised Father that she would not leave home until he came back from the war. He was in the Royal Army Ordnance Corps. He was badly shell-shocked and was nursed at Tin Town. Although he suffered from asthma he worked on the estate for many years.

About 1925 the estate cottage was condemned so we moved to a cottage at Balmer Lawn, where my sister-in-law, Mrs Head, still lives. My eldest brother bought a wind-up gramophone and we had comic songs, war songs and the family played violin, piano and melodeon. On Sunday we were only allowed religious records. Later we got a radio and the batteries were charged up at the Balmer Lawn Hotel. We had to sit up nicely at meal times and wait for our parents to begin – after grace.

Life changed greatly after the war. Before that there was more communal life. There were local dances in the Old Comrades and Kia Ora (NZ) clubs and the tennis tournaments at the Morant courts. My father helped to lay the beautifully sprung floor in the Morant Hall ballroom. We used to dance on Waters Green to the village band, and there was the annual village show with maypole and wild flower competitions for children. There was a more reverent approach to life in those days. My father used to say, "Sit at the table until the meal has got past the first waistcoat button!" and on Sunday afternoon walks we were never allowed to run! Happy days!

LES COOPER
I was born on 11 December, 1912, in Avenue Road, Brockenhurst. My father's parents were farmers at Moreton, Dorset. He came here to work on the railways as a shunter, but he was killed at night on the track in an accident. I was only seven years old. I can remember the upheaval that night. My mother was left to bring up my brother, my sister and me.

During the First World War as a young boy I can remember the New Zealand troops at Tin Town and the Indian troops waiting in Avenue Road to give us children chocolates. The Indians thought the world of children.

Did you know that Auckland Avenue was called that after the New Zealand town?

From the age of five to fourteen I went to the Village School. Mr Quinn was the Headmaster, Margaret Evans' father was the Deputy Head: we called him Jimmy White. He was very strict, but a good teacher and a good man.

As a boy I sang in the St Nicholas Church choir. There were 16 boys, 8 men, and 4 ladies in the choir. It filled the chancel. We included 2 Coopers, 2 Warrens, 3 Streets and Ken Martin. Lots of people went to church in those days. Why not so many now? The motor car I suppose. If a choir-boy attended every service for the quarter, he got 3/6d. The most I got was half a crown because my brother and I used to go down to my grandfather's Dorset farm. We were lucky because lots of people didn't get a holiday then – except railwaymen, postmen and a few others.

Has someone told you about the railways in the 1920's? They used to employ 40 to 50 men: the Stationmaster, Inspector, Foreman, two signal boxes (one was by Black Bridge), six to eight shunters, porters galore . . . At the top of Avenue Road they used to load up the cattle and horses on the cattle trucks. The railways employed more men than anyone else in the district.

After working at the garage I did chauffering for various families. It wasn't bad, but not an 8 to 5 job. You were always at their beck and call. Not big money. I didn't work for the Walker-Munros, but I was told that though they were not big money, they were good employers. My best chauffering job was for a lady who paid me ten shillings every time I drove her in her car to London. Unfortunately her son said that she was spending too much money and she left the area! I then returned to work in garages.

In 1939 at the beginning of the War, I worked in Wellworthy's for six weeks on pistons. It was horrible work and I hated it, so in 1940 volunteered for the Signals. Although I had worked with motor cars for years I had to be a cook – plus square-bashing. Also I had volunteered to be a motor cyclist. The Motor Cyclist Magazine had asked for Army volunteers to enlist as dispatch drivers. I did. Yet I only drove a motorcycle once during my time in the Army! Instead I became a driver in the Signals. I drove people, many of whom were trained as wireless operators, to go behind enemy lines. Lots of them were foreigners who had escaped from occupied countries. We weren't supposed to talk about any of it. I remember driving one corporal to Moss Bros, who, half an hour later, came out a lieutenant!

I spent some of my time playing football for the Signals Unit. That I enjoyed. The RAF were the best to play: they gave you a good tea, usually fish and chips.

When I think of pre-war I suppose the old days were harder but happier. People were poor then; but money doesn't bring you happiness does it? Also people now drive too fast. They come up through this village at 30-40 mph down Brookely Road. There's a limit, you might as well abide by it. The ponies, cattle and donkeys have as much right as we have.

They used to talk about different classes – upper, middle and working. That's rubbish. If a man does a good day's work and looks after his family he's as good as the royalty.

(EDNA COOPER, *his wife, then came in with Lucy, a lively young bull-terrier cross.*)
I used to live at Weymouth and we met on Les's grandparents' farm. At first in 1946 when I moved to Brockenhurst I didn't like it, but I've got used to it!

LES: For the last twenty years I've worked at Hayter's Garage and for the last 24 years we have lived in Mr Hayter's cottage which is over 300 years old. We're contented.
(Les Cooper's War Service is recounted in Chapter 7 – Ed.)

GEORGE JOHNSON *(brother of Les Johnson)*
Our grandfather came to Brockenhurst and worked as a carter for Miss Lovell at Hincheslea. Mother came from Bank. I was only four when my father (Frederick) who was originally in the coal business was killed in the First World War. His name is on the War Memorial at Wide Lane.

Childhood was very ordinary. I lived next door to my eventual wife. The village was very small, with many admirals, generals, etc plus maiden ladies. Now there are many newcomers. Not a village any more. No resentment. Newcomers all welcome as far as I am concerned.

We were very, very poor, but mostly everyone was. You daren't get up to mischief because every one in the road would know. We lived in a house with no electricity, no running water.

I went to the Village School till I was fourteen. Our Headmaster, Mr Armstrong, used to lose his temper completely. He should never have been a teacher. He beat one boy so badly in front of the children that two of the children had to drag him off and the child had to go to hospital. The doctor reported him, but nothing was done and he still continued for several more years before returning to Christchurch Priory.

Mrs Ormond, the builder's wife, was the best teacher – a lovely person.

In 1928 I tried for a job at Rhinefield House, but none was available. So I became an errand boy at Plumley's Stores for 12 months. After 12 months I got a job as a garden boy at Rhinefield House. There were 14 gardeners, 1 odd job man, 2 cover men (forestry workers) plus Ober Farm. In the House there was also a big staff.

In 1931 I moved to Sway to live with my sister and went to work where the White Rose now is, for Mrs Aston Talbot, as second gardener. I worked there for a few years. Then I went to Brock Golf Club, but after a year joined the Lancers to train as a cavalry man. I'd only ridden cart horses on Ober Farm. I had 12 months' training. I rode Australian Whalers – about 16 hands. I stayed for five years and came out of the Army in 1939 and did vocational training as a machinist, but I was on the Reserve and after six months was back in the Army, in the Queen's Royal Hussars. On 3 September I was in the canteen at Tidworth: within two months I was in Egypt with the Royals to deal with Arab bandits, mostly robbers.

(*War Service is recounted in chapter 7*).

I had six months in England then went out to Germany for six months in the Army of Occupation. We were first stationed near Belsen. A terrible experience. After the inmates were liberated two months before our arrival, they were using knives and weapons on the Germans. The first job was to disarm the inmates. Then we went to Wittgen, near Hamburg, to interrogate concentration camp commandants and guards – mostly SS. They were very frightened of us: we were armed and they weren't, but none was shot out of hand.

There was much devastation in Germany. I remember Essen. There didn't seem to be a house standing and the stench of bodies of men, women and children under the rubble was terrible. The Germans were beaten. We treated them as children.

I returned to England in a demob suit. I went into partnership with my brother as a landscape gardener.

Pre-war days were better days. Now it's the almighty dollar that counts. In those days money was not so important. People helped each other more – that was particularly true after the First World War. In those days you recognised others had more than you did, but you accepted it. I never had a bad employer.

GLADYS JOHNSON (*wife of George Johnson*)
I have lived in Brockenhurst all my life. My early memories include the boots I wore all the year round. I was about thirteen years old before I had a pair of shoes. My mother and a dressmaker friend made clothes for the children. Each of us had a panama hat with a differently coloured ribbon to show who owned which.

Children were expected to share the hard work. I remember carrying wood from Aldridge Hill and working with Father on the crosscut saw to prepare fuel for the open fire on which all the cooking was done. Before we had a range there was a small boiler on one side and an oven on the other. Mother had been a cook at the Forest Park Hotel so household skills were passed on.

We had a healthy diet of home-grown vegetables and I was fascinated as I watched the slaughter of a pig in a neighbour's yard. Cows in the Forest answered to individual names like Daisy and

Buttercup.
As youngsters my sisters and I had to share a bicycle and were never encouraged to go far from home. A trip to Southampton was a real highlight. Social activity in the village centred on the Morant Hall. Guide and Brownie plays, school plays and dancing to 'live' music provided by Mr Stevens, the printer, and his family, were all enjoyed.

Illness was always a dread. It took Mother two years to pay the specialist's fees when my twelve year old sister had meningitis. The Friendly Societies, like the Rechabites, were a great help.

I clearly remember hearing the declaration of war while sitting with the other staff on the staircase of the house in Surrey where I was in domestic service. I came back to Brockenhurst straightaway and was recruited for training in precision engineering at Redbridge. The factory produced mortar guns and Bailey bridges and operated twenty-four hours a day. It had several near misses as bombs fell on either side and frequently shattered the glass roof. After staying in a flat in Millbrook I returned home and travelled daily to work by train. In spite of a 6.38 am start I was only late twice!

You want me to compare 'then' and 'now'? I recall the truly fresh food and water, the open fires, the village comradeship and the beautiful embroidery work produced in the evenings. Father, who was a postman, worked very hard, like everyone else. I prefer the discipline of that era. Life was certainly better then!

LESLIE JOHNSON *(brother of George)*
I was born in Brockenhurst in 1915 and have lived in the village all my life and in the house 'Dunedin' for thirty-four years.

My father served in the 15th Lancers and was killed in the last month of the First World War. He is buried in Belgium.

Just before war was declared, I volunteered for the LDV. I was in my early twenties. Our main job was to stop the buses going between Lymington and Brockenhurst. We were armed with rifles. We were supposed also to have bayonets, but there weren't enough scabbards! Our job was to stop the buses and check all the passengers' Identity Cards. The drivers got fed up with us holding up the buses.

Soon after war was declared I was gardening at Greenoaks.

I volunteered for the Royal Engineers and trained at Shorncliffe Camp, near Dover. In my gardening jobs I'd become very interested in car engines and was encouraged and helped by one of my employers, Colonel Russell Jones, so I trained as an engineer.

At one time we were stationed at Lyndhurst. I told the officer that I lived at Brockenhurst and wanted to apply for a few days' leave.

When I returned I was told to report to the North of Scotland. The army did that sort of thing!

Eventually we got to Belgium. We stopped for a time near a First World War cemetery. I said to the Captain, "Could I go in because my father is buried there?" He said, "If you want to risk it." I got to the gates of the cemetery when a soldier rushed up to me and said that I must rejoin the others to continue the advance. I never saw my father's grave.

In 1945 we came back in the boats to Shorncliffe to the same camp from where we had mined the cliffs and put up pill boxes in 1940.

(Les Johnson died in October 1994. The rest of his experiences in the Services are recorded in Chapter 7 – Ed.)

MRS KNAPP

I was born in Southampton and came to Brockenhurst at the age of seventeen. I was in service in Major Ferguson's house in The Rise. That house is now the Watersplash Hotel. I was House-Parlour Maid and there was a cook and a kitchen maid as well as Nanna, the nursemaid. Major and Mrs Ferguson had two girls and a boy. They were a lovely family and treated us very well. I stayed there until I was married in the Baptist Chapel on Lyndhurst Road.

Father-in-law bought us a cottage in Burford Lane and I came there as a bride. My hubby was in building, my father was a gardener. There were four builders in the village, but there was plenty of work for them all.

I worked all my married life. I was in the college kitchen. It was a lovely staff group – all helping each other along.

I could have cried when that Morant Hall came down! They had a special floor for the Hunt Balls. I remember the long dresses. We made them ourselves. They were good times! You could go home at two in the morning and never felt frightened.

Before I came to Brockenhurst I worked in the British American Tobacco factory in Southampton. I remember 1912 when the 'Titanic' went down.

In the Second World War I worked in the school kitchen. The schools got a bit extra in the rationing, but food was always a problem. I remember helping Mrs Cartwright to put a sack of stuff up the chimney. She wanted a gas-proof room. I said to my friend when I went home that day, "I don't think there'll be a war. Do you?" She still pulls my leg about that!

I suppose us elderly people always say the old days were better. If we were young today, I expect we'd be just like they are now!

BETTY MARDON

My great-uncle, Mr Masters, owned the Island Shop. A few years after the war, he decided to open a sweet shop there. Lots of County School children as well as other people patronised it. We ran it very successfully for 13 years. Hard work, but worth it.

I suppose in some ways Brockenhurst was more snobbish in the old days, but then you weren't expected to mix with the grand families. For instance, there were two tennis clubs – the Village Club with two courts (started by Mr Jenons, the Ironmonger) near St Saviour's Church; and the New Forest Club with 15 courts which had many Wimbledon players like Crawford and McGruff playing there. Captain Sutton, for whom I worked at his Agent's office and who used to try to ensure that no 'cheap' houses were built on the Morant Estate, thought the world of these Wimbledon stars.

(Betty Mardon is also quoted in the Chapter 'Between the Wars'. Her husband Tom's wartime experiences are related in Chapter 7 – Ed.)

BASIL O'DONNELL

My father worked on the railway as a ticket collector. I was born in 1909 in Brockenhurst – the right-hand house of the two which now form the Cloud Hotel – being one of eight children. My father applied the strap if we misbehaved.

There was no electricity. Water was obtained from a well and the gas supply was such that on Sundays there was insufficient pressure to cook the dinner.

I can remember the Indian soldiers and being carried on their backs as a young boy and I watched them playing polo. This was in front of the Balmer Lawn where the present cricket pitch is.

A New Zealand soldier called Joe got to know my father while he was a ticket collector. Joe was stationed at Tin Town, now known as Tile Barn. He used to come down for a cup of tea and a chat, bringing me chocolate. Where they got this lovely stuff I don't know. He used to carry me on his shoulders and jump across the river. He double-dug my father's allotment.

I also remember seeing Zeppelins fly across.

As a Catholic family we had to walk through the Forest to Lyndhurst to go to Mass as there was no church in the village at that time for us.

When I left school at fourteen my first job was with a Mr Hibbs cleaning and repairing bicycles and their punctures and filling the acetylene lamps. My wages were 2/6d per week.

My next job, when I was about sixteen, was to work in the toy factory. In those days you could walk from the end of Meerut Road across nothing but fields to the Burley Road where the toy factory was, it being owned by a Mr Whittington.

Some time later a lady told my father she could get me a job in London. This meant that I needed a suit. So Billy Rook, the tailor, who lived opposite Streets, the ironmongers, made me a navy-blue double-breasted one, with drainpipe trousers, which made it difficult to get my legs through them. This job was as an assistant to the night porter. I found sleeping during the day difficult, so went rowing on the Serpentine.

I stayed there three years before returning to work at the toy factory until war broke out. Do you know that we made the crib used at Christmas at St Saviour's and Mr Whittington carved the Stations of the Cross in the church at Lymington? The factory eventually closed as the timber we used was not available, it being Canadian yellow pine.

When the toy factory closed I went to work as a gardener to a Miss Baker. Her own gardener, being on the Naval Reserve, was called up. She lived in a house called Marylands in Wilverley Road. I did not stay up there as I was expected to do the washing-up as well as the gardening.

I became one of the three full-time firemen in Brockenhurst, staying there until they closed down. What they did with all the valuable stuff there I don't know. I was then sent to Wellworthy's, joining the Home Guard at the same time. The HQ of the Home Guard was at the Tennis Club, where duties sometimes meant not getting back until 6.30 am and then straight on to Wellworthy's for work.

I was in three regiments during the War – the Duke of Cornwall's, Somerset Light Infantry and the 12th Devon Airborne. I also did some parachuting, but was considered too old, so went into gliders.

When I went into the army I was A1, coming out B7 and they gave me a 20% pension. All of a sudden they sent for me to go before a medical board in London. I saw a Major General, physician to George V. There were fifteen or so on the rostrum. They noted that I had a solicitor and should have no worries. They read out all my life history and halfway through the solicitor said, "My client withdraws". So they stopped my pension altogether. Many years later, when I had to have my knee pinned, I saw Sir Oliver Crosthwaite-Eyre, MP. He said, "I hear you haven't had a pension for over 25 years. It's just like flogging a dead donkey to get anything out of them. I will get you 40%." A fortnight later, I was sent to Bournemouth before two doctors, who said, "Good God, 40% for that – your only problem will be getting on and off a bus." They knocked it down to 20%. Later I went to see Patrick MacNair-Wilson, MP and then received letters from Roy Hattersley. From these I went before two old doctors on a medical board. One said, "I see old chap you are going to have a job doing your feet." He gave me an order for life to get my feet done. You know where I had to go? Eastleigh. It took me six weeks to get my money back and even after all that, all I got was 20%. (They have increased it now).

It took a long time, but the trouble is that there are so many rogues about so when you get a genuine case you don't get anywhere fast.

(Basil O'Donnell's war experiences are in Chapter 7 − Ed)

UNA PLACE

In the First World War my father was lather boy where Stan Schisan used to be at the Island shop. He used to go up to Tin Town, where the New Zealand and Indian hospitals were. The barber would go up to Tin Town to shave them.

Do you know how Fathersfield got its name? It was after 'Father' Keeping. He had the garage at Surrey Lodge. He used to come on his push bike and fall off every day after his visit to the pub. He was sloshed!

I went to Sway School and when I left at fourteen I worked for Colonel and Mrs Grace at Thornby, Armstrong Road. I was employed originally as in-between maid, but the Irish cook was so bad that I took over the cooking. Mrs Grace ran street collections for War Savings. Although I was paid 10/- per week plus keep, 2/6d of the 10/- was deducted to pay for a Saving Stamp.

One night a bomb fell in Sway Road − where Conway Cottage is now. I slept through the raid. There was a string of bombs. All of them missed the railway line and just the one hit the cottage smack in the middle. On another occasion a bomb hit Purkess's cake shop. It was a lovely new cake shop.

My sister, Gwen, was in the Land Army; she was billeted in Burley. They ploughed up the Common by the The Cloud and planted potatoes, also Whitefield Moor for potatoes and wheat. The moor, between Rhinefield Road and Burley Road, was used as a rifle range.

Brockenhurst County School was originally in Highwood Road (hence the cut between Avenue Road and Highwood Road). We used to call the children from there 'Brockenhurst Cabbage Stumps' because we never made it! You could only get to the County School by being above average or because your parents paid.

There was more snobbery then. I think that we're going a little bit too far the other way now − like your vicars and doctors and that, it's wrong to call them by their Christian names because then you've got no respect for them, or not the same respect. Teachers are sometimes called by their first names in school. That's wrong. I'm

40

a bit Victorian.

Buses were run on gas during the war. The buses towed a trailer with a gas cylinder on it. I used to see them chugging along the Lyndhurst Road. These buses were used mostly by Wellworthy. Lots worked for Wellworthy in those days.

TONY PURKIS

I was born in 1916. My father lived all his life on farms, looking after animals, while my mother, a cook, worked for Dalgety's and afterwards for Lord Montague (father of the present Lord Montague). Later he led a foresters' protest against the putting of padlocks on gates. The foresters won and the locks were taken off.

On my mother's insistence, I was sent to a private school in the Avenue, Brockenhurst but Father thought I was getting too soft so I was sent to the Village School and then when aged sixteen as a paying pupil at the local Grammar School. Afterwards I trained as a chef, became 2nd Chef at Canford Cliffs Hotel.

Then Captain Gandy, a Brockenhurst resident, recommended me as ship's boy on the Union Castle liner, 'Winchester Castle'. Dr Gaitskell, the village doctor, helped me to get a job with the Morant family at Brockenhurst Park. The best time of my working life. Very good employers. John Morant, a bachelor in his 20's, and his sister Beth, acting as Housekeeper, were the employers.

Frank Rashleigh, now in Carey's Cottage, was the butler, and Pat Whelan was my kitchen man until I joined up. It was a lovely old 18th century house. Very good social life – all the local gentry used to come. We used to have a Hunt Ball, Daffodil Ball and Spinsters' Ball in the Big House. There was room for all this. The Hall had 56 rooms and a bell for each room. The Big House was knocked down by the Berrys in the 1950's. I did all the catering – with fried eggs and bacon for breakfast for 150 to 200 people when there were House Parties. There was also a troop of local women on the staff, all friends of my mother. I wore a white coat, check trousers and big white hat. We enjoyed it at the time but I only returned for one year after the war. You wouldn't get the young to do it nowadays, nor are there people with the money to employ servants.

John Morant paid for me to have a course in French and later Continental cooking at Sloane Street. Marvellous training – Cordon Bleu. It entitled me to wear the Blue Ribbon in my hat. I love watching cooking programmes on television.

My assistant, Pat, called me at 7.00 am with a cup of tea and I got Mr Morant's guests' breakfast. Many shooting weekends – pheasants mostly, also partridge, snipe and occasionally rabbits.

Three gamekeepers reared pheasant for shooting. Mr Morant kept very detailed records of pheasants shot. Eight or ten beaters were given half a loaf of bread and half a pound of cheese when there was a shoot. The sportsmen were given lunch at Head Keeper's cottage at Dilton between Roydon and Dilton. I used to prepare Hay Box containers – usually steak and kidney pudding and loads of booze. I prepared the food but didn't personally serve the guests.

Many important guests came to shoot at weekends, such as David Maxwell Fyfe. *(After the war he became Home Secretary – Ed)* There were also tennis weeks. Thirty to forty would come down and play on the local courts. Guests included people like Fred Perry, Jack Crawford, Billy York and The Lascelles, who would all play in the tournaments.

I called John Morant 'Mr John'. Most unusually he called me 'Tony'! Mr Morant was very kind. They treated us very well, but, of course, we were a different species of human being!

I remember in 1939 Lady Kathleen Morant came down into the kitchen, she said, "How are things, Tony?"

"Not so bad, my Lady, but I need a kitchen boy or kitchen maid to help."

"I'll go and see Smith, the groom."

"Well, my Lady, don't tell him I suggested it."

She went over to Smith at the stables. "Smith," she said, "Tony wants a kitchen maid. Send your daughter to work here when she leaves school in the summer."

Smith was furious!

But in service the people who treated you worst were the upper servants. At meals the chef, the cook and the butler talked to each other, but no-one else among the staff of twelve spoke.

The Morants did a lot of good things in the village, usually without anyone knowing it. They were very good people.

(See Chapter 7 for War Service experience – Ed)

CONNIE PURKIS *(Tony's wife)*
Although not actually in Brockenhurst during the war, I lived nearby in Emery Down.

I worked on a dairy farm – we had quite a large herd. There was also hay to be made.

I cooked for the house and two or three Land Army girls, who lived in. I had no cooking instructions. We sorted it out for ourselves. I also helped bottle up the milk with other things that needed doing. Most of the milk was sent to a central depot. The Land Girls did the local milk rounds on milk floats – horse and cart. They would have to collect the required coupons for each delivery. Besides bottles,

42

GLENHOLM SCHOOL IN 1922.

cartons were already used in those days and I helped to clip them closed. The only butter we churned was for ourselves. We were not allowed to separate cream other than a small portion for our own use, but not for sale.

Everyone kept chickens – also pigs. Pigs were sent somewhere for slaughter and you had to give up half – and gave up ration coupons for what you were allowed to keep.

FRANK RASHLEIGH
I was born in 1910. My father was a carpenter in Southampton Railway Docks. He worked for the London and Southampton Railway. I had seven brothers and three sisters, that was eleven children from fifteen – four didn't live. I stand the last of the family, all my brothers and sisters have gone. That makes me eighty-four now. I came to Brockenhurst Park in February 1929 as a footman to Mr Morant. Not straight from school, I had one or two sorts of jobs – errand boy, in chemists and a bakehouse.

In my job I got up in the morning and if there were any visitors I used to have to look after them, valet some of them, call them with tea, lay out their clothes, take away their other clothes and do the dining room, of course.

Captain Sutton used to see about paying all the bills and pay the staff. Mr Morant did nothing like that. He was a great man for racing.

He used to ride himself quite a bit – point-to-point and hunting at least twice a week.

I learnt how to do hunting clothes, scarlet coats. That was the butler's job really. Old Carling, the butler, was a real old snob and I was having to do his work. Eventually he was caught out because Mr Morant had some very special old brandy, 1811, that he put out on special occasions. Old Carling used to swig this stuff and add some modern, but he got caught. So after five years he got the sack for boozing and Mr Morant gave me the butler's job.

Before the war the Morants were very good employers. All the estate workers had their cottages and about thirty shillings a week wages. The butler's job was only seventy-five pounds a year and the lodge where we lived. I married on that. I was there until war broke out.

John Morant was at Brockenhurst Park before the war. He had two sons, Edward and Simon, who is the race starter. He lives away up in Berkshire somewhere. When Mr Morant sold the house (it was pulled down) Edward had all the best features taken over to Roydon Manor. All the beautiful inlaid doors and half the staircase is there. When I go there, it's like Brockenhurst Park. Up to a little while ago I used to do dinner parties for them, but this ankle of mine is bad so I had to chuck that up.

When war broke out I was turned down because I had a bit of ear trouble and I got put into Wellworthy's, but up to that time I was an Air-raid Warden here in Brockenhurst. It was very nice; I was still living in the Lodge. My wife stayed there when I was sent to Wellworthy's in Salisbury. I used to come home every Friday night until Sunday night. My job there was making pistons.

At the factory in Salisbury where I was on a machine, they had lots of girls. There it was a necessity. They were a horrible lot. They would pull faints and things like that when I was on night shift. We found that the girls always took advantage. After a while I was made a tool setter, having about 12 machines. These girls knew how to put the machines wrong. I mean, when they wanted an hour's respite they would sort of put something wrong and I had to come and put it right. We were on shift work. We finished at 6.30 in the morning and the others started at 7.00 am. Coming from Brockenhurst we had to have lodgings there.

I had a son then, my daughter was not born until 1947. I did this right up until the end of the war.

The Morant's Park was occupied by troops. At the top gate the Welsh Fusiliers were near the Church. The Americans had the side near the Lodge. We were lucky and allowed to stay in The Lodge. My son had a wonderful time with the Americans. He spent all of his out of school hours in the camp with them.

Brockenhurst in those days was a close knit community. Well, of course, you see it was a retirement area even in those days. People like ourselves had to keep our place, we had to mind our p's and q's. In 1945 I went back to being a butler, but things had changed.

PETER REEVES

Born in 1921, I have always lived in Brockenhurst. For over thirty-five years I have been the grave-digger at St Nicholas Church.

I was born the other side of the Burley Road in North Weirs. I remember when the rifle range was moved from Beaulieu to near our home.

The Forest is my life. Give me a walking stick and I'm a happy man. See this stick? I've carved it from a fallen branch from the 1,000-year-old tree in St Nicholas Churchyard.

I've always had a dog – like this collie here. Once he came from home to the school searching for me. He broke through the glass window by the school stage. After that I used to keep him at the school.

When I left school at fourteen, I went to work for Purkess with John Purkess's father. I started by delivering groceries on one of the old trade bikes. In the mornings I helped Charlie Burt in the bake house. I also pushed an iron-wheel cart round the village. It was made by Sandford of Sway. I enjoyed it.

After two years there I worked for Mr Chalk, the fishmonger. We started at 8 o'clock in the morning and finished at 7 o'clock at night. You were working long after the other shops had shut. Old Mr Chalk, who was riddled with arthritis, was always working. He had no hobbies. When you arrived you'd find all the game, rabbits and poultry ready for sale.

I spent about two years there before going to the Forestry Commission. It was a reserved occupation and I could have avoided the army, but I said to them, "I've got to go". So I joined up in August 1941. To report at Salisbury Barracks I went by train from Brockenhurst. All my mates from the Forestry Commission were standing by the railway line waving to me.

(War Service experiences are recounted in Chapter 7 – Ed)

RON REEVES

My father was a carter of bricks for a Lymington builder and for several years worked on the railways. When he moved to this cottage in North Weirs, he gained the right to keep animals on the Forest. He

kept a cow for milk, a pig, geese, ducks and hens in the field nearby.
I went to the village school in 1929 when I was five. I always went
to school with 'the gang' which included Fred England and the
Samber boys. Mr Armstrong was my Headmaster. There were no
school meals in those days so we took our sandwiches. The school
gave us a third of a pint of milk every day. Often we'd take a big
potato which we were allowed to bake in the school fire. There were
twenty-five in my class.

I always wanted to be a vet, but I couldn't afford it. I used to mess
about with animals. I sometimes milked the cow when my father was
busy. I'd treat anything. The old lady next door had a chicken which
had swallowed a safety pin. I got it out and sewed up the chicken
again with a needle and cotton. I mended a canary's leg. A dog next
door had been kicked by a pony and had a broken leg. I mended it
by tying cabbage leaves round. People couldn't afford vets.

Just down the North Weirs road, the Chain brothers used to put
cord wood to cart to the station. Harry Burt used to take his cart
around the village, collecting rubbish and take it to Holland Wood
where the local dump was. Just up North Weirs, a hundred yards
from here there was a mound where First World War soldiers used
to dump their rubbish. People used to come and dig up old bottles
and the like.

I stayed at school until I was fourteen. Like every other boy, I
became an errand boy. I worked for Chalk, the fishmonger. He used
to keep a hundred pigs and two thousand day old chicks in part of
what is now the main car park behind Londi's. I used to help Chalk
to dig up that area to plant vegetables such as leeks, radishes,
mushrooms – anything. Holtom, the butcher, used to do his own
slaughtering near there.

When war broke out I just carried on as normal until I joined up in
December 1942. My father, Ted, who fought in the First World War,

said, "War isn't a very nice thing". Before the war I knew everyone.
Now I hardly know anyone – only the old ones. Now look at all these
houses. You have to think what was *there* before. Where Il Palio's is
there used to be a market place in the 1920's. The station had a
turntable for turning the engine round. Timber was taken to the top
of Avenue Road. There was a big shunting yard.

Every year they had a fair and flower show inside the gates of
Brockenhurst Park in Mill Lane. The children took wild flowers and
grasses. I took grasses. Everyone went down there. I enjoyed it.
There were steam engines and other things.

Before the war people were happier. We never had much but we
were happier. We always had something in our bellies. Things were
settling down really nice in the 1930's.

I used to go to Sunday School as a boy, but that was because I had
to. I'm not a church person. The Catholic Churches do more than the
C of E. Old Haslam, the vicar, was all right. He'd take the service on
the Sunday morning and then go up to the Foresters for a pint.

There's much more money about now, but not so much happiness.
I've had the best of things.

(Memories of Service abroad are given in Chapter 7 – Ed)

SAM and SID SAMBER
We were born up the Weirs opposite where the toy factory was, but
later we moved over to South Weirs. Seven boys and one girl we
were. We have been here in Fathersfield 50 odd years. They were the
second lot of council houses built – the first were in Addison Road.
Our sister made her home with us when she was widowed. We've
done the housekeeping for ourselves since she died. I was born 1905
and Sid 1907 – getting rather ancient now! Our father was a farmer
at Ober Farm that belonged to the Walker-Munros. New Forest Drive,
all that belonged to Ober Farm. How many years was that Sid? 39
years. It was a long way to walk from South Weirs. When he was
about 60 he decided he would have a bicycle and he rode then. He
said, "I don't want nobody to help me." Of course you know when
you first ride a bicycle, somebody else gets hold of the saddle and
helps you up but off he went. He was a big man over 16 stone.

We went to the Primary School. The teachers were very good and
fair. If you committed an offence fair enough, our older brothers were
strapped but by our time they were more relaxed. Our headmaster
was Mr Quinn. Between our brothers' time and ours, things altered.
We had a football team and a cricket team. We won a minors' league
two years running.

Sunday School was up at the Parish Church, we used to walk from

47

the Weirs twice a day, in the mornings for Sunday School and the afternoon service – of course at times we used to play truant!

As youngsters with our free time we made our own sport, we played football, cricket and when we got older played golf. We had our own nine hole golf course: all up South Weirs, round Worthys Farm.

First I went in the garden at Careys Manor. That was the Bowden Smith's then. I was there two years and then asked for a rise in wages. I thought I was worth it! But they wouldn't give me one, so I left.

In the end I went to Beachern Wood and that's where I finished up. Was there for 42 years. In those days Rhinefield House used to employ a lot of people.

At first I hardly ever saw Mrs Walker-Munro. My cousin who worked up there for three years saw her twice and spoke to her only once, but during the latter part she used to come out quite a bit, but before she was very reserved. But they were good employers. Oh yes! She used to call us her "wee little boys". She wanted a bridge over the Splash. Of course, the Council didn't want that. It would spoil the village.

We were at school in the First World War. We can sort of remember odds and ends. The Indian soldiers, they had the Forest Park Hotel. We used to go up the lane there and they would come to the barbed-wire fence and they would give us lads chupatties. All the troops were getting ready to get shipped to France. Mother used to make cakes for them.

SAM . . . I volunteered for the RAF in the Second World War but failed the hearing and got turned down. I was in the garden and carried on all the time. I also volunteered to go to the factories but nothing ever happened. I was in the ARP and First Aid Department, that sort of thing. When the siren went you dashed down from work to the village. We had bikes but there were never any accidents and we were hardly ever called out.

SID . . . I worked on the railway which was a 'reserved occupation'. My job was maintenance apart from the last ten to eleven years when I did store work and a lot of travelling for the railway as a courier. Correspondence used to come from Weymouth and from our offices in Eastleigh. Then for some reason they packed up Eastleigh and went to Wimbledon. I used to travel to Waterloo: if anything went wrong I would have to go on to the Wimbledon offices. I was on the Railway for 37 years.

STAN SCHISAN
My father was a Canadian lumberjack who had come to Balmer Lawn towards the end of the First World War to do forestry work. There he met my mother, who was a Gulliver. Although he returned to Canada, he finally came back to marry his sweetheart.

The Gullivers were an old Forest family. They lived off land 'stolen from the Forestry Commission'. My mother's father had made money out of selling butterflies – many of them rare. When they developed into chrysalises he put them in his well until they grew, chilled in the darkened damp, into butterflies. Many of them emerged deformed – three wings instead of four was not unusual. Collectors came from all over the world to buy the Gullivers' butterflies, especially the rare deformed ones! They made enough money from the trade to buy fine cottages, including the two white cottages in Rhinefield Road.

While Father was a lumberjack in Canada, an old Indian used to cut his hair. He befriended my dad and taught him how to cut hair. So when he came to work as a lumberjack he got to know Frank Murray at his barber's shop and thought he might eventually take up the trade, which he did and later took over the shop.

I left Ashley school 'discharged with dishonour' at fourteen and worked for my father. Vic, my school friend, joined me – he stayed at school six months longer than I did because he was brighter. In 1939 and 1940 he and I rode a tandem together. Vic now cuts hair in Lyndhurst.

My father sold his shop in Pitmore Lane for £300. We moved to Sway. Before the war a haircut for men was 3d, for boys 2d and a shave was 1d. My father gave me 2/6d per week pocket money with which I had to buy all my own clothes.

Cliff Rickman, my best friend, sat next to me in class. He got me that many hidings in school, it isn't true! He was a wicked little sod. One of his favourite tricks was putting carbide in water, making small fires in the inkwells. One day he set fire to the books under the desk. The Headmaster, a fair but strict man, striped our arseholes for about a fortnight. When Cliff had the stick, so did I.

When I was eighteen I was called up. In 1943 when I joined the navy, my ambition was to serve in the Motor Torpedo Boats. I felt I had the right practical expertise. I ended up as a sick berth attendant at Gosport. Even though I was quite near, I was not allowed home for two years. When nineteen years old, I was put on a draft for the Far East. I was given various injections, which got me down and I caught scarlet fever. This was the end of my hopes to see the world. Instead I ended up in the Isolation Hospital in Winchester. There were only two of us in the ward. One night we heard the drone,

49

drone, drone of a doodle bug. I yelled to my mate – "Oh, God, it's coming for us." Half the roof of the hospital was taken off, but nobody was hurt. Instead 173 trees were destroyed a mile away.

The only sailing I did in the navy was on the Gosport Ferry!

In 1945 I was working in Southampton nursing officers who had been in Japanese POW camps.

My father died just before I left the navy. I was very sorry not to be able to continue with nursing but I had to provide for my mother, two sisters and my brother, who was just a little nipper. There were no pensions or State help for them then. So I took over the two barbers shops.

ARTHUR STEVENS

My father, born in Lymington, was a printer. He obtained a very good post with his Uncle Bert who was a partner in a large London firm, so I was born up there in 1909. The smokey atmosphere of London did not agree with my father's health, so in 1913 my grandfather put up the money to set him up in a business in Brockenhurst. They took over the double-fronted shop opposite the post office which is now Londi's. One shop sold tobacco and stationery, the other sold sweets and mineral water. Right over the top of the premises, on the first floor, was a great big room in which there was a billiard table and card tables. This was known as The Institute. My father bought a small shed about eight feet by six, printing machinery, a frame of cases and other necessary things and started his printing works at the bottom of the garden. His first order I believe was for fifty bill heads for which he got half-a-crown.

When I was coming up to fourteen the Headmaster and all the school teachers wanted my father and mother to let me sit the exams for the Brockenhurst County School. Anyone could go there up to sixteen as long as you were prepared to pay the fees. Mother and Father were adamant. There was a good business going and I was going to be made a printer. I protested but in the end had to bow to my parents' wishes. They thought I should be apprenticed to someone rather than my father, so I went to Charlie Brown at Ringwood.

I used to leave Brockenhurst on a bicycle just before 7.00 am. From the bottom of The Rise, through Burley, the roads were almost all gravel up to Picket Post. Then it was a tarmaced road to Ringwood. I used to get there at 8 o'clock and then had to do a two-hour paper round and get back to the works by 10 o'clock. My job was often just treadling a printing machine. I had an hour for lunch and then back to the printing works till 6 o'clock; then biked back to Brockenhurst.

I was put into lodgings nearer the works. They were really old fashioned and I never picked up any type for the whole three years I was down there. My father said, "That's not the way to teach a printer." So I came back to complete my five-year apprenticeship with him.

I was a part-time fireman from 1940 until 1942 when I was called up into the Fire Service and served all during the war at Lyndhurst. When I was part-time, calling you out was very Heath Robinson to start with; all they used to do was call you up from Lyndhurst, that was the headquarters, if they wanted you, the leader of our brigade was on the phone and knew the local people's phone numbers to get hold of them. As soon as we got the sirens installed we were called out on these. The fire station was right at the top of Fibbards Road; it was located on the left of the cut through to the football field. It was a wooden building put up by the parish council in the old volunteer days. We also had fire bells for night time, for the siren was shut at night.

EMMY WATERMAN
I still live in the cottage on Waters Green which my grandparents bought for £150 in 1873.

I went to Brockenhurst Village School in 1912, the Headmaster was Mr Gendall who was also church organiser and school master. If the boys misbehaved they got the stick. The trouble these days is there is no discipline.

We looked up to our teachers in those days. All started to go wrong when teachers started dressing like their pupils. There was more discipline in the home because mothers did not go out to work.

In the First World War on Fridays all the school went up to Hincheslea to pick sphagnum moss for wound dressing in the military hospitals; we picked acorns for munitions.

On Sundays troop trains came to Brockenhurst station. I always remember one man crying out, "See to my leg – see to my leg". It was awful. The wounded were taken to Lady Harding's Hospital which we called Tin Town, because of the tin huts (near St Nicholas Church). The nurses' quarters were the other side of the road and they went over a footbridge to get to the hospital. Only the military were allowed up Church Lane. (*Other hospitals were in Morant Hall, Forest Park and Balmer Lawn – Ed.*)

One Monday afternoon the Conscientious Objectors arrived by train. They had to go up to the Tilery on Beaulieu Road where there were huts. Horses and carts met the COs at the station – the wounded troops on stretchers were jeering at them. When they got to the bridge near Balmer Lawn, soldiers and young people threw their luggage into the river. There were clothes and papers floating in the water, even a Bible. I remember one chap, his head in his hands, kneeling by the water saying the Lord's Prayer. The COs were put on forestry work. Towards the end of the war the lumberjacks took over the work and the huts. The COs just suddenly left. I don't know where they went.

People who grumbled about service didn't work for the right people. I always worked for very nice people – not the jumped-up johnnies.

I took the butler's place at a house in Lyndhurst. I always remember doing the lamps every other day. I am not very good at heights. I was terrified. We had a lovely servants' hall. I made a lot of friends. Now all my friends have died – except one – she and I write to each other regularly.

My next permanent job was at The Homestead, Broadlands where there was a retired vicar, Mr Clements and his son, who looked after him. I was very happy and stayed there several years. The old man got a bit funny – poor old thing. He started roaming. He had to have a nurse as well as his son to look after him. He bought separate bungalows in Balmer Lawn Road for his chauffeur and gardener.

I then went to Sway Place (now a nursing home) where I worked for about six years. While I was there my father died.

In 1941 I knew my age was coming up for call-up. I didn't want to go to Wellworthy's. It would have killed me. But Mr Prosser, the Stationmaster, offered me a job as a porter ready to take over as a ticket collector. When I first started work there I thought it would be dead. But it wasn't: we were very, very busy.

The men didn't like us women working there. Someone said if you tried getting past Emmy without a ticket she would chase you up the street! Well, I had to, I was doing my job. I used to let some of the soldiers through – poor devils. I'd just say, "Don't you dare tell a soul. I haven't seen you if they ask." They would be going up North and only had a few hours' leave.

If I wasn't working on the alternate Sunday I did work at the Army canteen at Morant Hall from 10.00 until 7.00. Often the soldiers stationed at Ringwood missed their rail connections and used to spend the night at the canteen. Mrs Haslam, the Vicar's wife, used to run it. There was a weekly dance in the Hall. That Hall should never have been demolished.

The WI used to sell meat pies at Ormond's Garage (now the Indian restaurant) every Friday. Lomonds, the Caterers from Southampton, used to provide the meat. The idea was that 'pie money' should be put towards building a village hall. That hall wasn't built, so after the war the 'pie money' was used for every good cause.

People didn't do so badly for food in the country. The men weren't there so the women did the gardens. We had chickens and a pig at the back. You gave up your egg ration in exchange for corn.

When the Americans came all the girls went mad – except me. They had so much money to throw around and they had NYLONS! Those girls from Wellworthy's came here on the train. I thought, they don't realise what they're letting themselves in for.

CHAPTER 3

BROCKENHURST AT WAR
1938-1945

A Chronological Account

Each year includes: –
A Diary of National and International Events – The Editor
Introduction to the Year – Geoffrey Hawkes
Local News from the *Lymington Times* – compiled by Douglas Ferry
Brockenhurst Notes
Local Memories and Eyewitness Accounts

1938

Diary of National and International Events

March	Austria incorporated into Third Reich. *Anschluss* – union of Germany and Austria.
September 29	Munich Agreement between Hitler, Mussolini, Chamberlain and Daladier. Czechs had to surrender Sudeten borderlands. Chamberlain declared: "Peace in our time". British rearmament began seriously. Radar developed secretly.

In 1938 Charlie Chaplin produced and acted in one of his best films, 'The Great Dictator'. In many ways it was a whimsical portrait of Adolf Hitler; it had the Fuhrer's posturings and outbursts, his megolomania. And yet Charlie's famous moustache, sad and somewhat pathetic, belonged more to our own Prime Minister, Neville Chamberlain. 1938 was Hitler's year. The Third Reich had the ascendency in Europe, annexing Austria, dismembering Czechoslovakia

54

piecemeal and preparing secret war on Poland. Crushed by the speed of events, Chamberlain sued for peace, as if determined to find something good in Nazi Germany. On September 30 he signed the Munich Agreement with Hitler and the French Prime Minister, Daladier. It was to be 'peace in our time', and a wave of euphoria swept through Britain. Chamberlain had somehow got the better of this once forlorn Austrian – now the world's most powerful man. But, events were soon to prove otherwise.

From the *Lymington Times*

After the *Anschluss* between Germany and Austria, Britain began making preparations for a war. Our story begins therefore in July 1938, the last almost normal peacetime summer.

Brockenhurst from the 11th to the 16th of that month had its biggest annual social event, the New Forest Club's open Lawn Tennis tournament. This had been held continuously since 1913, and drew players and spectators from far outside the Forest area. The entry was 'first-class and larger than in past years, and includes many well-known and "ranked" players whose names are familiar at Wimbledon', including the NZ men's champion.

The weather was fine throughout, except for some rain on the Friday, and the tournament was followed as usual by a ball at the Morant Hall on the Friday night, where the attractions included Jack Jackson's Band from London and Diana Miller 'of radio fame, who has appeared in so many London cabarets'.

Capt Sutton, the Morants' Agent, who was one of the most influential people in village life at that time, was in charge of the secretarial work, and the floral arrangements from the greenhouses at Brockenhurst Park were arranged by Mr G Meaden, the Morants' head gardener.

In August the second big event was held – the New Forest Dog Show. This again was the 'biggest ever', there being 1,577 entries and 727 dogs taking part. 3,000 people (more than the total population of Brockenhurst!) were expected at this event.

But Brockenhurst was beginning to lose some of its independent 'village' status. On 1st July the 30-year-old Brockenhurst Gas Company was taken over by the Bournemouth Gas and Water Company, and gas ceased to be manufactured in Brockenhurst. The price was to be reduced from 1/6d to 11½d a therm, and the product would 'now be of uniform quality and pressure'(!). A new Gas Showroom was opened in Brookley Road as part of the deal.

And at the Parish Council meeting in September it was announced that control of the village Fire Brigade would pass to the New Forest

RDC at the end of the year. The Parish Council was to receive £684 compensation, and there was some debate a few months later as to what it should be spent on. A swimming pool at Balmer Lawn seemed to be the favourite, though this never materialised and the money was still held in a fund five years later in 1943.

In November advertisements were placed for the erection of the new Brockenhurst telephone exchange. There were 273 subscribers in Brockenhurst – 'well over 10% of the population in that delightful village' gushed the *Lymington Times*, though it was later pointed out that some areas in the Borough had a higher proportion than this.

At the midnight communion on Christmas Eve 1938 the new £450 Hammond electric organ at St Saviour's church was played for the first time, by Mr WD Braithwaite 'whose efforts, with those of Capt Sutton, have been largely responsible for the raising of the money by subscriptions'. This instrument was to serve St Saviour's for nearly 55 years until it was replaced in 1993.

And as the final big social event of the year the annual Childrens' Ball was held on 28th December at the Morant Hall, when 100 young people attended from all parts of the New Forest.

So pre-war Brockenhurst continued on its way, but preparations for the war were proceeding. There had been a panic at the time of the Munich crisis in October, and slit trenches were hastily dug in Lymington and elsewhere, Council workmen being taken off other work to assist volunteers.

A forgotten sequel to the Munich agreement was that a number of British Legion ex-servicemen were selected to go to the Sudetenland plebiscite areas for police duties to maintain order, and VG Ballard, Lieutenant, KOYLI, of Brockenhurst was amongst their number. But having trained and set sail the shipload of volunteers had to anchor off Southend waiting for the 'International Commission' to report, and the personnel eventually returned home, the project having been abandoned.

Clearly however the government did not believe that there was to be 'peace in our time' and the preparations went on at an increased pace.

The County Council was made responsible for Air Raid Precautions, but delegated this to local Councils (without however providing any funding, a not unfamiliar situation today). As 1938's peacetime council budgets had contained no provision for this there were some problems!

ARP soon became embroiled in local government politics and jealousies, compounded by official confusion. During the rest of the year the newspaper reported almost continuous rows on Lymington Council, with various councillors and officials complaining, resigning, or threatening to resign. A real problem was that different officials were responsible for the AFS (the fire-fighting wing of the ARP organisation) and for the regular fire brigade, and there was a similar situation with ambulances, but there was rather too much injured self-importance about.

The first consignment of gas masks (respirators) arrived in Lymington in mid-September, and 'squads are being trained to assemble them'. Air Raid Wardens were supposed to visit every-body's houses and fit them, and official announcements gave the impression that this was all done very quickly and smoothly, but news items in the paper, as so often, tell a slightly different story. Well into the following year some people were complaining that they still had not been fitted.

And a man wrote from 'the RDC area adjacent to the Borough', saying "When people were . . . distributing gas masks my wife . . . offered her help. But she was blandly informed 'Oh, but you don't belong to the Women's Institute . . !' "

GAS MASKS

Many politicians and citizens feared that when war came poisonous gas attacks would occur.

Brockenhurst took the issue of gas masks very seriously. This remarkable extract from *The Brockenhurst Bulletin* (15 October 1938), which was 'A Monthly Magazine of News and Interesting Items' printed and published by John R Stevens. Price 3d. It shows how seriously the threat was taken.

The international crisis descended on us with the respirator census still unfinished. For this there was really no excuse and the less said about it now perhaps the better. It was not expected that we should have to assemble our own respirators, but this difficulty was successfully overcome by Admiral Currey and those who helped him. The real difficulty arose from the fact that when the respirators had to be distributed there were still a number of people who had not been fitted and that some of those who had been fitted had not been fitted properly. One consequence is that there are at present about one hundred large size respirators in store whereas there are a number of people who require medium and small size who are without respirators. Arrange-ments are being made to fit all those who have not been properly fitted and it is hoped that anyone who is doubtful whether his respirator fits properly will apply to an air-raid warden for advice. In the meantime it may be repeated that the correct *size* is determined by the position of the eyes (which should be in the middle of the window when the face piece is lifted well up

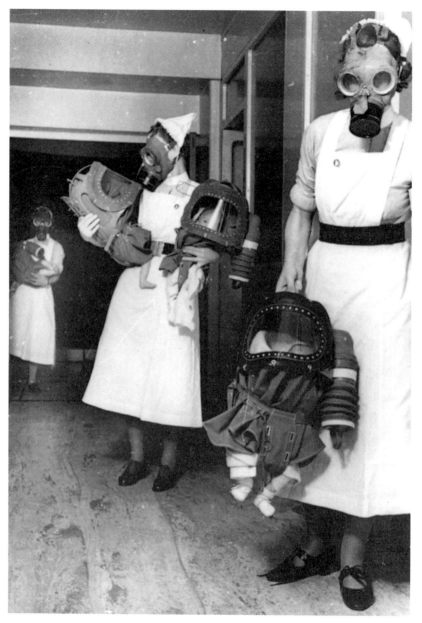

GAS MASK DRILL. PHOTO BY COURTESY OF THE TRUSTEES OF THE
IMPERIAL WAR MUSEUM.

on the face so that it makes good contact under the chin) and a *proper fit* by subsequent adjustment of the straps. It is to be noted that the air breathed out passes out of the respirator between the edges of the rubber face piece and the wearer's face. If the respirator is too small or if the straps are adjusted too tightly the effort of breathing out will be increased.

As respirators are now in the hands of the public and it is not known when they will be withdrawn the following notes on their proper care are given.

1. When not in use the respirator should be kept in a cool dark place.

2. It should be put on and removed carefully by the straps. It should *not* be removed by grasping the container (or the edge of the rubber under the chin) and lifting it off upwards.

3. If the outside of the respirator should get wet from any cause or the inside damp with moisture from the breath it should be dried with a soft cloth. *If water gets into the container it will be ruined.*

4. The respirator should not be hung suspended from the straps.

5. Care must be taken at all times to avoid damage to the transparent window.

The eight members of the Decontamination Squad attended a special decontamination course at Lyndhurst. The keenness shown by the squad has been most favourably commented on.'

GERALDINE ROBERTS comments:
Gas Masks came in various shapes and sizes. The largest were for the small children. Babies were put into a kind of flexible body suit, strapped to a frame. When children grew out of this complex 'suit' they were given a red 'Mickey Mouse' mask which had two round 'eyes' and a 'nose' acting as a valve. Most civilians had the black mask with a single window, which inevitably got steamed up, and a round tin-shaped filter. One was supposed never to be parted from it, because, in fact, it was Government property. In theory, one could be fined £5 for damaging it!

Those with real breathing problems could apply for the 'Helmet' respirator, which covered the whole head. Air Raid Wardens and other members of the Civil Defence Services, wore something rather similar to the Mickey Mouse version, though less excitingly coloured. Finally, there was a Service Design. This was presumably more efficient than the other versions, and allowed for greater ease of movement.

BEFORE WE GO

1939

Diary of National and International Events

March 16   Bohemia and Moravia (rest of
                Czechoslovakia) annexed by Hitler.
                Anti-Polish campaign began in German
                press.
                British Territorial Army doubled.
April 1   End of Spanish Civil War.
     7   Italy seized Albania.
   27   Conscription introduced in Great Britain for
                ages 20-21.
May 25   Italy and Germany signed pact.
                Anglo-Polish treaty. Great Britain promised
                to help Poland if attacked.
August 23   German-Soviet Pact signed by Von
                Ribbentrop and Molotov. Threat of world
                domination.
   28   Netherlands mobilised.
   31   British fleet mobilised.

SECOND WORLD WAR

Friday September 1   Poland invaded by German forces.
                Britain and France mobilised.
   1-4   Evacuation schemes put in motion in
                England and Wales.
     2   Compulsory military service for all men
                aged 18-41.
Sunday 3   11.00 am – British and French ultimatum
                expired.
                WAR DECLARED BETWEEN BRITAIN
                AND GERMANY.
                Australia and New Zealand joined in
                declaration of war.
     4   *Athenia*, a British liner, sunk by submarine.
                South Africa declared war on Germany.
     6   First enemy air raid on Britain.
   10   Canada declared war on Germany.
   11   British troops on French soil.
                British Expeditionary Force (BEF) under
                Lord Gort.

17   Russian troops crossed Polish frontier along entire length. Russian and German troops met at Brest Litovsk.

27   Warsaw capitulated.

29   Germans and Russians signed Pact and approved partition of Poland.

October 14   *Royal Oak*, British battleship, sunk in Scapa Flow. 810 lives lost.

November 30   Finland attacked by Russia.

December 11   Italy left League of Nations.

13   Battle of River Plate – German warship, *Graf Spee*, engaged by British cruisers, *Exeter*, *Ajax* and *Achilles*. After four days *Graf Spee* was scuttled in Montevideo harbour.

14   Russia expelled from League of Nations over invasion of Finland.

EUROPE AT WAR

At 11.00 am on September 3 1939, British listeners tuned into the BBC to hear an announcement to stand by for a speech by the Prime Minister, Neville Chamberlain: at 11.15 am he came on the air, his voice tired and strained. Britain had called for an undertaking from Hitler to withdraw German troops from Poland, which had been invaded on September 1.

"I have to tell you now that no such undertaking has been received", the Prime Minister said, "and that consequently this country is at war with Germany".

A lull in international relationships followed the announcement, a period known as the 'Phoney War' in which Brockenhurst experienced the first effects of petrol rationing and saw the first homesick and disorientated evacuee children arrive on our railway station. The radio which brought the news of the declaration of war became a national lifeline: petrol shortages and blacked out streets meant that we spent a lot of evenings at home and few people missed the nine o'clock news on the BBC Home Service. Through those broadcasts and a door-by-door delivery of leaflets we learned how to secure our homes against air-raids, where to find the best food bargains (and how to cook them) and how to put up Anderson shelters in our back gardens. Soon, however, that same radio was to carry news of different import. The 'Phoney War' of preparation and little else came

"..... WE ARE NOW AT WAR WITH GERMANY."

to an end and we, as a nation, began to understand as first Denmark, and then Norway, the Low Countries and France fell to a new wave of Nazi onslaughts, exactly what the term 'blitzkrieg' meant.

A war not of our choosing was about to reach Britain's shores and invade in its own way every homestead in our country.

From the *Lymington Times*

There were still some eight months of peace ahead when 1939 dawned, but there was a feeling that time was running out.

The headline in the first issue of the *Lymington Times* however was OUTBREAK OF TYPHOID FEVER AT BROCKENHURST! This was intended to scare, as there had been a big outbreak at Croydon caused by the water supply. But the NFRDC said there was no need to be alarmed as this was an isolated case in one family and was 'quite different to Croydon'. It seems to have been a storm in a tea-cup, as no follow-up to the news item ever appeared.

There was continuing disquiet over the state of the Forest after the blizzard at the end of 1938, and complaints from many, including the indefatigable Capt Sutton, that the Forestry Commission were not doing enough to clear it up.

And in June there was another piece of unpleasant news when St Nicholas Church was broken into, 'for the third time in ten years'. Hopefully unconnected with this, Brockenhurst had acquired a new policeman in May, PC Cherrett.

Social events continued almost as usual in the run-up to hostilities. There were 300 guests at the New Forest Hunt Ball at the Morant Hall on 14th April, and in June Brokenhurst Manor Golf Club celebrated its Silver Jubilee with a dinner dance and a 4-ball match between well-known professional golfers (including Henry Cotton) on the Saturday.

Indeed, during the last few weeks of peace the programme of social events in the village seemed to intensify. The Hampshire WI Federation held its produce sale at Brockenhurst on 13th July with over 1,100 entries, the annual Summer Dog Show was held on 29th July with a record entry of over 1,400, and the 4th Annual Ball of the Rhinefield Polo Club was held 'at the mansion of Major and Mrs R Walker-Munro at Rhinefield'.

And at the beginning of August the usual Tennis Week took place, though it seems to have been a more low-key affair than in 1938 and was upset by the weather. The report in the paper does not mention attendances or anything much about the social events.

However, the County Junior Open Lawn Tennis Championship was held as usual. Mr Lermitte, the Committee Chairman, presented the prizes, and 'filled all the challenge cups with champagne which the winners drank, to the amusement of the onlookers'. (Perhaps some of these inebriated juniors are still around today?)

And on 23rd August the 17th Annual Gymkhana, arranged by the RAOB Hunt Lodge, was held at Tilebarn Farm – watched by 800 people.

The Bishop of Winchester advised people to "take their holidays and forget about dictators", but unfortunately Hitler had been very much in peoples' minds for most of the year.

War preparations in the area in 1939 had three aspects – military build-up, civil defence, and evacuation of schoolchildren from the cities.

In May it was announced that the War Office planned a TA Reserve (National Defence Companies), whose duties would be to guard oil and petrol depots, railway junctions, bridges, tunnels, etc against sabotage, and generally engage in home defence. As this precursor to the Home Guard seems to be little known today it might be worthwhile giving some of the details.

It was intended to enlist men in the age range 45-51, together with any younger men unfit for normal military service. Enlistment would be for four years, for home defence only. The NDCs were to do their own training, with a commitment to six hours drill per year (!) in peacetime for which payment would be made at TA rates, but they would be called up by the War Office when an emergency arose, and would be paid a bounty of £5 on mobilisation. The New Forest NDC was to comprise·some 230 men and six officers, the latter having already been chosen from among local notables.

The NDCs however do not seem to have been a success; two months later a letter was published from Lt-Col RG Crighton, OC Hampshire NDC, rather desperately appealing for volunteers.

Meanwhile, on 3rd June, it was registration day for young men aged 20-21 conscripted under the new Military Service Act. These 'militia men', who had to register at the Labour Exchange in Lymington, were required to do six months intensive training with a Regular Army or Anti-aircraft battalion, followed by three years with the Territorials or three weeks annual training with the special reserve (although of course this peace-time scheme was replaced by a more general call-up once war actually started).

However, on Sunday 16th July 'cheering and special trains were a feature of local railway stations as Britain's New Army travelled to join their Regiments'.

Young men were exempt from conscription if they could prove they were conscientious objectors (there were none from this area) or if they had joined the Territorial Army before 27th April. Not surprisingly, it was announced in June that the 5th/7th Bn. Hampshire Regiment of the TA had 'done exceedingly well in its recruitment campaign', having doubled its strength in just over two months (!) – from 592 in April to 1,246 on 12th June. Six new TA units were formed, including a 20-man one in Brockenhurst.

Territorial Army camps had always been held in the New Forest each year, but in 1939 these were on a much larger scale than usual and 30,000 men were to camp at Burley, Beaulieu, and East Boldre during August. The local paper said that 'Lymington was invaded by the Army, with scenes reminiscent of 1914'.

Major the Rt Hon Anthony Eden took time off from his official duties in mid-August to join his regiment (2nd Bn The Rangers KRRC) at East Boldre for a fortnight's training. His 600 men travelled from Waterloo to Brockenhurst in two special trains, and were taken by lorry as far as Hatchett Pond where they were met by a military band.

On Sunday 13th August some TA soldiers returning to London from Beaulieu 'had an alarming experience, when their motor-bus failed to clear the railway arch at Balmer Lawn, the roof of the bus being ripped from end to end'. Fortunately there were no serious casualties, an NCO at the rear having shouted to the men to duck, and amazingly they all proceeded on to London in the remains of the bus, accompanied by a police convoy.

August 1939 was very wet, and the TA camp at East Boldre was affected by floods on several occasions, 7,000 men being washed out on 3rd August. They were billeted in 'farm buildings and schools in Lymington, Beaulieu, Brockenhurst, Boldre, and East Boldre'.

Meanwhile Civil Defence matters were in hand, with appeals in January for ARP volunteers including dispatch riders and boy runners (16-17). And in March a meeting was held at Lymington to explain the ARP administration to the public. Hampshire was divided into seven areas plus the County Boroughs, and Area No 7 comprised the Borough of Lymington, the New Forest RD, and Ringwood and Fordingbridge RD. This was in charge of a salaried Assistant County ARP Controller, Col Daniels, and there was another paid officer Capt Jarvis. All other workers were volunteers. It was stated that 65% of ARP was paid for by the Treasury, the balance coming from the County rate.

ARP exercises and training sessions took place all through the spring and summer, disclosing (as might have been expected) many serious failures of communication. There was a mock air raid on Lymington in June, and a trial blackout of the whole of southern England on the night of 9th/10th August.

Traders were warned that they must 'group their vans under the National Service Scheme – or they won't get any petrol if war comes'.

In January the distribution of cardboard boxes for gas masks began – these were 'issued unassembled, and the Head of the Household must see that they are put together properly'. And in August the authorities had to remind people that a fine of £5 would be levied for not taking reasonable care of gas masks, 'which were Government property'.

But in this rural area it was the projected evacuation of school-children and adults from the cities which was causing most concern.

At the end of 1938 the Public Health Committee of the NFRDC had recommended that billeting of refugees should be entirely voluntary, 'otherwise refugees should be placed in camps'. The matter was referred back, and Dr. Des Voeux thought the proposal would be very dangerous – 'rich people will refuse . . . while the poor, with much less room, will have them'.

In reply to expressions of concern in February, the paper said that the Government's latest scheme was to provide camps for evacuated civilians, which could be used as holiday centres in peacetime. The local MP, Major John Mills, confirmed this – he 'regarded billeting generally as an emergency measure to be replaced as soon as may be by the provision of camps and the use of larger empty houses . . .'

On Saturday 2nd September the *Lymington Times* said that the Germans were reported to be bombing Poland, and contained news of the arrival of Southampton refugees in Lymington. But most of the paper was taken up with a description of the new Brockenhurst County School, which was to open on 19th September.

The school had cost £32,400, and was the largest secondary school building in the county and the third to be completed 'since the war' (with a few hours left to go this must have been the last time this expression was ever used by anyone about the 1914-18 conflict!)

This edition of the paper also contained details of billeting of city schoolchildren in the NFRDC area 'in the event of the evacuation scheme becoming operative'.

Nearly 6,000 children were expected, mostly from Portsmouth, and their arrival would be spread over two days, two trains a day being scheduled at each of Brockenhurst, Beaulieu Road, and Lyndhurst Road stations. The scheme was very complicated, and for some reason most of the children destined for Brockenhurst had to detrain at Beaulieu Road, and Sway children at Brockenhurst, and they were conveyed to their reception points (mostly village schools) by Hants and Dorset buses. The programme was as follows:

1st day	Brockenhurst Station	560 Boldre, **100 Brockenhurst**
	Beaulieu Road	**800 Brockenhurst**, 150 East Boldre, etc
2nd day	Brockenhurst Station	600 Sway, **60 Brockenhurst.**

Mr AEN Ashford, Clerk to the Council, was the officer in charge, but the children were to be met by voluntary helpers, the recently-formed Women's Voluntary Service being particularly involved. The children were all to be issued with 48-hour rations before being conducted to their billets.

In fact only 2,385 children arrived in the New Forest RDC area out of the 5,814 expected, and most of the emergency rations had to be sent back unused to the Ministry of Health who were master-minding the operation.

Advertisements in this last peacetime paper included stirrup-pumps at 24/6d each from Manns Bros, New Milton, and Pye radios to rent at what seems a rather expensive 1/9d weekly average (considerably more than a building craftsman's hourly wage).

The next edition of the *Lymington Times*, on 9th September, was announced as 'Wartime Edition, 1st Week' and was drastically cut from the usual 12 pages down to 4. From now on newspapers were subject to strict censorship, for example place names could not be mentioned in connection with news items if it was thought they could be of assistance to the enemy.

In the first few weeks of the war draconian restrictions were introduced in all walks of life, which were soon relaxed as the fear of intensive air bombardment receded and were replaced by more permanent and realistic arrangements. All cinemas were closed at first, but after a week the Government decided to allow them to open in towns which were not regarded as vulnerable.

The Bournemouth Gas Co announced that the normal pressure of gas would be reduced if an air raid warning was received, and people in churches, cinemas, etc were 'advised to stay put when an air raid warning sounds unless duty requires them to leave or if they live nearby, say a 5-minute walk'.

Tradespeople were having problems. Foleys, who advertised fruit and vegetables every week, asked for customers' kind indulgence – 'there is no shortage of produce but there are difficulties with transport'. The Goverment issued an order that shopkeepers must pay cash for all goods before they could remove them from store or have them delivered, so they in turn appealed to customers to pay accounts promptly. And it was agreed by the shops in the area that they would close 30 minutes after sunset.

The NFRDC Food Control Committee was set up comprising 10 people, one of the four tradespeoples' representatives being Mr RG Purkess of Brockenhurst. Another well-known village trader was also in the news with the announcement of the death of Mr WE Holtom, the butcher.

By mid-September details of petrol and food rationing were announced, the scheme giving supplementary rations for adolescent boys – but not for girls!

At the end of the month came National Registration Day, when the names of all people who slept in the house on Friday 29th September had to be filled in on an official form. (The registration numbers which people were then given are still used today, over half a century later, on their NHS medical cards!)

By the end of September many Southampton evacuees at Lymington had gone home, as the threatened air-raids had not taken place, but Portsmouth children now had their school permanently in Brockenhurst and the arrangement was causing some friction.

At the NFRDC on Monday 25th September it was pointed out that some poorer residents of Brockenhurst could not feed adolescent evacuees on the 10/6d weekly Government allowance (or 8/6d where there were two or more in the same house). They were billeted in cottages where the average wages of the working people were 35/- to 42/- a week. Admiral Currey compared these payments with the 2/- per night allowed for members of the ATS who were billeted, and thought that children's parents should contribute.

The Clerk to the Council admitted that many parents were indeed able to contribute, 'but if they had publicised this the scheme would have had less chance of being successfully carried out.'

However, in early October the government announced that parents would have to contribute 6/- a week towards the cost of their children in reception areas (or a lesser amount according to their means).

Civil Defence was also causing problems. Members of the AFS (Auxiliary Fire Service) had been called up at the outbreak of war, but when the feared blitzkrieg did not materialise they were stood down again. This caused a good deal of hardship, as their previous employers were not required to take them back and some had already taken on new staff to replace them. At the Parish Council meeting at the end of November the Co-ordinating Fire Officer for the district, Mr HW Heppenstall, said that on 14th November the total strength in Brockenhurst was 10 retained firemen and 18 auxiliary, 12 who were paid for full-time service were under notice.

Under the headline BROCKENHURST WITHOUT ARP AMBU-LANCE it was reported that Mr Fields-Clarke, the local ARP officer, told the Parish Council that he was worried about the absence of a permanent ambulance in the village, and the non-provision of a local cleansing (anti-gas) station – the nearest one was at Lymington.

The Chairman of the New Forest ARP Committee, Rear-Admiral HS Currey, told the Parish Council that there were now only three ARP ambulances in the whole Rural District, the 'hired vehicles having been dispensed with'. When asked what had happened to the New Forest ambulance stationed in Brockenhurst he replied that 'this is not an ARP ambulance. The reason it has not been seen around is because the driver is ill.'

It is clear that the auxiliary ARP services and the regular fire and ambulance services were still not well integrated, and that there was some rivalry between the respective organisations.

In the 21st October issue a good deal of the limited space was devoted to news of local men involved in the sinking of the battleship *Royal Oak*, Signalman RG Chalk of Brockenhurst being one of those missing. It was said that he was born and bred in the village, where his grandfather had a fishmonger's business, and his father had a fruiterer's business.

The blackout was a constant source of news, various people in Brockenhurst being charged with showing lights. A serious effect of the blackout was the danger of motor vehicles with restricted lighting running-down forest ponies on the roads (at that time none of the main roads was fenced). Capt Sutton suggested that white stripes should be painted on ponies' hindquarters and in the area of their saddle-girths.

By 9th December 75 forest ponies had been killed on the roads during the year, 30 of these during the three months since lighting restrictions began. The Verderers appealed to owners of pastures to let commoners' animals graze them at a nominal charge, to keep them off the roads.

And as a more amusing blackout story it was reported that problems were arising on Waterloo-Bournemouth trains with people crowding into the restaurant cars which had full lighting with darkened windows, whereas ordinary carriages had 'blue lights which just make it possible to see across the carriage'.

BROCKENHURST NOTES – JOHN PURKESS

The Portsmouth Southern Secondary School for Boys arrived in Brockenhurst on September 1. They were billeted throughout the village. They arrived ill-equipped for the village road and path conditions in wet weather, many never possessing Wellington boots. They also thought it a dump, being without a cinema or a fish and chip shop.

69

BEFORE WE GO

September 3 was a beautiful sunny day. The Brockenhurst County High School had moved during the summer holidays into its new premises on the Lyndhurst Road and the Highwood Road buildings were empty. To accommodate the 'visitors' Brockenhurst pupils went to lessons in the mornings and the Portsmouth boys used the building in the afternoons. This continued for most of the first term whilst the desks, etc were brought from Portsmouth to equip the Highwood Road buildings. The Portsmouth boys continued to use some of the Lyndhurst Road facilities throughout the war.

Avenue Road saw regular movements by Rank Flour lorries as they filled the indoor riding school at Avenue Riding Stables with sacks of flour, in case the Solent Mills were bombed. This was situated on a site behind Gates Garage.

Shortage of petrol necessitated the restriction of bread deliveries to three days a week, a service that continued throughout the war by Purkess, the baker's.

Fire Watching rotas were arranged and the watchers were accommodated in a room in Malta Cottage, on the side of Fermain in Brookley Road. These premises were also fitted out and used to sell bread and cakes after Purkess's bakery shop was bombed.

The Hampshire Girls' Orphanage was evacuated to Marden House in Rhinefield Road. We arrived at school one morning to find all these new girls in blue uniforms in all the classes.

Extract from the minutes of the Brockenhurst Horticultural Society Committee meeting on Friday, December 9:
'In view of the outbreak of hostilities, the question of continuing the Annual Show Exhibition was debated and it was moved by Mr Wheeler, the Hon Secretary, and by Mr Larcombe and unanimously agreed that in view of the war the society cease to hold its Annual Exhibition until such time as peaceful conditions return. A meeting to be called at a later date when considered desirable.'

The next meeting was called on February 9, 1945!

ALEC PURKIS – *an evacuee in Brockenhurst. A Wasp remembers* –
On September 1, 1939, aged 12, I was evacuated along with about 350 other boys from my school, The Portsmouth Southern Grammar School, to Brockenhurst. Our train went to Salisbury where we waited two hours for the bus to take us to Brockenhurst. It's funny how I can remember these things. We were dropped at Grigg Lane, trooped along the Sway Road and lined up opposite the school, where the Village Hall now is. Ken Martin, the chemist, was running, helping things along. One of the young Girl Guide reception party was a Margaret Purkess from North Weirs, who eventually became

70

my wife! With three other boys I was escorted by the Girl Guides to the Morant Arms – which turned out to be full. We waited there two hours while arrangements were made for us to lodge at French's shop. Each of us was given a food parcel which included a packet of ginger biscuits, Cadbury's chocolate and a tin of condensed milk.

We stayed at French's shop for three weeks and then I was moved to North Lodge, Mill Lane, the home of Mr and Mrs Frank Rashleigh and their little boy, Philip. That was a lively welcoming place to be – like the rest of us they didn't think that I'd be there long because the war would be over by Christmas!

For my last year or so I lodged with Mr Whittington of Edgemoor, Burley Road. There he had his famous toy factory. He made the ark and the animals, replicas of the royal coach for King George VI's coronation. The other Portsmouth boy with me was an avid jazz listener. I remember him going into the sitting room and telling Mr Whittington not to listen to all that classical music, which interfered with his jazz! Flissy White, his diminutive cook/housekeeper, was very good, but not too generous with the rations. When we got home from school we'd get thin cucumber and tomato sandwiches and little else. I was always hungry.

However, we got on well with the Brockenhurst lads *(and at least one of the girls – Ed)*

MARGARET PURKIS (nee Purkess) confirmed the good relationships: I enjoyed the arrival of the Wasps, as we called the boys in their black and yellow striped caps and blazers.

ALEC continued: Although it was a bit of a cultural shock coming from a big city to a village, I enjoyed it. I must have done because we have come back to live in Woodpecker Cottage.

(Other recollections by evacuees can be found in childhood memories of Post War Residents – Ed)

CONSCIENTIOUS OBJECTORS

Before the end of the year several Brockenhurst people had joined the forces. Here, and nationally, the declaration of war and the need to fight had been accepted almost unanimously. Not quite, though, because during the Second World War about 60,000 men applied to be registered as Conscientious Objectors (COs).

Perhaps because of their harsh treatment in the First World War COs were now regarded with tolerance.

Some who had been guaranteed conditional exemption from military service became forestry workers. One local man was sent to Ashurst. He has provided this information:

During the war the woodmill operation was enlarged at Ashurst and more men, and some Land Army girls were working there. They were mainly engaged in collecting cut timber from different sites and turning it into railway sleepers. It was hard work in all weather conditions and once engaged the workforce could not leave.

It had some of the atmosphere of a lumber camp with the sawmill making its familiar noise and the workers taking the midday meal in a log cabin. The meal consisted of sandwiches brought from home and to warm them they would be put on top of the black boggy fire until the heat began to scorch them. At other times meals were taken at the locations where timber was being collected. Much of the timber came from the Burley area.

Among the work force were two or three conscientious objectors to the war. One or two stood by the position taken by Quakers in the First World War when many of them had spent long terms in prison. Basically their objection was a religious one formulated around the instruction of Jesus that we should love our enemies and do good to those who abuse us. In 1914-18 67 COs died in prison and 30 were taken to France and sentenced to death for refusing to take up arms. During 1940-45 the COs fared better but some of them still served prison sentences before appearing before another tribunal and being directed to work on the land. Some had a political and humanitarian objection to the war among them an International Socialist who believed in the brotherhood of man.

So far as we know three COs were at the Ashurst site; two for most of the duration and one for only a few months.

WHITEFIELD MOOR UNDER THE PLOUGH.

1940

Diary of National and International Events

Early 1940   Little activity. Continuation of 'Phoney War'.

April   Germans occupied Denmark and invaded Norway. Overrun in a few weeks. Neville Chamberlain forced to resign: Winston Churchill became Prime Minister of Coalition Government.

May 10   Germans invaded neutral countries of Luxembourg, Netherlands (overrun in 5 days), Belgium (overrun in 14 days). German Panzers advanced rapidly into France, splitting Allied armies.

27   Evacuation from Dunkirk of British Expeditionary Force and French 1st Army. Britain fought on alone.

June 10   Italy declared war on Britain and France.

July 1   Germans occupied Channel Islands.

August 13   Fleets of German bombers began to attack SE England. Battle of Britain.

September 7   Very heavy London air raid.

15   Battle of Britain ended.

November 5   Heavy Atlantic convoy losses. German 'pocket battleship', *Admiral Scheer* sank HMS *Jarvis Bay*.

14   Coventry attacked by German bombers. Cathedral destroyed.

December 2   Bristol bombed.

29   City of London suffered severe German incendiary attack. Many Wren churches destroyed.

THE DEEPENING CONFLICT

In 1940 'Gone With The Wind' starring Clark Gable and Vivienne Leigh reached local cinemas. It was also the year of 'The Wizard of Oz' with Judy Garland in the lead role. Both films were an instant success, as were such songs as 'There'll Always Be An England', and 'We'll Hang Out The Washing On The Siegfried Line'. The films and songs were morale boosters during a year in which Britain evacuated its troops from Dunkirk and the Blitz of London began. Invasion fever gripped the country. Road signs disappeared from Lymington and Brockenhurst, and as Paris fell to the Germans, the Local Defence Volunteer Force was formed. By July, at Churchill's suggestion, this was renamed 'the Home Guard' and by that autumn 500,000 men had volunteered to watch over our coasts, public buildings, roads and railways. The cartoonist, David Low, summed up the mood of the nation. His famous drawing of a clifftop foot soldier on the edge of an angry sea, his arm raised, fist clenched, with the caption 'Very well, alone!' caught the spirit of Britain's resolution in the face of German onslaught.

From the *Lymington Times*

In January the local butchers' shops advertised that all monthly accounts were suspended, and all weekly accounts had to be settled by the Wednesday – the shopkeepers were of course having to pay cash themselves, by Government order.

But this was the time of the so-called 'Phoney War', when nothing much was happening in the way of military activities.

The evacuee debate boiled up again, and feelings obviously ran very high. The paper of 17th February reported:

SCANDAL AND DISGRACE

Brockenhurst Up in Arms over Portsmouth Evacuees

Residents Break Down Under the Strain

The terms 'scandal' and 'disgrace' were used in criticism of Portsmouth City Council in the lack of interest which that authority has shown regarding their secondary school evacuees who are billeted in Brockenhurst.

The criticisms were made in a very frank discussion which took place at Monday's meeting of the NFRDC. So many complaints had been received from householders that the Clerk (Mr Ashford) said the only solution was the establishment of hostels to accommodate the boys and some of the staff, the remainder to be placed in carefully selected billets.

Rear-Admiral HS Currey said that there were 275 boys and 55 (!) masters and staff from Portsmouth in the village. The billeting allowance of 10/6d single and 8/6d for two billets meant a tax or levy of £10-£15 a week on the householders, which at the end of the year meant that Brockenhurst residents would pay £500 over and above ordinary rates and taxes, yet the parents of the evacuees were so wealthy that they could buy and sell the village three times over and not feel it!

74

Continuing, Admiral Currey said that many elderly householders had broken down physically and mentally under the strain of looking after these children, and no fewer than 35 medical certificates had been received from people who had broken down under the strain. 'It is a scandal!' he declared.

The good Admiral and his associates seem to have got a bit carried away. Mr. May, the headmaster of the County School, took a more sympathetic, and perhaps official, view when he addressed the school prizegiving on 16th March:

. . . the Headmaster remarked that as everyone knew, the Portsmouth Secondary School had been evacuated to Brockenhurst. It was decided some twelve months ago that in the event of evacuation one school should have a long morning and the other a long afternoon. However, because the number of evacuees had been smaller than anticipated it had been possible, by using both buildings, to resume their full-time programmes of work, and they were now at full pressure.

"I need not tell you," continued Mr May, "what a blow it was to have to share our new building with another school, but any sacrifice we made has been made gladly, and the two schools have worked together without the slightest friction. Further, any sacrifice we have made has been small compared to that by Mr Jones, his staff, and his pupils from Portsmouth."

(For a Portsmouth boy's own account see Alec Purkis page 70)

In the old school they had had 320 pupils, but by reason of private evacuation from other schools they now had 390. (The Portsmouth Secondary School boys, of course, were not enrolled in Brockenhurst school and are not included in these figures.)

It was reported that many evacuees in the area went home for Easter, and caused heavy railway traffic when they returned.

The winter had been very cold, with over 20 degrees of frost recorded, and the Ministry of Mines waited until April to increase the coal ration from 4 cwt to a maximum of 5 cwt a fortnight! But even so these were maxima, not a guaranteed ration, and coal merchants were asked to 'distribute their stocks fairly between customers'.

In April the New Forest Agricultural Society suspended their annual show, and halved the subscriptions, and would consider a further reduction in a year's time 'if the war still lasts' – the First World War 'over-by-Christmas' syndrome was obviously still around! The Horticultural Society also decided not to hold a show in 1940, though this seems to have been due to their difficult financial situation as much as to the war – the 1939 Show had made a loss, and the number of subscriptions was down.

However, the WI was thriving, and the Brockenhurst Group of

nine Institutes held its 19th exhibition on 24th April, although the number of entries (650) was down on the 1939 total of 800. This was stated to be due to the deletion of some classes. In those days there were numerous classes for children, including one for needlework for the girls at the County School.

During this period one or two news items of local personalities appeared. The decapitated body of Mr JP Corkill, the 39-year-old proprietor of Careys Manor Hotel was found on the railway line in February – it was thought he was suffering from concussion after an earlier road accident when he skidded on some ice.

It had also been reported in January that Brockenhurst had nearly 100 names on its Roll of Active Serving Men in HM Forces, and that this Roll was read out periodically in church.

But at the beginning of May (the same weekend that 26-year-olds registered for military service), the Germans invaded Holland, Belgium, and France, and the 'Phoney War' was at an end; from now on it was to be the real thing.

A certain amount of panic set in . . . the paper had to warn that householders who received evacuee schoolchildren without the sanction of the Billeting Officer would not get the Government allowance, and that children arriving from Southampton were not sent with the approval of the Southampton Education Committee.

By 18th May it was reported that there had been a 'magnificent response' to Anthony Eden's radio appeal the previous Tuesday for enrolment in the new Civil Defence Corps to deal with enemy parachutists (in contrast to the poor response in peace-time to the propsed TA National Defence Companies). There had been 61 enrolments in Brockenhurst and 206 in Lymington, more than could be immediately used. This organisation was soon renamed Local Defence Volunteers (LDV) and then (by mid-July) the Home Guard.

At the same time Capt Sutton proposed a 'Pony Corps' to patrol the New Forest – he pointed out how impossible it was to cover the area by road or on foot – and he got a number of volunteers for this enterprise, which was commended by the LDV commander for the New Forest area, Brigadier Francis.

By 25th May Parliament had passed legislation 'giving the Government complete control over every person and all property in the country, and enabling it to direct any person to perform any service required . . .'. But in the same same issue of the paper Keeping's Garage was still running its pre-war advertisement for new Morris cars – total war was taking a little time to sink in!

The paper was restricted in mentioning wartime movements of forces and civilian personnel, but it was reported that 50 Newfoundland lumberjacks 'working near Brockenhurst' (they were actually camped at Pignal Hill enclosure) were entertained to a meal by Sway WI, and by the autumn Capt Sutton was arranging weekly concerts for them and 'others brought into our midst'.

In June the Brockenhurst County School held its 29th annual sports. The Headmaster asked parents whether it was right for the school to continue to run outside activities, or whether they should abandon them for the duration ('cries of No, No'). Encouraged by this response extracts from plays and opera (Dido and Aeneas) were publicly performed by the children on 24th and 25th July, and a carol service was given at Christmas.

On 29th June Southampton was bombed ('according to the German High Command' – the paper was not allowed to state facts but could quote enemy allegations), and arrangements were made throughout the country for parents to sign forms for their children to be evacuated overseas for the remainder of the war. 90 enquiries were received at Brockenhurst County School and 35-40 forms were filled in; 17 children were undergoing medical tests by the beginning of July. (These figures would refer to the whole New Forest catchment area of course, not just the village.)

At the end of July the Government announced the formation of Voluntary Information Committees formed of local bigwigs 'to listen to what you say'. A meeting was held in Brockenhurst on 20th July to discuss measures for 'improving and maintaining the morale of the population, and reporting on and correcting rumours, etc'. There was a storm of protest both in the local and national press at this ill-founded intitiative, and its 'committees of snoopers and sneaks'. In an attempt to improve public relations these committees were renamed the Home Front League, and they held a number of public meetings during the autumn, but criticism continued.

Meanwhile it was not only cities like Southampton that were being attacked from the air. There had been a number of cases during the summer of Brockenhurst people being summoned for breaking the blackout with their garden bonfires, and those who thought such prosecutions unreasonable must have received a nasty shock, for on 17th August the *Lymington Times* reported:

Nine bombs fell on a South Coast village in the early hours of Wednesday morning (14th); they all fell more or less in a straight line within 440 yards but no-one was injured!

One damaged the central section of a British Legion timber-built hut, and another shattered the front of a baker's shop.

The British Legion steward (Mr R Hardiman), who was sleeping in the club, had a remarkable escape, for although the force of the explosion threw him out of bed on to the floor, and brought a pair of antlers which were nailed to the wall above down on top of him, he escaped unharmed. The bomb demolished the centre of the hut and made a hole about 16 feet across, and almost as many deep, in the foundations, but left undamaged a couple of billiard tables standing on one side of the crater and the bar on the further side of it. About £30 of the stock of this was lost however due to the bottles crashing to the ground.

Mr KJ Martin (the chemist) a member of the AFS on duty close to the hut at the time the bomb fell, said that it was a whistling one. He listened to its shriek, wondering where it would fall.

He immediately glanced at the building, and saw that the line of the roof, as seen against the sky, was incomplete in the middle. 'The club's in two halves!' he shouted to his mate, and ran across to the section where he knew Mr Hardiman was sleeping. To his relief he found him shaken but uninjured.

Children Very Calm

The occupants of the baker's establishment had an even more remarkable escape, for the whole front of the building was torn away. The owner Mr R Purkess, and his wife were sleeping in one back room and two little daughters aged 10 and 8 in another.

"I heard a terrific crash and knew that part of the house had gone," said Mr Purkess, "and without waiting to dress we ran into my little girls' room and found them sitting up in bed wondering what had happened but very calm and not crying at all. We hurried them down the stairs in the front of the house – the treads were all covered in debris – and then I went back for clothes for them.

"Then I went into the house and opened a door towards the front part to get my telephone but found the way blocked with debris, and someone from outside shouted to me to come no further. The children finished the night in their grandmother's opposite."

Another inhabitant of the village who was undismayed by Jerry's visit was Joey, a twelve-year-old canary belonging to Mrs Pitt who was away from home at the time. Joey was found in the morning after the raid hopping about in his overturned cage on the floor of one of the rooms of the vacated house. Ten feet from the wall on which his cage had been hanging was a bomb-crater 12 feet across, but apart from causing Joey's fall it had only brought down some plaster in the house and cracked one pane of glass.

"Joey started to sing again a few hours later," commented Mrs Sanger the caretaker, "and he doesn't seem to have been unduly disturbed by the incident!"

One of the bombs burst a water main, but the damage was quickly repaired, and another fell in a doctor's garden. A surprising feature was the minor amount of glass broken.

(Personal accounts of Brockenhurst's air raids
are in the Brockenhurst Bred section)

The Brockenhurst raid was followed by a much more serious one in daylight a week later (23rd August) on a 'South Coast town', identifiable in photos as New Milton, and sporadic attacks followed night after night on villages in the area which cannot be identified from the newspaper reports. On the night of 17th November in particular there were a number of local incidents, and: '. . . some HE bombs were dropped near a house called Hincheslea, and an incendiary bomb came through the roof and ceilings. Many windows of the house were broken.'

In the last edition of the year, on 28th December, the *Lymington Times* reported on Brockenhurst Parish Council: Chit-Chat and Minor Dissension Must Stop – Rear-Admiral Currey speaks out at Brockenhurst. Mr Fields-Clarke had tendered his resignation to the NFRDC as Head Warden (again!) owing to controversy over providing a siren in the village. He was not in favour of a siren, but understood that a petition with 900 signatures asked for an audible system of air-raid warning. If Brockenhurst wanted a siren he would not stand in the way, but he resented criticism of himself.

The Chairman, Admiral Currey, said he thought criticism of Mr Fields-Clarke was most unfair. The ARP organisation in the parish had complete confidence in him, and most of the critics were people who had not taken the slightest trouble to assist in ARP work. The Parish Council then unanimously passed a vote of confidence in Mr Fields-Clarke and asked him to retain his post.

But two or three months later it was reported that Mr Fields-Clarke had finally resigned on the grounds of ill-health and Lt-Col WH Samuel was now Acting Head ARP Warden for Brockenhurst. He was officially appointed as Head Warden in June 1941.

BROCKENHURST NOTES – JOHN PURKESS

June – Two dugouts were constructed in Black Bridge field overlooking the main road to defend the village from advancing enemy from Lymington. One can still be seen.

August 13/14 around 3 am The first bombs.

One either side of the field, now the site of Gates 'new' garage, one falling alongside the 'old' garage damaging it.

The next outside the conservatory of Wide Lane Cottage, raising it an angle of about 30 degrees.

Next was down the front of Purkess's Bakery shop. Reg Purkess met Mr. Stevens, the printer, on his way down to inspect the damage about 4 in the morning and arranged for the notice to be printed: 'DON'T LET HITLER SPOIL YOUR APPETITE, BREAD & CAKES

BEFORE WE GO

FROM THE DAILY EXPRESS, AUGUST 15, 1940.

Cakes today as usual, says bombed baker

W *HILE British fighters played Old Harry with Nazi raiders in the air yesterday, things were also happening on the ground below. Here are some of the things that happened. Here, too, are other stories, ranging from the heroic to the comic, but all expressing the thumbs-up spirit of Britain in a blitzkrieg.*

A SOUTH-EAST village baker was wakened earlier than usual and found that a bomb outside the shop had blown in his front window.

First thing he did was to persuade his wife to go to sleep again.

Second thing he did was to scrawl a big notice: " Don't let Hitler spoil your appetite. Bread and cakes as usual "— and stick it in front of his shop.

Then he got on with his usual day's baking.

Expected to starve

A YOUNG Nazi airman woke up in a south coast hospital after his crash. Presently he was brought a meal—generous helpings of fish freshly caught in the Channel, potatoes, greens, butter, fresh fruit and cream.

He goggled in amazement as the loaded tray was put in front of him. " But why are you so kind ? " he asked. " You give me all this food when you have no food yourselfs ! "

Swim to England

STORY told yesterday of the last moments in troopship Mahomed Ali El-Kebir, sunk by a U-boat a few days ago:—

When all the rafts and boats had gone, thirty officers and men remained on board. They were wondering what to do. A naval petty officer said: " Come on, mates, there'll always be an England. Let's swim to it."

With that he dived into the Atlantic. Others followed, and were picked up by England's warships.

Necklace

THE steward at a British Legion club in the south-east of England was asleep when a bomb fell

SHARE YOUR AIR RAID STORIES

SHARE your air raid experiences with the other readers of the Daily Express.

Send us your stories of stoicism, humour, and adventure during the siren hours.

Tell us how you are facing up to the threat of bombs ; what your life in the new front line is like.

Address your letters to
Thumbs Up,
Daily Express,
Fleet-street, London, E.C.4.

through the roof. He found himself sprawled on the wreckage of the bed. A pair of antlers hanging on the wall had fallen round his neck. Otherwise he was unhurt.

No yellow canary

OBSERVED : Two captured Nazi airmen eagerly reading English newspaper accounts of the battle. . . . A taxi-driver stopping his cab to pick up two beetroots flung into the road by a bomb. . . . A canary in an overturned cage, seven feet from a bomb crater, singing like mad.

Baronet-M.P. fined for showing a light

Sir Percy Harris, Liberal M.P. for South-West Bethnal Green, was fined £5 at Acton, W., yesterday, for allowing a light to be seen in the black-out at his home, Morton House, Chiswick-mall, W.

Police Constable Perry, of the Thames Police, said that the light could be seen a mile away

80

MR PURKESS'S BAKERY DEVASTATED BY A BOMB, AUGUST 15, 1940.

AS USUAL'. These were produced and were on sale at the usual time in the grocery shop. How heartbreaking for youngsters seeing the workmen shovel piles of sweets, from the broken jars, into the crater. Illegal photographs exist of the damage, the policeman on duty having been lured to the back and provided with some refreshment, whilst Mr JW Martin used his camera.

The British Legion Hall received the next hit, right in the middle. The steward was sleeping there at the time.

Another bomb fell near Careys Cottages.

November 30/December 1 – A number of bombed out families from Southampton came down by train and were accommodated in the Wesleyan Schoolroom in Avenue Road before alternative accommodation could be found.

Lumberjacks from Newfoundland came to work in the Forest and they built a traditional North American Log Cabin Camp on the road leading to the Victoria Tilery. There is a hut there now, but not one of the original cabins. Unfortunately some were destroyed by fire after the war, when it was used by youth organisations.

Our forces retreated from Dunkirk in May. Vivid memories of that time from John Woollett are in Chapter 7, but COLIN TOWNSEND-ROSE recalls a local legend:

A whole lot of troops were turfed off the train at Brockenhurst. Miss Bowden-Smith, who was living at the Thatched Cottage, declared that she would give tea to each of the several hundred troops who had been evacuated from Dunkirk. Without help, she did just that. She was pouring tea continuously for hours. When she finished she had the same amount of tea as she had when she began. At the time this was called a miracle.

Her mother, old Mrs Bowden-Smith, had an ear trumpet. She sat in front of our family at St Nicholas Church and sometimes got me to speak to her. I was terrified. At Careys Manor, where she lived, there was always a smell of burnt feathers on the top floor. I was told that it was caused by Mrs Bowden-Smith going up to inspect the maids' bedrooms with her ear trumpet held by one hand and her candle in the other hand, and she couldn't avoid causing minor fires in the bedding. It is said that she haunts part of Careys Manor.

By August, the Battle of Britain had begun. The village school had no air-raid shelter at the time, so when the siren went, the pupils were told to go straight home. One village boy, TERRY WINGATE, remembers:

Having been sent home, I became aware of our neighbour, Mr Spencer of garage fame, gazing skywards shouting imprecations. On looking up I saw a ME 109 with a Spitfire on his tail, turning furiously in and out of a small white cloud. The turning circle of both planes was about the same. There were short staccato bursts from the machine-gun fire from the Spitfire but he couldn't nail him. As I watched I was well aware they were spiralling directly down to us at every turn. The adrenalin was really pumping through us and both of us oblivious of any danger. Finally the 109 was left with no choice, he either had to make a break for it for home or crash. He chose home, going straight across the green like a scalded cat and across the grammar school playing fields with the Spitfire jockeying on his tail.

Unfortunately all good things have to come to an end – some kind of benefactor had an air-raid shelter built at the school and we had to sit in a dungeon-like gloom until the air-raid was over.

BOMBS IN BROCKENHURST AREA

It was not only the big towns which were attacked. Extra care was taken to enforce the blackout, with several people from Brockenhurst being summoned for not extinguishing their bonfires properly at night.

Even so, nine bombs fell on or near the village on the night of August 14. Amazingly no one was hurt that time. In occasional raids later, there were some casualties though accounts vary as to how many exactly, and certainly Jean Gentle of Woodlands Road, was killed.

Not surprisingly, most people living here at the time can remember where most of the bombs fell on Brockenhurst and have their own tales to tell.

ARTHUR STEVENS gives the following list: One at the bottom of Careys Cottages, this was a 500-pounder and never went off; another in a garden in Fathersfield; one fell on top of the British Legion Club which was where Brookely Court is now. The next one fell right on top of Stan Purkess's house which was where the shop's car park is and another fell where Gates workshop area car park is now. Then, one on the big house called the Briars at the corner of Avenue Road and Sway Road on the left towards the junction killed two people; another in this area fell on or near the railway. All of these never caused any fire.

JOHN PURKESS adds his boy's eye view to his earlier account:

Before the siren arrived in Brockenhurst around 1941 or 1942 the school was phoned from the Morant Hall in Lyndhurst Road (behind the now Balmer Lawn Garage) and the air-raid warning given to us by a prefect.

My uncle was Air-Raid Warden for Brookely Road. Before the siren was put up near the Hall all wardens carried whistles and bells to announce warnings and all clears. One warden, John Larkin, used to go round with a long bean pole, tapping on the windows of houses and shouting, "Raid!". My mother was often on call opposite a lady who had no phone. So when the phone call from the manual exchange came announcing the all clear my mother would run over and tell her and they'd both rush down to the First Aid Post at the Morant Hall, which the lady ran.

When our Bakery was destroyed and my uncle was in charge of the shop, there was an evacuee who was living with us for safety; fortunately he was away for a week in Portsmouth! My uncle's family were unharmed sleeping in the back bedrooms. On December 1, 1940 loads of refugees bombed out in Southampton arrived and were put up at the Methodist Hall.

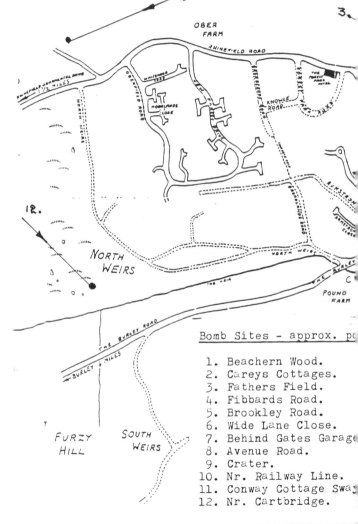

Bomb Sites - approx. p(

1. Beachern Wood.
2. Careys Cottages.
3. Fathers Field.
4. Fibbards Road.
5. Brookley Road.
6. Wide Lane Close.
7. Behind Gates Garage
8. Avenue Road.
9. Crater.
10. Nr. Railway Line.
11. Conway Cottage Sway
12. Nr. Cartbridge.

MAP SHOWING WH

BROCKENHURST AT WAR 1938-1945

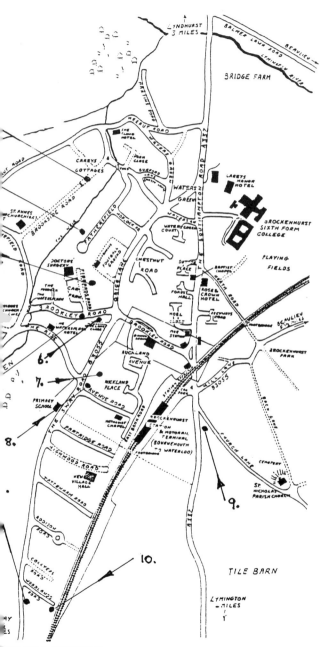

BS FELL LOCALLY

Mr Lodge, the foreman shunter, told us they were taking shelter under the railway wagons during one raid. When the German planes had gone, he looked at the labels on the wagon. They were marked 'Danger – Ammunition'!

As a boy of ten I remember often watching Southampton being blitzed. On one occasion I saw from my bedroom window a raider being hit and coming down in flames near Dilton Farm, Roydon way. From Black Bridge we saw planes going over to bomb New Milton.

JACK HANSON recalls one of the raids:

While I was working at the Foresters we had a stick of bombs. On another occasion we spent one night in our air-raid shelter when we thought they were bombing Wellworthy. In fact they gave Shirley Holms a hell of a pounding. The planes probably followed the railway line hoping to hit Wellworthy's munitions factory.

JUNE DRAYSON recalls just two of the raids:

This sounds awful, but it really was most amusing at the time. There was the baker, if I remember right, woke up to find he had dropped from the top floor to the bottom. The house had been hit in such a fashion that when they woke up they found themselves below. No one was killed, though later the bomb at the station did kill two families who were there to meet their husbands and fathers who came home to find them obliterated – very sad. I remember singing in the choir at St Saviours Church for the funeral of one of those killed.

COLIN TOWNSEND-ROSE living as a boy at Little Prescotts:

A bomb landed on Wide Lane Cottage; although the crater was six-feet from the Conservatory, yet only one pane was cracked. The house was split in two. Another bomb landed on a cottage in Sway Road and two old ladies were killed. During that night I slept under the dining room table.

One period I remember is what seemed continuous air raids. Lots of bombs were dropped over Shirley Holms. One landed on a cottage and one car was blown by bomb blast onto another one in the garage. They caught fire and more of the cottage was destroyed. When it was rebuilt it was named Phoenix Cottage. My mother used to work part-time at the ambulance station and she was kept busy.

Other local bombs I remember were three very near the level crossing gates, leaving two craters and one unexploded bomb. In 1944 there were also two flying bombs. One landed on Whitefield Moor near Puttles Bridge; the other one north of New Park, four hundred yards from the A337. I collected, so I rushed over there and found the tail piece of the flying bomb which I was going to carry home on my bike. Unfortunately the village policeman arrived and took it from me.

The biggest bomb round here was a high explosive which made a forty-foot-wide crater on the left of Rhinefield Road just before the A35.

Incendiary bombs landed in Wilverley Enclosure; the fires got into the peat and smouldered for over two weeks.

Three bombs landed at Mowlams Mead and I filled my saddle bag with shrapnel.

A number of the lads used to go in search of pieces of shrapnel and souvenirs from planes that were shot down. DAVID CHAMBERLAIN felt that during the war everything seemed to happen on a Saturday or Sunday morning:

We would get on our bicycles and go to the scene of the various crashes. We used to go round to collect the perspex from which you could make brooches and things.

One boy is remembered by BRIAN PLUMLEY because he had a knack for 'finding things':

Once he and I went up by Aldridge Hill. There was a load of little stunted fir trees, Scots Pine, I think. He used to look along there and see where the branches were broken off, dig down in the ground and find an incendiary bomb intact. Round the bottom of them was a piece of tape about two inches up. If you pulled the tape off there was a row of holes and you could put a bar in the hole and you could carefully undo them and take out the percussion caps. Fred's father was a blacksmith. He had an anvil. We put several of these caps on the anvil and hit them with a sledge hammer. The sledge hammer went up in the air! We all ran and there was a cloud of smoke everywhere. Everyone came out of their houses. We were told not to do it again! There were quite a few dropped around in the Forest. Nearly everybody in Brockenhurst had an incendiary bomb as a door stop!

(A map showing where the Brockenhurst bombs fell is on Pages 84-85.)

THE FIRE BRIGADE IN BROCKENHURST

JACK HANSON, *a vital member of the Brigade, tells of his early life and how he became involved:*

I was born in Romsey in 1910. In 1920 my father, who had worked for the brewery became the landlord of the Railway Inn (now the Snakecatcher) and we moved to Brockenhurst.

On leaving Brockenhurst Village School at fourteen, I worked on the family farm, rented from the Cadland family at Fawley.

When my father died in 1933, I had to leave the farm and, as my father had done, became a publican; first at the Railway Inn, and when we found it too big, we moved to the Foresters.

A lot of the Territorials from Beaulieu Camp used to come to us for beer and sandwiches. They were hungry I can tell you. That was a busy time.

In 1938, when I was twenty eight, I joined the Brockenhurst Fire Brigade because they were calling for volunteers. My job was to drive the fire engine – given by the Walker-Munros of Rhinefield House, which later was kept here in Fibbards Road along with the two wheel pump trailer. It had a crank handle and you had to keep a lamp under the engine. We learned our fire fighting through practices.

One night in April 1940 we were called out to a fire at Southampton, where the German planes were bombing the waterfront. We were sent to Dibden Church which was ablaze. But there was no water; the water mains had been damaged. We just had to watch it burn. If we had had our trailer pump then we could have helped, but we didn't get one till later. Soon afterwards the Fire Service was moved to Lyndhurst.

The other Fire Service members, all friends, were: Harold Head, Ted Hayward, Ken Martin, Gus Plumley, Arthur Stevens.

The Fire Service was not called out for the air-raids over Brockenhurst because the bombs didn't start fires.

1941

Diary of National and International Events

January	Australians captured Tobruk. Later Benghazi and other North African towns. Germans sent troops to Libya.
March	USA Lend-Lease Bill to help Allies, signed by Roosevelt.
April 6	Germans invaded Greece and Yugoslavia.
May 24	Empire forces withdrew from Greece.
June 2	Clothes rationing began in UK.
22	Germany attacked Russia.
October 16	Soviet Government under Stalin left Moscow to escape Germans.
November 14	Ark Royal sunk.
18	Eighth Army's first offensive in Libya. HMS *Dunedin* and HMS *Barham* sunk.
December 1	Food Points rationing scheme introduced.
6	Japanese attacked Pearl Harbour. Many US ships sunk. USA entered War.

8   Japanese landed in Malaya.
9   Eighth Army freed Tobruk.
10 HMS *Repulse* and *Prince of Wales* sunk by
    Japanese off Malaya.
25 Hong Kong surrendered to Japanese.

THE GATHERING STORM

On the grey Atlantic and in the blue sky over Britain an epic battle
of survival was fought in 1941. The Blitz on London had reached a
new intensity in May with a raid by the German Luftwaffe which left
a third of our capital's streets impassable and 155,000 families without
gas, water or electricity. Sleeping Londoners crowded the platforms
of Underground Stations, while huge conflagrations burned in the
streets above them. And yet by day the battle for supremacy in the
air was being won and at sea, albeit against mounting losses, the vital
convoys of food got through. That spring, Ernest Bevin, Minister for
Labour, announced the call up of women, and in December after the
bombing of Pearl Harbour, America entered the war. The conflict was
now truly global: in Churchill's words, it was "our darkest hour".
And yet theatres kept their doors open, and each Thursday on the
BBC between 8.30 and 9.00 pm there was laughter in the face of
the gathering storm as Mrs Mopp and the immortal Colonel
Chinstrap in Tommy Handley's 'ITMA' entertained the nation. As a
nation we learned to laugh at ourselves and in that humour there was
was determination that nothing the enemy could do would ever
destroy us.

From the *Lymington Times*

On 16th January there were some air attacks in the locality ('on a
South Coast village' – probably not Brockenhurst), and night attacks
along the South Coast took place on 2nd and 11th May. On 25th April
a large number of refugees from bombed towns arrived in the area
late at night, some 171 being accommodated at Rest Centres in the
Borough of Lymington alone. But thereafter enemy air raids gradually became more desultory and months often went by without any
local attacks being reported. An Air Training Corps was founded at
the County School, a flight of 50 boys being inaugurated on 8th
March of whom about half were Portsmouth lads.

And at the school annual prize-giving in March the Headmaster
said that 'a year ago one-and-a-half acres of ground in front of the
school were ploughed up, and four acres since, and the pupils will

by their own efforts keep themselves and the Portsmouth School in vegetables all the year round. 450 dinners are served daily . . .'

From Lady Day gas went up by 1d a therm to 1/1d, but on the whole inflation was kept fairly well in check during these war years.

During May a War Weapons Week was held nationally. Lymington held its Week at the beginning of May, but the Forest villages held theirs beginning on Saturday 17th May, and the paper was able to give unaccustomed coverage to this as the excitement in the Borough was finished.

The NFRDC area aimed to raise £150,000 (a figure equivalent to some £7,000,000 today), but each village had to determine its own target. Brockenhurst's official target of £20,000 was less than £7 a head but Mr May (the County School Headmaster, speaking for the village committee) said they aimed to beat this. The paper said Brockenhurst was 'fired with enthusiasm to beat Lymington's figure of £15 8s 0d per head'.

A full programme of events was organised in Brockenhurst throughout the week, with a procession, a big dance at the Morant Hall on the Saturday evening, and a cabaret and concert on the Wednesday evening including the 'Moderniques' dance band. There was a packed audience of 600 people, with many others unable to gain admission.

But alas, all was in vain. Although Brockenhurst led in the earlier days, by the end of the week Lyndhurst had achieved a total of £58,121 against Brockenhurst's £46,702, and was congratulated by Capt Sutton on a 'capital' result. Brockenhurst had certainly hit its target of beating Lymington on a per capita basis, having raised £15 11s 0d per head, but came only third in the New Forest after Lyndhurst and Minstead.

Also at the end of July Colonel Hamersley appealed for men to join the Home Guard. He pointed out that no inducement had been needed at the time it was formed, but response must have been poor, as in the end a form of conscription had to be introduced.

On 16th August a heinous crime hit Brockenhurst, when three-farthings (about 0.3p.) was stolen from the St Nicholas offertory box by a 20-year-old soldier from the Royal Warwickshire Regiment who broke into the church. Mr Jenvey, the sexton, had emptied the box the previous night but left a halfpenny and a farthing in it. The soldier was unfortunate enough to be charged with Sacrilege, 'a most serious crime in the eyes of the law' according to the Recorder, and was sentenced to seven months imprisonment (!) for this and the 'less serious offences' of stealing a pair of overalls and a jacket from New Park and the Morant Hall.

But the military had in mind better ways of employing soldiers'

WAR WEAPONS WEEK.   BROCKENHURST.
MAY 17TH—24TH, 1941.

OFFICIAL PROGRAMME OF EVENTS.

17th, Saturday.	11 a.m.	**Opening Ceremony** at Morant Hall. Speakers—Colonel J. D. Mills, M.P., Colonel V. W. Roche. Followed by a **Military Display** in the Car Park and a **PROCESSION** through the village.
	2.30 p.m.	**Cricket Match**—Brockenhurst v. Army.
	7.30 p.m.	**Grand Dance, Morant Hall**—Moderniques Band. Prizes 4 War Saving Certificates. Entrance 2/6.
18th, Sunday.	11 a.m.	**United Service** at the **Parish Church.**
19th, Monday.	8 p.m.	**Special Boxing Exhibition** at **Morant Hall.** Tickets 3/-, 2/-, 1/-. *(by permission of A.B.A.)*
20th, Tuesday	6 to 9 p.m.	**Table Tennis** (Knock-out) **Competition** at the **New Forest Club.** Entries 6d. to be made before 6 p.m. at the Estate Offices or at the Club.
21st, Wednesday.	2.30 p.m.	**Whist Drive** at **New Forest Club.** Entrance 1/-
	8.0 p.m.	**GRAND CONCERT & CABARET.** at **Morant Hall.** Stage Band, Community Singing, Songs, Tap Dancing, Pipers, Comic Sketch, etc. Entrance 3/-, 2/- 1/-. *The War Weapons Week Draw will be made during the evening.*
22nd, Thursday.		**All day Golf Competition** (Open) at **Brokenhurst Manor Golf Club—PUTTING IN GAS MASKS.** Entrance 6d. Prizes-War Savings Stamps, etc.
	7.30 p.m.	**Whist Drive** at **Morant Hall.** Entrance-1/3d. Prizes
23rd, Friday.	6.15 & 8.15 p.m.	**Cinema** at **Morant Hall**-" Oh Mr. Porter " (Will Hay), Mickey Mouse, etc. 6.15 p.m.—Entrance 1/-, children 6d. 8.15 p.m.—Entrance 2/-, 1/-, 6d.
24th, Saturday.	2-5 p.m.	**Children's Sports** at **County High School.** An array of Sideshows. Entrance—Adults 3d., Pupils 1d.
	8 p.m.	**Special Dance** at **Morant Hall**—Moderniques Band. Entrance 2/6. Prizes—4 War Savings Certificates.

During the whole week there will be an Open Golf Competition at Brokenhurst Manor Golf Club.   Entrance 1/- a Card.

All profits on Entertainments during the Week will be invested in Government Securities for the Brockenhurst Nursing   Association.

91

spare time, and a letter in the paper in August said a Royal Artillery unit would appreciate football and hockey fixtures. And on 4th October the Army Welfare Officer, West Hants, wrote thanking people for games for the troops, 'especially Mr Tiller in Brockenhurst and Mr Wakefield in Ashley and the pupils in their respective schools'.

Earlier in the year Alderman Marshall, on Lymington Council, complained that 'new railings had been erected around the Secondary School at Brockenhurst', and Councillor Stubbs (who was in fact Chairman of Governors of the school) explained that these were not new railings 'but had been collected from hedges around the school' (as if they were rosehips or blackberries?). However, by October an NFRDC advertisement appeared requisitioning all iron railings, posts, bollards, gates, etc, which were not of special artistic merit or historical interest.

On the 16th August an advertisement by the Borough appeared in the *Lymington Times* seeking accommodation for 70 secondary schoolboys aged twelve to sixteen in Lymington town – 'the usual government allowances would be payable'. And on 6th September the paper announced:

70 scholarship boys who will attend the evacuated Portsmouth Secondary School at Brockenhurst arrived in Lymington on the 4.15 pm train on Tuesday . . . billets were found for them all. They were welcomed by the Mayor and the Scout District Commissioner.

On Tuesday 23rd September Field Marshal Sir Cyril Deverell visited Brockenhurst County School and inspected the ATC (there was as yet no Army Cadet Force at the school). The boys were being trained in signalling by Major PB Allott (retired), who was also Lymington's Deputy ARP Officer, and they 'would shortly be attached to the Home Guard and were to establish a complete system of communication along the coast from Southampton to Bournemouth.'

But not everybody was happy with the way in which schoolchildren were being instructed. At the New Forest Conservative Association meeting in Brockenhurst in October Mrs Goodenough asked 'whether it was not a fact that a great many school teachers were putting socialistic ideas into the heads of their pupils'. The chairman replied soothingly that he did not think that in this area there was much of that kind of left-wing propaganda.

The very successful Points Rationing scheme started on 17th November – 'you can buy tinned foods from any retailer, whether registered with him or not' said the local paper.

There were signs that as the war progressed bureaucracy was tightening its hold on the country. This was to become even more obvious the following year, but in November 'fines amounting to £5 and £4 0s 6d costs were imposed on Miss Ethel Cumberbatch, aged 80, of Black Knoll, Brockenhurst for selling butter without a licence, failing to cancel coupons, and for selling cream.' The goods had been sold to employees and to a friend, Mrs. Baring of Beachern Wood. Miss Cumberbatch had always done this, and it was difficult to get her to understand the new regulations – it was admitted that as she was not a trader she would not have received the leaflets about this.

At the beginning of December there was an unfortunate accident on the main Brockenhurst-Lymington road 'near St. Austins', when an Army lorry overturned and two RA soldiers were killed, 14 others being thrown out of the truck and injured in varying degrees.

And the year ended with Brockenhurst High School Carol Service on the 18th December in which the school choir of 80 was augmented by staff and members of Lymington Parish Church choir, and a total of 500 pupils and parents sang.

BROCKENHURST NOTES – JOHN PURKESS

Shelters were built alongside the Church of England school on two sides, the South and West. Most pupils were disappointed that they were not constructed underground, the floor being no more than 30 inches below ground. We used to sit in there during raids, complete with gas mask, and had some sort of lessons or sang community songs. We were all instructed to have a block of chocolate in our gas mask box for refreshment if we were detained at school long after hours. We were only allowed home during a raid if a parent came and collected us.

The prisoner of war camp was built at Setley, about quarter of a mile south, on the opposite side of the road to the Oddfellows Inn (The Filley). It was home to Italian prisoners to start with, who used to work in the Forest and were moved in open trucks, about twenty prisoners with one guard. There did not seem to be reports of any escaping. Later, after D-Day, German prisoners were there.

To increase food production the War Agricultural Committee set up a depot at Hollands Wood and proceeded to clear large areas of the Forest Lawns for food production. Before they started, the areas of Black Knoll, Whitmoor, Longslade Bottom and Wilverley Plain were all covered in gorse. These were cleared and ploughed and produced large quantities of potatoes and other crops.

Allocations of drinking chocolate and milk powder were given to children. We all went down to the supper room in the Morant Hall to collect our share.

An air-raid siren was installed behind Morant Hall.

Canadian troops billeted at the Balmer Lawn and Careys Manor gave a Christmas party in the County School hall for all the children of Brockenhurst.

BROCKENHURST HOME GUARD

The Local Defence Volunteers (LDV) was inaugurated by Anthony Eden, the War Minister, in May 1940. It was to supplement the relatively few and desperately over-stretched regular troops. Two months later the name was changed to the Home Guard. There was no pay apart from travelling allowances. The original equipment consisted of a rifle, bayonet, steel helmet and arm-band. By the summer of 1943, men could be compulsorily directed to the Home Guard, which grew to nearly two million. It was disbanded on December 31, 1945.

STANLEY PORTER recalls that in 1942 there were 102 members of the local Home Guard.

How like Dad's Army was it? Some we interviewed said it was; others disagreed vehemently. Below are three representative views.

JACK BLANDFORD, father in law of Iain Hayter:

At the beginning of the war I was forty-three but was declared unfit for the army. At the time, and for eleven years altogether, I was working for Dr Freeland, the local GP in his house, Harting. He had no electricity, telephone or mains water supply.

Because I couldn't join up, I became an Air-Raid Warden which had priority over all my other duties and took up a lot of time.

Later I joined the Home Guard and was a 'full blown private' throughout. But the Home Guard also took up a lot of time. Every Sunday morning we had to parade at the Morant Hall, perhaps for a few hours and sometimes we had rifle practice (we got rifles provided by the Americans) or grenade practice on Hincheslea. Oh yes, other times we had skirmishes (exercises) with the Marines stationed at Balmer Lawn. They fired live ammunition at us from 100 yards but because their sights were set at 600 yards, the bullets went over our heads!

'Dad's Army', the BBC programme, makes me wild. It wasn't a game. They're poking fun at something that was serious.

The Home Guard had to be there for any occasion whether, at the beginning of the war, it was to search for enemy parachutists, or to support the army.

WALLY KNOTT had a different view. He was in the Railway Home Guard:

A few months before the Second World War was declared I received a letter saying that in the event of war you will not be called up for the army as your job is of national importance. Things like that makes you think, so I thinks to myself. I do's this and do's that, what more can I do for my country? That's why when the time came I joined the Home Guard, ended up a corporal and doing four years in all. We were trained by army officers, Sergeant-Majors from the Royal Marines, Pompey, in drill. Also in armed and unarmed combat. Us Home Guard from Brockenhurst railway got the signal and telegraph department to make up from signal pieces a moving target which bobbed up and down. We practised firing at it. All this practice took place in what we termed the old turntable turn out: our training was mainly at weekends, using the school playgrounds.

One particular night we set off and marched down the Sway Road. It began to snow pretty heavy and we carried on to the junction and turned left to get onto the moor. We were to have another talk on hand grenades and practice throwing. The prisoner-of-war camp was there on Setley Plain, the chap in charge of us said, "Hark at them enjoying themselves. Here are we after a hard day's work out in the bloody cold. Let's shake the buggers up." So six of us had to get out our grenades, told not to forget our drill, prepare ourselves, show, pull, throw and down – bang! bang! bang! – all the camp lights went out and the camp silent. Our instructor said, "Don't forget what I told you. There is only one good German and that's a dead un!"

Another evening, having finished our training we were marching down the road getting near the Morant Hall, I could see some army officers. So I said, "Look out lads, march to attention!" And on passing them did the right drill very smartly, eyes right, etc. There was Eisenhower, so we were told afterwards. The next night I think it was, Mr Fenner said he had a letter congratulating the Home Guard on its smart and efficient turnout, signed Eisenhower.

One morning I was up early getting ready for work to start at Bournemouth when I heard a low-flying plane. Opening the back door I saw a German plane very low flying over. I could have easily shot it down with my sten gun. Glad I didn't try for I wasn't supposed to keep live ammunition at home.

Some time just prior to that day, a bomb had dropped next door, halfway down the gardens of 18 and 19, making a hole 15 feet diameter and about 3 feet deep. Nothing grew there again for a long time.

MARGARET EVANS suggests that sometimes the local Home Guard made the television programme look authentic:

I remember one story. There were few cars on the road and those that were, especially after dark, would be challenged. A particular Home Guard gentleman, equipped with a rifle and torch, stopped a car one night and asked for the driver's identity. In order to take the Identity Card he asked the driver to hold the rifle while he took the card and examined it!

The village was, of course, in total blackout with no street lights or lights from houses. This led, on occasions, to Home Guard members challenging cows and horses!

A PLANE CRASH – Raider shot down at Pilley

On the night of the 7th/8th July during a raid on Southampton, a small number of enemy aircraft were shot down, one of which, a Heinkel HE111H-5, from 3/KG28, came to ground at Slade Farm, Pilley. The beginning of the end for this plane began at Middle Wallop when at 2345 hrs on Monday, 7th July, Beaufighter, B2143 of 604 Squadron, took off with Flying Officer Crew at the controls, and Flight Sergeant Guthrie on the radar. When they attacked the Heinkel its entire tail section sheared off causing the aircraft to enter a flat spin. On hitting the ground the wreck caught fire and burnt fiercely. The aircraft was works number 3992 and crashed at 0135 hrs on Tuesday morning. The Beaufighter had returned to Middle Wallop by 0240 hrs on Tuesday.

Of the five crewmen, two were killed in the crash while three managed to bail out. Two of the parachutists were taken prisoner by soldiers manning the searchlight post at Crockford Clump. Although the remaining crewman's bloodstained parachute had been found about 1½ miles away from the crash site near Brockenhurst, it was not until five weeks later that his badly decomposed body was found when Mr Long of Haywards Farm, his brother and his two children, Max and Tony, were clearing ponies from the field when thirteen-year-old Tony came across him. When Tony enquired whether he could have the Luftwaffe wings the airman was wearing, his father told him that you don't rob the dead, implying the use of a little respect. Imagine the anger of the lad when the Men from the Ministry came to take the body and one of the first things they did was remove the wings, using his father's knife.

The tail section was not found until two weeks after the crash and was found by a Frank Drodge, who was indulging in a bit of poaching. He was in the woods near Dilton Farm shaking some

96

BROCKENHURST HOME GUARD, 1942.

small trees when the tail fell down beside him.

When the Air Ministry came to investigate the rest of the aircraft, it was noted that the 7.9 mm tail-gun was missing. A Mr Duplessey from Rodlease House in Boldre, who was in the Home Guard, had removed the gun and ammunition for the Home Guard use as they did not have a machine gun at the time. The police then began to search for the gun and it was as if they had an idea who had it as often they would come and visit. Once they were even treated to a cup of tea on the sofa while the gun was lying underneath them. The gun was kept for about a year when it was returned to the Air Ministry.

Two lads who indulged in souvenir collecting at the time even made some cash out of it. Before the tail was removed one of the swastikas was hacked off and hidden in some furze bushes, by Tony Long and Bob Berry, who also had the tail wheel. Later in the war, while talking with a US Major at the airfield, the lads mentioned their souvenirs and the Major offered to buy the swastika, which he did for half a crown for each lad.

(This article has been written and researched by Richard Reeves, a student – Ed)

1942

Diary of National and International Events

January 2   Japanese took Manila then landed in New Guinea.
February 9   Soap rationed.
15   Singapore surrendered to Japanese.
April 5   George Cross awarded to Malta.
May 30   1,000 bomber raid on Cologne.
Canterbury bombed by Germans.
July 16   RAF's first daylight raid on Ruhr.
August 11   Malta convoy: loss of HMS *Eagle*, *Manchester, Cairo* and one destroyer.
September 6   Germans halted at Stalingrad.
October 23   Allied victory at El Alamein.
Allied offensive in Egypt began.
November   Retreat of Rommel's army.
Russians held out at Stalingrad.
27   Germans entered Toulon.
French fleet scuttled.
December 24   French Admiral Darlan assassinated.

THE CONFLICT SPREADS

In January 1942 the first GIs arrived in Britain from America. Soon they were to be seen in Brockenhurst, though not yet in great numbers. It was the year of Vera Lynn singing 'The White Cliffs of Dover' and of Irving Berlin's 'White Christmas' sung by Bing Crosby. At the same time, in the autumn of the year, the German assault on Russia reached Stalingrad and the long bitter siege of that city began, a siege which was to claim the lives of 750,000 Russians and 400,000 Germans. Such contrasts were, and are, the stuff of war. 'White Cliffs' and 'White Christmas' gave the dreams of peace we all, as Allies, shared: the searing whiteness of the Russian winter, seen in glimpses on the Pathé newsreels at the cinema, gave the actualities of a war now entering its grimmest phase.

From the *Lymington Times*

The year opened with a discussion on wells. The Parish Council had submitted a list of 5 wells in the village to the NFRDC in order to see whether they should be cleaned out at public expense for use in case of emergency. The matter was referred to the Health Committee with executive powers, and they must have decided in favour because at the next meeting Admiral Currey said that heavy rain was liable to cause pollution in these forest wells and the public were advised to boil water for drinking.

In January Dr FW Kenchington, the Assistant Agricultural Officer to the Hampshire War Agricultural Committee, announced plans to convert 20,000 acres of Crown Lands in the New Forest into cattle ranches to support a herd of 10,000 heifers. A Government grant of £5 per acre had been obtained towards a 1,000 acre experiment in the Beaulieu area.

'As to the future Dr Kenchington declared that if the Forest was to be handed on to the next generation something must be done about it at once; something which would improve its drab, dark, monotonous landscape, something that would remove the bogs nobody could walk over, something that would clear the jungles nobody could walk through!'

However, six months later the Verderers Court discussed 'the suggestion that the New Forest Pastoral Development Scheme might be suspended due to lack of agricultural machinery' and Dr Kenchington's vision of a brave new world seems to have disappeared from the news thereafter.

The County School held its annual prize-giving in March – Councillor Stubbs, the Chairman of Governors, congratulated the school on its vegetable garden. Mr May, the Headmaster, drew attention to the voluntary work at the School and said that as well as the ATC a detachment of Rangers would be formed for the girls and a Cadet Corps for boys aged between fourteen and sixteen.

The weekly Morant Hall dances continued, but the June advertisement had to ask Patrons to 'please note that there is no conveyance back to Lymington after the dance'. However, two months later there was a really major event:

Morant Hall
Friday 14th August
8 pm to 12 midnight. Actual broadcast 10.20 pm
BROADCAST Dance Cabaret
Gillie Potter
Jackie Hunter (American Radio Star)
Melville Christie and his Dance Orchestra
with Eva Beynon and David Henri

Tickets in advance 5/6d   HM Forces 4/6d
At the door 7/6d

99

The local paper informed readers that Melville Christie's Orchestra 'is on the air 2 or 3 times a week'. Gillie Potter was a well-known broadcaster of humorous monologues.

Meanwhile back in March the Warship Week had opened in the New Forest on the 21st (a fortnight after Lymington again), and undaunted by his experiences Capt Sutton once more challenged Lyndhurst to beat Brockenhurst, whose official target was again £30,000 of National Savings.

The NFRDC area as a whole exceeded its target of £400,000 for the adoption of HMS *Wilton* by £16,000, but once again Lyndhurst carried off chief honours with £85,564 (about £30 per head of population) as compared to Brockenhurst's £43,479 (£15 5s 8d per head), although Brockenhurst had handsomely exceeded its target.

As well as sponsoring all these National Savings the Brockenhurst Committee 'sent a cheque for £502 as a free gift to the Treasury. Of this figure £255 came from the Gift Shop, £134 from draws, £52 from the Church of England School as a result of their concerts, dances brought in another £34, while whist drives, football matches, treasure hunts, cinema, and donations made up the balance'.

Multiplying these figures by about 35 or 40 to get the 1990s equivalent the village had obviously made an enormous effort (nearly £10,000 in 1995 terms from the Gift Shop, for example). The NFRDC area as a whole however had failed to beat Lymington's National Savings total on a per capita basis, and the Rev EW Powell lost the wager which he had made with the Mayor of Lymington the previous year and had to supply him with a new hat.

Later on in the summer the Brockenhurst branch of the British Legion Club raised £100 for the Merchant Navy Comforts Fund in a fortnight.

One edition of the paper reported 'the extraordinary case of a Midlands business man offering to supply a titled lady, the wife of a brewery director, with farm butter, cheese, guinea fowl, chicken, and chocolate in return for a supply of whisky for his farmer friends . . .'

The lady concerned, Lady Brickwood, who was staying at Little Prescott, Brockenhurst, promptly informed the police, and the man was fined a total of £50 for the various offences.

At the beginning of April the New Forest Association for Moral Welfare held its annual meeting, and reported that 62 of the 85 cases it had dealt with in the year concerned unmarried parenthood, the other 23 involving 'difficult juveniles'.

The new ration books which were issued at the end of May contained 'mystery coupons' – the guess by the paper that these would be for sweets and chocolates turned out to be correct.

100

In June Col Mansel Jones VC of Weirs End, Brockenhurst, died aged 71. He was the Chairman of Lymington Hospital, a pillar of the Conservative Association, had been treasurer of the New Forest Asociation for many years, and was very active in local affairs. His funeral at the Parish Church was an impressive affair with full military honours. Men of the Royal Fusiliers (a regiment which appears to have been stationed locally at the time) fired three volleys over the grave, and the enormous list of mourners in the local paper seemed to contain the names of everybody of significance in the neighbourhood.

At the end of August, No 606 (Brockenhurst County School) Flight of the ATC spent a week under canvas at a famous RAF station 'somewhere in England'. And at this time the RAF, alone of all the Services, ran a weekly job advertisement in the paper for men aged 42-55 for thirteen different trades from Armourers to Shoemakers. This advertising was strange because men within these age groups had already been required to register for service, the forty-nine-year-olds being called upon in August.

During August there were one or two isolated air attacks on New Milton/Lymington ('a South Coast town'), the first for some months.

Because of restrictions on the use of mechanically-propelled vehicles there was a big interest in the August pony sales at Beaulieu Road. About 130 animals were sold, and 'mares and colts, which before the war would have fetched only a few guineas each, went up to £26 5s 0d', and buyers attended from far afield – Brighton, Shrewsbury, London, etc.

And in the 26th September issue the *Lymington Times* was complaining about the proposed introduction by the Regional Fire Guard Commissioner of compulsory fire-watching in the Borough:

The compulsory fire-watch order is not applicable to the whole New Forest area – for instance, Beaulieu, Lyndhurst, Brockenhurst, and Boldre are not included in it, and residents in these villages will not have to register for this duty.

This does not mean that fire-watching is not undertaken in these places, in fact . . . there is an excellent voluntary system in operation in these villages – as indeed there is in those areas where compulsion is now being applied.

On Sunday 15th November the Government ordered church bells to be rung throughout the land to celebrate the victories in North Africa – until then they had been kept silent to be used as a warning of invasion, the likelihood of which was now remote.

But the war was not over yet! The NFRDC also announced 'Every householder . . . must complete a copy of the household fuel assessment form (Form RR1), and return it without delay to the Local Fuel Overseer', and coal supplies were to be restricted to a maximum of 12 cwt per household for the months of November and December and a total of 15 cwt for the first three months of 1943.

Christmas travel conditions were grim, as the railways were not allowed to put on extra trains to supplement the meagre war-time service. Although the 5.30 pm from Waterloo on Christmas Eve was made up of no less than 20 carriages they were all packed with people.

BROCKENHURST NOTES – JOHN PURKESS

After private motoring was stopped in June, supplies of petrol were restricted and only obtainable from two garages in the area – the Imperial Garage at Lyndhurst and the Pennington Cross garage.

To get supplies for the delivery vans at Purkess, the van would have one or two 10-gallon drums aboard and go to Pennington to collect the rations.

Despite shortages three out of the four Purkess vans kept deliveries going. The fourth van was cannibalised for spares.

FOOD RATIONING

In the First World War food rationing was not introduced until February 25, 1918. In the Second World War the Government had introduced rationing by January, 1940.

On the Saturday of the first week Reg Purkess took home bags of coupons, which, although separated, had to be counted. This was done by threading them on to cotton and putting a marker on every hundred. An endless job. On the Monday he employed Rose Carter and her sole job throughout the food rationing era was to keep control of coupons, points and the returns.

Brockenhurst, like other country villages, benefited from farm produce to supplement rations. Nevertheless rationing was strictly and fairly enforced throughout Britain under the brilliant leadership of Lord Woolton, who became Minister of Food in 1940. His Ministry inspired us to eat raw carrots on the dubious premise that they helped night vision! The Editor's sister, Jill, still remembers the jingle: –

> "Those who have the will to win,
> Cook potatoes in their skin,
> Knowing that the sight of peelings,
> Deeply hurts Lord Woolton's feelings."

Also encouragement to slimmers: – "A large untidy corporation is far from helpful to the nation."

ROSEMARY TAYLOR gives this summary of wartime food:

I was nine when the war started. We lived about two miles from Reigate, in Surrey, and moved into our newly-built house just two days before the outbreak of war. The gardens, back and front, became vegetable plots from the start, and a small chicken run was soon established at the top end of our third of an acre. The eggs from those six hens formed a vital part of our wartime diet, and helped us tolerate the revolting smell of the weekly boil-up of vegetable waste which was the hens' staple food.

From January 1940 on, ration books became a vital essential of everyday life. The first issue contained mysterious coupons which were gradually to become called into use. The first rationed foods were butter (4 oz per week), sugar (12 oz), and bacon and ham (4 oz). As a child, the butter ration made a powerful impact, particularly at a later stage, when a 2 oz allocation was kept on one's own individual little dish. At meal times this could be used at one's own whim, spread on bread minutely thin, or in more careless abandon. The shrinking piece was most jealously guarded against theft or vandalism.

Meat was rationed from March 1940, by price at around 1s 10d per week, which could buy a little over 1¼ lb weight. Offal, poultry, game and fish were not rationed, but rapidly became very expensive and tended to disappear 'under the counter'. Other fats soon joined the coupon class. Tea, the national beverage, was considered vital for morale and lives were risked to ship supplies for the weekly ration. Jams, tinned and bottled preserves were allocated at 1 lb per head per month. A great blow was the cheese ration, at only 1 oz per week, though manual workers were soon allowed more to make their traditional and essential lunchpacks. Eggs were 'subject to availability', often one per week, supplemented by rationed dried egg powder, mostly used in cooking. Milk was controlled, sometimes down to ½ pint a day, though children at school had additional supplies.

Bread was not rationed then, but the all-prevailing white loaf gradually turned grey as National Wheatmeal bread was introduced. Vegetables were never rationed and formed a vital, healthy bulk to everyday diet. 'Dig for Victory' allotments sprang up everywhere and rosebeds became kitchen gardens. On the whole people fed reasonably well, given skilful handling of what was available. British Restaurants were opened, serving two course meals with strange dishes such as Woolton Pie, at very reasonable prices. These supplemented rations and gave exhausted housewives a break from meal-planning. Nationwide, food prices were subsidised and kept to within 20% of pre-war prices. The Government handling of food supplies was very successful and a great deal better, so our elders told us, than that of the First World War.

MORE ABOUT FOOD

For children and sometimes their parents the quest for food could be an adventure, as GEORGE GATES remembers:

I was at school at Boldre and, it being some miles from my home, my parents had bought me a bicycle. My headmaster, 'Jim' Newman, used to take advantage of this.

He was in the midst of setting up the school meal service and would often call for my attention in class. "George Gates, get on your bike and fetch these things for Cook."

I would be given money and a list of requirements. Invariably, because of wartime shortages I would need to do a tour of the Pilley shops, and if I was not successful at Shelley's, Drudge's or Mrs Dawkin's, then I would race down to Boldre Post Office in an attempt to buy the missing items. By the time I'd pedalled all the way back up Pilley Hill to the Boys' Clubroom at Church Lane, where these premises were used as a kitchen and dining room, Mrs Smith, the cook, would usually be in a dilemma, worrying that I might not turn up in time with ingredients for the dish of the day, but generally very pleased with the goods or substitutes which I had been able to muster.

BERYL BROWNING tells of food swapping:

We lived next door to a very large family. There were nine children and they did not need their full rations of, say, tea, margarine and sugar; we were only two of us. My mother used to swop what we had in abundance with them and it worked out fine. We were never, or were my friends as I recall, short of food. There was always a pig and chickens in the garden and the neighbours had chickens. The local lads used to go and get rabbits. We lived on rabbit stew – with lots of swedes and turnips. There were, I think a lot of people who did *not* have enough food. We in the country were well fed and very healthy. There was a smokery at the bottom end of Lymington High Street that used to smoke the pig for us when slaughtered. It was shared with neighbours.

CASUALTIES OF WAR

It would be easy to think that the tragic aspect of war largely missed Brockenhurst. Not so. In the village there were many wives waiting for news of their husbands and mothers of their sons. Separation was often for years; so was the heartache and worry. Often the worst part was not knowing what was happening to a loved one.

That was what NURSE MYLES went through. She was the District Nurse then living in Partridge Road. She was also the midwife, who, in the 1920's and 1930's, had helped to bring into the world many whose memories are recorded in these pages. She was not only respected, but loved by people in the village; loved also by the gypsies whose camp was at Number Ten Gates at Latchmoor. She was also their midwife, nurse and friend. "They trusted her absolutely and thought the world of her," says GEORGE JOHNSON.

He had known the Myles family all his life. 'Leslie' Myles whose brother, Bertie, was handicapped, was his contemporary and school friend.

In 1933, the two of them, desperate for work, decided to volunteer for the army. Together they joined the Lancers, served with distinction in India for six years and were demobilised in 1939. After a few months working at Wellworthy's factory in Lymington they joined the Royal Dragoons (The Royals). They were sent out to the Middle East as part of the Eighth Army *(see Chapter 7)*. They served in the

THE LATE JACK DUNKINSON AND 'LES' MYLES.

Royals until in 1942 George was invalided home. Meanwhile Leslie was with the Eighth Army, which, following the victories in North Africa, crossed to Italy. He survived the advance northwards against furious German opposition and must have been longing to return to England. He was killed on the German border.

George, convalescing in England, was very distressed to learn of the death of his friend. He went to see Les's mother, Nurse Myles. To those who didn't know the Myles family it would have seemed like just another sad consequence of war. To the people of Brockenhurst her tragedy affected them all. As for Nurse Myles she never got over the shock.

She was not, of course, the only person in the village to experience such a loss. BILL DUNKINSON tells of how his brother JACK, and others were killed:

The Germans were invading Crete with landing crafts. Commander A'deane, who lived in the Thatched Cottage in this lane was Captain of the destroyer *Greyhound*. He used the *Greyhound* to ram the landing craft. The Germans then dive-bombed the *Greyhound*. The Royal Navy sent in another destroyer and two cruisers; *Fiji* and *Gloucester* – my brother's ship. All were sunk.

Jack, aged twenty-one, was a big fellow over six foot. A marvellous athlete and an outstanding boxer. He never smoked or drank. His death was a tragedy. It broke my mother's heart. She never got over it and even now I still think about him every week.

There were so many in Brockenhurst who were killed. In Sway Road the St Clair family lost three sons. Jack Short (another old Forest family who lived near the Fire Bell), Pat Painter, Harold Cleveland, Les Myles, Reg Meaden, Ron Read, Alf Shiletto. They were all my mates, all nice men, all young. A tragedy.

Incidentally I don't think that many Brockenhurst people know that Commander A'deane was awarded the Albert Cross. During the German landing on Crete when his destroyer was being bombed, he heard a sailor in the water screaming for help. He dived off his ship trying to save him and was drowned. Mrs A'deane and my mother shared their terrible loss.

1943

Diary of National and International Events

January 18	Leningrad 16-month German siege ended. Russians stated well over 600,000 had died.
23	Tripoli occupied by Eighth Army.
27	American bombers made first attack on Germany.
31	Remnants of German Army surrendered at Stalingrad.
May 7	German resistance in Tunis finally overcome.
16	RAF 'Dambusters' Raid on Ruhr.
July 10	Allied invasion of Sicily.
25	Mussolini overthrown.
August 17	Sicily in Allied hands.
September 3	Allies (including Eighth Army) invaded Italian mainland.
7	Italy surrendered. German Army – in strength – seized Rome.
October 1	Naples captured by Allies.
November 6	Kiev taken by Russians.
28	Churchill, Roosevelt and Stalin met at Tehran.
December 2	UK – men directed to coal mines 'The Bevin Boys'.
26	German battleship *Scharnhorst* sunk.

THE TIDES OF WAR

In 1943 Frank Sinatra sang 'All Or Nothing At All' and Gary Cooper and Ingrid Bergman starred in the film 'For Whom The Bell Tolls'. The two titles, although unintended, summed up much of what was happening on the war front that year. It was indeed total war – all or nothing at all. In April, German troops attacked the half million Polish Jews crammed into the Warsaw Ghetto, systematically destroying their houses street by street and sending the survivors to concentration camps. Few escaped. And yet on January 31, German armies besieging the city of Stalingrad had surrendered to the Russians, and, in September Italy formally surrendered to the Allies. The tide of war was beginning to turn. Enormous efforts were made on the Home Front to keep the momentum going. Part-time work became compulsory for all women in Britain between the ages of 18 and 45. During 1943, at its maximum strength, the Women's Land Army numbered more than 80,000 women. Their green jerseys, brown breeches and felt hats were a familiar sight in the New Forest, and the women, working in all kinds of weather, sometimes alongside Italian and, later, German prisoners of war, made a vital contribution to the eventual overthrow of the Nazi aggressors. A bell rung by many hands was beginning to toll for Hitler and his allies in Europe. A bell rung not only by airmen, seamen and soldiers in the front line, but by a whole nation at war with a common enemy.

From the *Lymington Times*

The New Year opened with a bureaucratic concession – during the months of January and February (hardly the most attractive time of year!) people would be allowed to visit the Isle of Wight without having to obtain permission, though they were warned that they would not be allowed to take up permanent residence there.

And the columns of the *Lymington Times* were enlivened in January by a correspondence about the shortage of batteries for bicycle lamps. A gentleman wrote in to say that the problem was that the bulbs in bicycle lamps were still of the pre-war rating, and that if weaker bulbs were used the batteries would last longer. His case was not helped by his confusing watts and amps, but a number of people wrote in general support. One shopkeeper reader felt 'a partial solution to the problem is to stop pleasure cycling at night. When one has to say 'no batteries' to customers all day it is annoying to see . . . batteries being wasted at night by people bent on pleasure'.

The thought of people deliberately cycling for pleasure at night in January shows what a tough people we must have been then, especially as during that month there were night air attacks on a neighbouring 'South Coast town' in which people were killed, and also a severe three-day gale in which trees were brought down and roofs stripped! News of the gale was not allowed to be released until a fortnight after it happened, such was the official mania for secrecy. At the end of January Mr R Purkess died, at the age of seventy-six.

And the unfortunate commoners were having a hard time, because added to the problem of various areas of the Forest being taken out of use 'for war purposes', an outbreak of foot-and-mouth disease on a local farm meant that all animals pasturing in the Forest had to be taken in by their owners.

Miss Barnett's charity concert at the Morant Hall at the end of February was affected by the sickness of many of the usual artistes – war weariness and the winter weather were having an effect on people, though the Portsmouth boys from Arnewood Towers presented a very successful play.

On 6th March Lymington began its 'Wings for Victory' week, another National Savings event in which £242,405 was raised in the Borough. Although this received very extensive coverage in the paper the references to events and challenges in the NFRDC area, which had been a feature of previous such weeks, were missing.

Brockenhurst County School held its annual Speech and Prize Day on 31st March. Mr May said that the standard of work was still being maintained in spite of war-time difficulties, but pressure on accommodation was now greater than ever before – the School had 530 pupils. And there were 318 boys in the 'Southern Secondary School for Boys, evacuated to Brockenhurst and billeted at Brockenhurst, Sway, Lymington, and New Milton.'

Under the gripping headline 'Murder and Suicide!' the paper announced in June that a special meeting had taken place in Brockenhurst (as in Sway) to consider building a public hall as soon as possible after the war, perhaps in conjunction with playing fields. A Mr J Spracken commented "'if you are going to build a hall the size of the Morant Hall it is going to be a case of murder and suicide." It was mentioned that there was some £700 available from the sale of the fire appliances, and a committee was set up – little did those present realise that it was going to take some forty years for these plans to come to fruition!

Women's events were in the news – Brockenhurst WI celebrated its Silver Jubilee, and an exhibition was held in July at the Morant Hall of plans of homes designed by members of the Hampshire Federation of Townswomen's Guilds and judged by a 'leading architect'.

During July the RDC received a plaque from HMS *Whirlwind*, the destroyer which had been adopted during Warship week, and this was installed at the Council Offices. The Chairman expressed a hope that after the war a suitable building would be erected to house this and other mementos of the war.

And the RDC Highways Committee asked the County Council to replace the bridge leading to Boldre Church, which had collapsed under the weight of a Bren Gun Carrier and killed its crew.

In October, Wessex Electricity's advertisement reminded people that they must not use their electric fires between 8.00 am and 1.00 pm – 'do some physical jerks instead' was the helpful advice.

Although it could not be said at the time, the build-up for D-Day was on its way, and in the reporting of road accidents mention is made of military activities at two local hotels – in September there was a collision involving vehicles coming out of Careys Manor, and on the morning of 19th November a double-decker bus 'carrying 52 passengers and towing a gas generator swerved on two wheels' to avoid a military vehicle driven by a Canadian soldier coming out of the Balmer Lawn Hotel.

And 1943's final and unwelcome item of news, on Christmas Day, was that from 1st January 1944 the price of the *Lymington Times* would go up one halfpenny to a penny-halfpenny.

BROCKENHURST NOTES

October 7 new railway sidings put in at Brockenhurst station. Preparation for D-Day.

AIRCRAFT CRASHES

At 1715 hrs on Friday, August 13, 1943, a Halifax and a Wellington were involved in a mid-air collision over Arnewood Court. The Wellington was one of five diverted to Beaulieu airfield after an anti-shipping patrol. The Halifax had just completed an air test and was in circuit coming in to land at Holmsley South airfield.

Both aircraft were flying at 700 feet through patchy cloud and poor visibility and circumstances caused the accident. The Wellington immediately went into a dive and crashed into a field near Silver Street, Hordle and the wreckage slid into a small gravel pit. The Halifax flew on for a bit, but then caught on fire and dived onto the railway coach home of Peter Jenvey at Flexford, South Sway. Both crews and Mr. Jenvey were killed in the accident. (*The Editor remembers pieces of plane falling over Hazelhurst.*)

On August 30, 1943, another Beaulieu based Liberator BZ785 crashed in the locality.

This time the aircraft was a Mk V coded 'L' from 811 Czech Squadron, RAF. The aircraft crashed, on a training flight, near the airfield dispersal sites.

As a local story goes, Mr Hart, a farmer at Dilton, was smoking his favourite pipe when the plane came over the farm with one engine on fire, taking·the top off a fir tree then crashing into Dilton Copse. The explosion blew Mr Hart off his feet and knocked the pipe from his mouth, but when he picked himself up from the ground he was more worried about finding his pipe than the flaming bomber that had just crashed nearby. The crew of six were killed.

(Researched and written by Richard Reeves)

GEORGE GATES writes:

I witnessed two air crashes in the Parish. The first one was on a bright summer afternoon, when one of our fighters chased a German bomber from the direction of Sway, over Battramsley, where it was hit by the Spitfire's continuous 'rat-a-tat-tat' gun fire.

The other crash was on a dark November evening, when a Liberator, laden with depth charges destined for U-boats, developed engine trouble and used its 'Leigh' light to seek out space in the village to 'ditch'. After losing height on a curving course over Boldre Church, the plane struggled on over the black iron bridge of the Sandy Down/Rodlease footpath. At Riversdale where I was watching the drama, it curved on a greater angle back towards the river, where it finished up on the other side in the field below Friars Wood.

The tremendous explosion killed all of the brave crew. When all the wild yellow daffodils bloom at Friars Wood each springtime to me they are a natural monument to these unfortunate men.

OUR ALLIES AROUND BROCKENHURST

By 1943 a large number of Allied troops and Air Force personnel were stationed in and around Brockenhurst.

IAIN HAYTER, then a young boy, remembers one encounter with them:

The Americans were camped outside the Balmer Lawn. My friend and I called in one morning. They said, "Come on in, kids. Have some chocolate! You want some lunch, kids?" We did. I remember the meat and vegetables mixed with peaches.

In the afternoon my mother wondered where I'd got to because I never missed a lunch. In the end they went to the policeman who found us queuing for supper at Balmer Lawn. We'd been there all day!

Meanwhile Iain's parents had founded the WHITE RABBIT CLUB

for British and Allied Service men and women in the Brockenhurst area. Here HUGH SUTHERLAND, then a RAF pilot stationed at the vast Beaulieu aerodrome, describes how he joined this remarkable organisation:

I went to the regular dance held at the Morant Hall opposite the Rose and Crown. During the Paul Jones a girl said that she knew a woman with a Scots' accent like mine. She thought that she might like to meet me. So it was that I met Kath Hayter – Iain's mother – who, like me, came from Inverness-shire. I also met Harry, her husband.

Despite the desperate struggle they had in keeping Hayter's garage going with only one taxi and no petrol to sell, they opened their tiny house to all servicemen and women, mostly, but not exclusively, from Beaulieu aerodrome. Everyone could have hot drinks, food and a bed for the night. There were only two bedrooms in the house. *(The house is still there near the petrol pumps. – Ed)* Membership of the White Rabbit Club gave you entry to the house. One of the qualifications for membership was whether you'd had a pee in the tiny garden fronting Brookley Road. You often had to use the garden because the one lavatory wasn't enough for the twenty to thirty airmen, who were given such fantastically generous hospitality. You were allowed in provided you wore one of the tiny white rabbits which Kath Hayter made for the lapel. Apart from British members there were lots of Canadians, New Zealanders, Australians, Americans, Poles, Czechs and other nationalities. It's a mystery how Kath and Harry held on with their business and yet could be so generous. They gave security and a sense of belonging to hundreds of people from all over the world. Members of the WRC were a well-decorated lot: over 20 DFCs, 10 DFMs, 6 DSOs and one very rare Conspicuous Gallantry Medal.

Many of us can never repay the amazing generosity and kindness of Kath and Harry Hayter. It's because of the affection which I received in Brockenhurst that my wife, Peggy, and I came to live in the area.

I've also come to realise what an enormous contribution the White Rabbit Club, in this small Hampshire village, made to the war effort. It became famous throughout the world.

Many others remember with gratitude the wonderful Christmas and New Year children's parties, given by the Canadian soldiers who were stationed in the area. The Americans were also renowned for their generosity.

Naturally, though, there could be occasional friction between the locals and allied troops.

MISS JM DOUGLAS was living with her sister. Her brother-in-law

112

TWO AMERICAN SOLDIERS WITH STAN REED.

was Chief Air Raid Warden for the area and she remembers him telling her of one real tough old forester. The old man said, "The Americans seem very decent, but those white ones they have brought along, I don't like them." He found that the black Americans were at heart countrymen, who knew about forest ways and how to live in the countryside.

THE PRISONERS OF WAR

Interestingly very little has been said against the POWs. Miss Douglas tells of the same old forester that one day he was talking to a German POW with signs and a few sentences of gutteral English. The German kept exclaiming, "Bang, bang, bang...". Later he explained, "I did not like fighting. I am glad for me it is all over."

Immediately after the war I was travelling out to my brother in Cyprus. At Genoa my trunk had completely disappeared. An Italian porter offered to help me. When, some time later he appeared with my trunk, I wanted to tip him for his trouble. He refused. "No, no, no. I was a POW in England during the war. The English people were kind to us and I just want to repay some of that kindness."

BERYL BROWNING also remembers the prisoners at Setley:

They were very lovely men and I could not understand that they were supposed to be cruel and did such wicked things. They worked on the local farms and mixing with the local people, but always had to be back at camp at half past four or five of an evening. They used to come to school where I was at Pilley. One particular gentleman used to come and walk home from school with me every evening and we chatted all the time. We became great friends. When he was due to leave he came and knocked at our door and actually asked my mother for a photograph of me to take home. For some reason I did not understand, she refused him, and I can still remember being quite sad about this – this lovely man!

This camp at Setley was a complete settlement on its own – halls, electricity, sewerage, everything. After the prisoners left, the local people were housed there and they stayed there for many years. It was completely flattened in the 1960's.

One prisoner's name that has cropped up several times and always accompanied by a compliment, is that of MAX MÜLLER.

BRIAN PLUMLEY speaks for others:

He was a fine man. Everyone liked Max. I was fond of Max. He was just doing a job, that was it. He was caught and behaved properly. Max always had a German shepherd dog with him. He stayed on after the war and worked for Holtom and Pascoe, the butchers, as Manager.

WALLY KNOTT remembers:

I was working on the level crossing gates one day and heard old Max coming down the road and saying, "March like the Breetish, march like the Breetish. Left, right, left, right, left, right. March like the Breetish. That's better, that's better."

MOLLY MÜLLER, widow of Max, now living in Brockenhurst again, has given us information about her greatly respected husband:

My husband was born in Germany in 1913 in Aschaffenburg-on-Main. His father was an engineer in precision engineering; I think that is what they would have called him, but he died quite young. I remember Max saying that his grandparents had a smallholding and they used to go out and do the hay-making and gather in the different crops. They would all get together, in which family house I don't know, but they had this great big wooden table in the kitchen and the plates were carved into the table and the children used to have to help scrub the table when they had all finished; it was amazing really. This must have been when my husband was tiny. Somewhere I have a photo which my sister-in-law sent and my daughter is the spitting image of him at this age.

In Germany to be in the butchering trade, they had to start right from slaughter-man up through to the top. His brother came home on leave from the army, all dressed up and Max kept on about wanting to go into the army, but his mother said, "No, when you have finished your apprenticeship, then you may go in". I can't remember when he went into the army, it must have been before the War. He was a PT instructor. He fought in Russia, but was captured in France after D-Day. He had a very, very hard time in Russia: there weren't many of them that came out. I can remember him saying he wasn't in France that long before being captured. He was captured by the Canadians – they thought they had the popular German boxer, Max Schmeling, so everyone called him Max and the name stuck to him, but actually his name was Ludwig Wilhelm. He was in charge of Setley camp: he used to have to go round the camp and keep everything in order, including sorting out all the food. There were hundreds there. He was very popular, but very strict.

I would imagine the camp must have closed when my husband was discharged because I have this dilapidated discharge form dated 31 December, 1948.

All the ex-German POWs, when they returned to Germany, were made to see the concentration camps. They could not believe it. They had no idea what was going on, even their own people at home didn't know about them. It was terrible.

We kept in touch with quite a few of the ex-POWs. We used to have gatherings: they used to come to tea and have singsongs. We had a mouth organ; my husband played the accordion as well as the mouth organ for them; sometimes they would have spoons and sing along in German. We used to have lovely get-togethers.

Mrs Müller described how she met Max:

I was born in Westfield Road, Lymington on 27 April, 1927. After leaving St Thomas's School, I eventually worked in a cafe, now called 'Jack-in-the-Basket', and then went to Wellworthy's. Max was

WOOD CARVINGS MADE BY A GERMAN P.O.W. AT SETLEY CAMP.

lodging on my route home from work and that's how we met – he courted me with a box of tomatoes!

COLIN TOWNSEND-ROSE's home in Tile Barn Lane was near the POW Camp at Setley:

The Italians, who were there first, were a noisy lot. We could hear them swearing, shouting and singing. They were taken into the Forest to hunt. I remember one occasion when I was riding my pony I got off to talk to some of the Italians. When I got home I realised that I had dropped my wallet. A few days later it was returned to me by a POW. I was thrilled because it had my Identity Card – precious in those days. I went to see the Italian and rewarded him with a ten-shilling note. He gave me a penny whistle which he had made out of soft wood. It was accurately tuned and I kept it for many years.

Then the Germans arrived. The German commander was Max Müller, who was a charming chap. He married an attractive young lady from Brockenhurst and settled here. We had two Germans working for us cutting down trees, splitting and carting our logs. They were so strong that they broke our axes. Hans was another wonderful chap. I remember his story. He deserted from the German army on the Eastern front; he couldn't stand it. He walked thousands of miles back into Germany, only to be captured by the British three miles from his home and ended up in Setley. A tragedy for him.

When on our farm he insisted on doing all the heavy work (he was in his early twenties) because, as a farmer's son, he thought that I should not be put off farming. I wasn't. Years later my mother went to a wedding in North Germany and Hans drove hundreds of miles just to see her. I still remember him well, even his brilliantly polished boots. I've never seen boots polished like this.

1944

Diary of National and International Events

January 22	Allies landed at Anzio.
May 18	Cassino (Italy) Monastery captured by Allies.
June 4	Rome captured by Allies. King of Italy abdicated.
June 6	D-DAY INVASION OF EUROPE (over 4,000 ships).
8	Fierce battle for Caen.
July 9	Caen captured by British troops.
20	'Bomb plot' on Hitler's life.
August 1	Warsaw uprising.
15	Allies landed in South of France.
25	Paris liberated.
September 3	Allies entered Belgium.
8	First V-2 fell on England.
11	Allied forces in German territory.
17	Airborne troops landed near Arnhem.
October 3	Warsaw rising crushed by German troops.
25	Battle of Leyte Gulf. End of Japanese sea power.
December 6	Greece – Civil War.
16	German counter-offensive in the Ardennes.

THE EBB TIDE

"Once more unto the breach, dear friends, once more;
Or close the wall up with our English dead!"
From Act 3 Scene 1 of William Shakespeare's King Henry The Fifth.
In 1944 Laurence Olivier directed and appeared as the victorious King in the film version of the play. That momentous year, Britain with its allies was once again fighting on the 'vasty fields of France',

on this occasion as a liberator and with France as an ally. D-Day had finally arrived on June 6 when 4,000 ships crossed the English Channel to launch more than 150,000 men on the shores of Normandy. On August 25 General De Gaulle entered Paris and shortly afterwards on September 3 Brussels was liberated from the Germans. Olivier's heroic portrayal of the warrior King captured the mood of 1944. The tide had truly turned against the Axis aggressors. Rome had fallen to the Americans in June and in the same month in the Battle of the Philippine sea, the American Air Force established a lasting supremacy in the air over the Japanese. And yet it was a year of bitter losses and a titanic struggle lay ahead, with theatres, opera houses and music halls closing in Germany in preparation for what both sides in the conflict realised was the final act of a darkly tragic period of history.

AN EDITORIAL NOTE ON D-DAY – 6 JUNE

Most of Europe had been occupied by the Germans since 1941. For over two years Stalin had been pressing his Western allies to assist the Soviet Union in its struggle for survival. The peoples of the occupied countries (at least nineteen) were desperate to be freed from a brutal tyranny of almost unimaginable cruelty.

General Eisenhower and most of his team of victorious Commanders – some of whom used the Balmer Lawn Hotel – were placed in charge of the most formidable task hitherto contemplated – the Liberation of North-West Europe. The most meticulous plans were made, including the construction of artificial harbours and in March 1944, after intensive Anglo-American air operations against the German aircraft industry and fighter force had assured the Allies of air superiority, the pre-invasion air assault was launched against targets in France and the Low Countries.

When the British, Canadian and American armies came to touch down on the Normandy beaches on June 6, 1944, they found that the German powers of resistance and reinforcement were decisively weakened. However, a very tough struggle was still to follow.

From the *Lymington Times*

Over Christmas and the New Year a number of parties were given for local children all over the area by Canadian soldiers. From this and other items in the paper – traffic offences, weddings – there were clearly a large number of Canadians stationed in this part of the world.

And under the headline 'Making the Forest into Farms' it was

reported that the Court of Verderers had been presented on 2nd January with a 'Ministry of Agriculture Scheme for enclosing parts of the open wastes of the New Forest for food cultivation and with the object of improving the pastures'.

The proposal was to take about 1,000 acres, grow three annual crops on them, and then sow down grass, throwing them open again in four (or five) years at the Verderers' discretion. In the Brockenhurst area there would be 92 acres taken at Wilverley Post NW and 165 acres at Wilverley Post SE, 111 at Whitefield Moor west of Ober Farm, and 214 acres at Black Knoll.

Capt Sutton pointed out that 'drainage, clearance, etc, was simultaneously imperative for the improvement of existing lands' (i.e. those not involved in the Scheme). But he said that although the Commoners Association opposed enclosures in general, they accepted the present proposal as a wartime measure.

In April the Brockenhurst Choral Society gave selections from 'The Messiah' in aid of the Orphanage. This Society had not appeared previously in the paper, and may well have been newly-formed or perhaps re-formed.

At the beginning of March there was a presentation by his colleagues to Mr Prosser, the former Brockenhurst stationmaster, who had been promoted to the similar position at Bournemouth. The spokesman at the ceremony was Mr PJ Horlock, JP, who was station foreman and who was very active in village life.

On Monday 5th March 'queues lined up at every greengrocer's shop, when oranges were once again on sale . . .' But a literal 'black' market was exposed in April when three men were sent to prison for stealing half-a-ton of coal which was being unloaded from railway wagons at Brockenhurst for Portsmouth Secondary School.

On 18th April an enemy aircraft 'believed to be a Junker was shot down at Exbury in the early hours of the morning, and German air activity seems to have stepped up somewhat as on 15th May there was a raid on a 'village in the South which had experienced previous bombing incidents but which suffered its first fatal casualties'.

A problem arose in May when cattle were being moved from Beaulieu Manor, and one of them was killed by a Services vehicle. The military refused to pay compensation as there was 'no negligence on the part of the driver', but Sir George Meyrick said this was immaterial as cattle had a prior right on the roads in the Forest, and Capt Sutton said he would take the matter up with the appropriate authority – but as so often with newspaper stories the outcome never seems to have been reported.

But now the whole area must have been busy with soldiers and equipment of all descriptions in preparation for D-Day in June, because the 'Prohibited Area' status of the district was being more strictly enforced. In April there had been a series of check-ups on people arriving in the New Forest area by train at the weekends, carried out by the police, the Special Constabulary, and the military. ID cards were inspected,and four people were refused admission to the district and forced to return home. These included someone who had come down all the way from Cumberland, and a girl from Brighton who had come to visit her soldier fiancé (who, it turned out, had in any case left the area).

And as June approached security became even tighter and local people were prosecuted in large numbers for failing to carry their ID cards – every week 60 or 70 names of people who had been fined 5/- or 10/- at Lymington Court appeared in the paper.

However, after D-Day conditions relaxed. The Annual Meeting of the Hampshire Federation of Women's Institutes was held in Winchester in mid-June, having been postponed from 17th April at the request of the Chief Constable 'to reduce travelling'. And within a month the ban on visitors to many coastal areas, including Bournemouth, Ringwood and Fordingbridge was lifted, although the New Forest, Lymington, and New Milton were still banned areas and visitors from outside were not allowed.

However, this well-meant concession provoked a storm of abuse locally, as people from Christchurch, Highcliffe, and Ringwood were now living outside the controlled area and therefore could no longer visit New Milton or the New Forest, which they had been able to do all through the darkest days of the war and during the run-up to D-Day. Many of these people had social commitments in those areas. The police were meeting trains, inspecting ID cards, and sending people home.

The problem was finally solved from 25th August when the restrictions were lifted altogether, although it was pointed out that people still had to carry their ID cards. At the same time another restriction was removed – it was no longer necessary to immobilise motor vehicles by removing the distributor arm when not in use.

Meanwhile, back in June Brockenhurst County School had held its annual Sports Day, and the following month 'topped the County for scholarship successes', obtaining three out of the 12 which were awarded. No other school got more than one.

Accidents continued on the Lymington–Brockenhurst road in 1944. In July a double-decked Hants & Dorset bus coming from Lymington overturned after colliding with a van at St. Austins, Boldre – 19 people received cuts and bruises but no-one was seriously injured. And two months later an ATS girl who was riding in a US Navy lorry coming from the Brockenhurst direction was killed when it ran into some trees near the New Inn *(now The Hobler)*.

On 21st August Mr Jenvey, the C of E sexton, found a mailbag in Church Lane on his way home from fire-watching at St Nicholas which should have been on the up midnight mail train in transit from Lymington to Southampton. The bag was empty, but in the morning the police found £3,700 in notes in packets some 20 yards away – the equivalent of well over £100,000 today. The thieves, who had abstracted the bag from Brockenhurst station, had thrown these packets aside in the dark in helping themselves to a 'few registered letters of little value'.

In September the blackout regulations were eased, but this concession, which should have been a pleasant event, was turned into a nightmare by official muddle and confusion. For some reason the revised requirements for 'half-lighting' were not supposed to be printed in the newspapers, but were to be announced by official posters. The *Lymington Times* grumbled 'the press are prohibited from telling the public in a straightforward way what they can and cannot do . . .'

Nobody seemed to be able to find the official posters (*Lymington Times* finally ran one to earth outside Milford-on-Sea police station) and meanwhile the papers printed garbled and different versions – the Mayor of Lymington announced that from 17th September (the end of double summer time) the level of obscuration required was 'so that objects in the room are indistinguishable from outside', though

121

full blackout was to be instantly reinstated if an air raid alarm sounded! However, the police and wardens were still trying to enforce the law, and it was suggested that people should telephone the police to find out exactly what was required!

In fact the transition on the Home Front from total war to something rather less was catching officialdom wrong-footed all the time. On 23rd August there was an exceptionally heavy rainfall in the area, but the censors would still not allow the paper to mention this until its issue of 16th September!

In the same issue were two items of particular interest to Brockenhurst – one was the discovery of a 'secret pound' in the woods near White Moor, which it was thought had been used for stealing cattle, and the other was the death of Mr Reginald Purkess in Boscombe Hospital (at the age of forty-eight).

In the next issue of the paper it was announced that there would be no compulsory billeting this year for the 50 new entrants to Portsmouth Secondary School, as Marden House at Milford-on-Sea had been converted into a hostel for them, and was to be run by one of the masters and his wife. Although this was to be welcomed, Milford was hardly the ideal location for daily travel by children to Brockenhurst by public transport.

As so often, however, officialdom had finally sorted things out too late to be of any use – by December Lymington Council were discussing the possibility of accommodating war-workers in 'the two hostels at Milford which have been vacated by Portsmouth School boys on their return to their home town'!

In fact the Lord Mayor of Portsmouth and the Lady Mayoress visited Brockenhurst County School in December to thank all local foster-parents, and in replying Mr May mentioned that 'after Portsmouth had taken over the old Brockenhurst Secondary School buildings a number of rooms in the New School had remained at the disposal of the visiting school for various purposes.'

Several schoolboys appeared at a special juvenile court in Lymington in November in relation to offences in Brockenhurst. Five of them aged 14 or 15, of whom two were Boy Scouts, admitted stealing 700 cigarettes from a hut at Balmer Lawn on Sunday 21st October – 'we did this for want of something to do in Brockenhurst, just for excitement!'

In November the authorities decided, quite rightly, that air attacks on Britain had come to an end, and the papers were allowed for the first time to give chapter and verse for all that had happened. The *Lymington Times* gave details of almost every incident that had taken place in the Borough, but only a sketchy account was given of air attacks in the NFRDC area.

The New Forest had received no less than 2,700 bombs, 25 people had been killed, and 42 properties destroyed. Of Brockenhurst it was merely said 'Brockenhurst was raided in August 1940, and had its share of 30 or more incendiary attacks which were made in the New Forest area during the period under review.' The paper also noted that on 8th July 1941 a plane had been brought down near Boldre.

And the Home Guard was finally stood down, with ceremonial parades on Sunday 2nd December, but not before the Brockenhurst platoon had enjoyed their annual smoking concert at the Railway Inn *(now the Snakecatcher)*. Also it was noted that the second Police Ball held at the Morant Hall was as great a success as that of two years previously.

Just before Christmas, on 16th December, the intensive mail activity at Brockenhurst station around midnight attracted thieves again, and a mail van was stolen by soldiers and 'found a few miles away damaged by a collision, and with two mailbags missing.'

The final Brockenhurst news item for 1944 under the headline '£4,000 for Playing Fields – Brockenhurst to buy 7.5 acres' concerned a special parish meeting in December which

having received a further report from the Playing Fields and Village Hall Committee, passed by 38 votes to 3 a resolution recommending the raising of a loan not exceeding £4,000 for purchasing 7.5 acres of land in Grigg Lane at a cost of not more than £3,000, and draining sufficient of that land to enable football and other games to be played there. It is intended that the land, which includes an excellent site for a village hall, shall remain a centre of recreation in perpetuity.

The following evening the Parish Council agreed to approach Hampshire County Council for consent to the raising of the loan. A request was also made for another two dozen council houses in the village.

BROCKENHURST NOTES

May   Build up for D-Day.
Bombs landed in Sway road opposite petrol storage.

July   Doodle Bug landed near Ober Bridge.

DOODLE BUGS (V-1s)

ARTHUR and SAM SAMBER remembered the doodle bugs:
There was a doodle bug, which fell at White Moor and one at New Park. I saw that one − I was by the back door. It was coming over from this direction and there was this noise; so I went to the door and saw this flame − the blast hit the house − also one went into North Weirs.

D-DAY

Even in May local papers were reticent about reporting the huge influx of troops into the area. In any case, the reporters themselves may not have been fully aware of the extent of the build up since we now know that vast numbers of men, and quantities of equipment, were skilfully hidden in and around the Forest. The locals, of course, realised that something was up. For instance, some roads were being widened and concrete laid down to take the tanks. The result of this work is still in evidence here and there, as in Pilley. It is from personal recollections that we can best build a picture of the days leading up to June 6, D-Day.

Apparently, according to BRIAN PLUMLEY:
They had this metal track with holes in it and lay that all down. They had square concrete blocks just like boxes of chocolate. These were put down. They widened the road up to Forest Park, down Rhinefield Road, through Bolderwood to the Canadian Cross. That's where they had their last service before they went off down Beaulieu River.

(The Canadian Cross can still be seen and Armistice Day poppies are laid there each November − Ed)

124

WALLY KNOTT recalls:
For about a week before, both sides of the Sway Road from the Primary School to the junction was lined with lorries. It was a restricted area, only those living there were allowed access. Also parts of Lymington Pier were sealed off. I can tell you, there were thousands of troops in and around Brockenhurst.

Hollands Wood also had them. In Brockenhurst Park there was what they called a wire cage, troops being isolated there for about four days before being sent overseas.

BRIAN PLUMLEY says:
When I was riding to work in Lymington by all these tanks, there were all these Americans washing, shaving and throwing packets of 200 cigarettes at you, tins of pineapple and all sorts of things. I used to have a little bag on the back of my bike for most of the nights while they were there.

DAVID CHAMBERLAIN:
I remember how the soldiers would grease all the engines, put all the inhibiting stuff on, then, there was a false alarm. They never knew when they were going. They were forever preparing the vehicles – and they would be stood down. As far as I know, they stayed with their vehicles all the time.

But nothing stayed the same for long.

MARGARET EVANS:
One would go to bed at night and wake up in the morning to find all sorts of vehicles, including bren gun carriers and tanks, which had filled the side roads off Sway Road; or conversely one would go to bed with the roads filled with vehicles to find they had all gone by morning! It was quite eerie, as one heard no sound of them during the night.

COLIN TOWNSEND-ROSE recalls:
The Roydon Estate had a huge camp full of troops. Part of the camp was a Sealed Camp where no one was allowed out, because the men inside had been given details of battle plans upon landing in France.

In the copse near our house I said to my brother, "Look at those tanks hidden in the trees." They were there all right – waiting for D-Day. I could see them because I am colour blind. I could see under the camouflage. Sometimes my mother driving home would be confronted by a tank in our road. She had to drive into the hedge. Eight out of ten tanks got stuck in the bog at South Weirs.

Over at Hatchet Pond there are still, I think, two parallel concrete ramps on which army transports were immersed in water to see if they were properly waterproofed.

Some thoughts on life around Lymington at the time of D-Day, as related by DR BASIL THORNTON, who practised in Lymington

125

and Brockenhurst.

The build up: Things began to liven up when they started to widen country lanes and put in hardstandings. One way systems were created which made it very difficult for me to get around and I did not have the petrol for lengthy detours. I found that if a route was not guarded by a 'Snowdrop', an American Military Policeman, there was a fair chance that there would be no oncoming traffic and I could nip through the wrong way and get away with it!

Along the verge of Sway Road in Brockenhurst, they had lines of vehicles being made amphibious by the application of a kind of soft sticky silicone grease (good for plumbing repairs, if you could get a bit).

About a week before D-Day, all personnel were gathered in Briefing Camps hidden all over the Forest. They were briefed on their coming tasks and objectives and how they were expected to carry them out.

There was a camp across the Beaulieu-Lyndlehurst Road and as I would have had a long detour, I insisted on being allowed to drive through, which I was, but with a sentry on my running board, his rifle at my ear and directions not to look right or left but keep my eyes on the road.

In the briefing camps all personnel were arranged into groups with their vehicles and equipment, ready for embarkation. We had one soldier in the theatre at Lymington Hospital with an appendicitis at this time. He had an armed guard to ensure that he said nothing!

To illustrate how difficult it was to get around the area in those days – I had a confinement at a farm beyond Sowley – and set off over the level crossing, through the toll bridge, signed the book at the Causeway Control Point giving a reason for the journey, went past Elmers court, opened and closed the gates on either side of the runway of Pylewell aerodrome, which ran across the road, then through the forest gates at Broomhill, and through another runway with gates by St Leonards' Grange. Needless to say, I was too late for the birth of a baby girl, who, by the way, I still meet occasionally.

Of course, there were few civilian doctors about and life was very hectic. A day could start with anaesthetics at Lymington Hospital, followed by surgeries at Lymington or Brockenhurst, a round of visits in East Boldre, afternoon surgery in Sway, which was in the front room of a private house, and visits or more surgeries in the evening.

With all this moving around, I was perhaps uniquely placed to see the build up to D-Day and its effect on the area.

On D-Day minus one, I was visiting a patient at a cottage on the shore by Pitts Deep and had the impression of being able to walk right across to the Island from craft to craft, the Solent being so full of them.

I slept through the exodus, having been very busy the preceding days. The enormous air armada passing over at low level to avoid enemy radar, left me quite undisturbed, but everyone was talking about it the following day.

In the next day or so, I was walking down Belmore Road on a warm sultry evening and could clearly hear the gunfire from the Normandy beachhead.

1945

Diary of National and International Events

January 17	Russians captured Warsaw.
21	Russians in Silesia, East Germany.
26	Auschwitz liberated by Soviet troops.
February 4	Yalta Conference.
14	Dresden bombed.
March 6	Cologne captured by Allies.
April 1	Americans invaded Okinawa.
5	Japanese Cabinet resigned.
11	Russians entered Vienna after 7 day battle.
12	President Roosevelt died (unexpectedly).
27	Russians and Americans linked up in Germany.
28	Mussolini and mistress shot by Italian partisans.
30	Hitler killed himself and mistress.
May 2	Germans in Italy surrendered. Berlin captured by Russians.
3	Rangoon (Burma) captured by British.
8	END OF SECOND WORLD WAR against Germany. VE Day celebrated.
June 26	United Nations Charter signed at San Francisco.
July 26	British General election. Huge Labour majority – Churchill succeeded by Clement Attlee as Prime Minister.
August 6	Atomic bomb on Hiroshima, which was laid waste.
8	Russians declared war on Japan and advanced into Manchuria.
9	Nagasaki – second atomic bomb.

14   JAPAN SURRENDERED unconditionally to
     Allies.
15   VJ Day celebrated.
September 2   Victory over Japan completed.

CALMER WATERS

On April 18, 1945, The Berlin Philharmonic Orchestra gave its last concert of the war, Wagner's 'The Twilight of the Gods', and less than a month later Germany surrendered to the Allies. Hitler, faced with defeat, had committed suicide in his Berlin bunker on April 30 and in the small hours of the morning of May 7 General Jodl signed an Unconditional Surrender in the same railway coach which had witnessed the signing of the Armistice in 1918.

Winston Churchill had demanded unconditional surrender and had got it. It was indeed a twilight for fascism, for on August 14 Japan surrendered after the explosion of the second atomic bomb on Nagasaki.

Across Europe, in Russia, in North America and Australasia the celebrations rang out, firstly on VE Day on May 8, then on VJ Day on August 15.

From the *Lymington Times*

Major Mills, the New Forest MP for many years, had announced that he did not intend to stand again, and Lt Col Oliver Crosthwaite-Eyre was nominated as the new Conservative candidate. The new man was a Roman Catholic, and this provoked an extraordinary letter to the local paper from The Protestant Truth Society pointing out that Germany and Italy were Catholic countries (and implying that Hitler and Mussolini were members of that Church), and questioning the new candidate's loyalty to the British Crown!

The result of this, of course, was a predictable rush of support for Col Crosthwaite-Eyre and a good deal of free copy to fill the *Lymington Times*.

But the main item of concern, as the war in Europe entered its last few months, was transport arrangements for servicemen on leave. It was now possible to arrange leave on a more generous basis for soldiers in the BLA (British Liberation Army) and other services, and these men of course were given railway passes to the nearest station to their home. However, they often arrived late at night after several days travelling, and the newspaper took up the case of a BLA soldier who had to walk from Brockenhurst station to Pennington with all his kit.

128

A local taxi service then wrote to the paper pointing out that:

we meet all trains at Brockenhurst whether ordered or not, and nobody is left behind except the people who have to wait for the first train in the morning to Ringwood, Wimborne, etc, which are outside our radius. Parents, wives, and relations would help much by telling the service people that there is a WVS Canteen open all night at Brockenhurst for their benefit where they can contact a taxi and have something warm while they are waiting.

However, the paper spoilt this idyllic vision somewhat by suggesting that perhaps soldiers did not always have the fare for a taxi journey of several miles! The situation was not helped by some of the 'coldest weather for 50 years', or by the fact that the last train from Waterloo was habitually unpunctual.

Indeed, the paper picked on another case a week or two later, when a serviceman whose family lived in Lymington was stranded at Brockenhurst at 11.00 pm because the taxis did not have enough petrol – 'they don't get any extra for participating in the get-you-home scheme.'

A Major Martin, from Southampton, arranged with the WVS at Ringwood to supply private motorists to take men home from Brockenhurst. The WVS would issue petrol coupons for this, which would have to be countersigned by the stationmaster at Brockenhurst.

By mid-February it was stated that General Luckock, the local Army Welfare Officer, had had a long talk with Mr Nobbs, the Brockenhurst stationmaster, who had 'made out a splendid guide for his night porters as regards who to call up, and has arranged that pending the arrival of a car the man should be directed to wait at the WVS Canteen at the Morant Hall'.

And on the 17th February the paper noted the 'Death of Local Hairdresser, well-known in Sway and Brockenhurst'. This was Mr CA Schisan (fifty-four), who had opened a hairdressing saloon at 'The Chambers' (later known as the 'Island Shop').

(see Stan Schisan – Brockenhurst Bred page 49.)

On 24th February it was noted that compulsory fire-guarding was to end, and all equipment out on loan was to be returned to the local council!

By a single vote the New Forest Defence Association decided to seek temporary enclosure of 250 acres of the New Forest for cultivation in addition to the 750 acres which the Verderers had agreed with the Ministry of Agriculture (though it will be remembered that the newspaper report of this at the time had spoken of 1,000 acres). This was to be 'subject to the new sites being chosen in consultation with the Association, and thrown open again, with all other enclosures under the Scheme, not later than Lady Day 1949.'

At the end of March it was announced that under the new Education Act which came into force on 1st April Brockenhurst was to be the Grammar School for the district. Mr May said that 120 scholars would be admitted each year, based on the results of an examination, and the abolition of school fees 'would break down snobbery'. To some parents who objected to this encroachment of Socialism he pointed out that parents had been paying £15 a year per child whereas the cost was £35 per year, so they were already being heavily subsidised.

At the end of April Mr FW Kimber, a Brockenhurst postman, was awarded the Imperial Service Medal on his retirement for his forty-one years service in the Post Office.

In the edition of 28th April, with VE Day now only a week away, the newspaper complained that 'last week-end was the first time in five years of war that people could not get potatoes', and suggested rationing.

The editions of 12th and 19th (297th and 298th wartime editions) carried news of the VE celebrations in Lymington and Sway respectively, but there was no news of Brockenhurst. The Lymington bonfires got a bit out of hand, but the police wisely adopted a low profile (though some people criticised them for this).

And the Verderers were concerned about the possibility of increased use of the New Forest for tank exercises, now that 'with the end of hostilities private people could turn the military off their land.'

On 11th August, with the ending of the war against Japan, the *Lymington Times* carried for the last time the masthead note 'Wartime Edition', with the supplementary note ' – 310th week'.

How depressed its readers would have been, as they looked forward to better times, had they known that they were not yet even halfway through Britain's period of shortages, austerity, and rationing, and that things such as bread rationing still lay ahead in the future!

BROCKENHURST RAILWAY STATION

This is mentioned particularly in 1945 reports from the *Lymington Times*. It is appropriate to stress that the station was of immense importance throughout the war. As in the First World War, thousands of service men and women used the station for getting to local army camps and aerodromes; others changed trains there.

The station also had a crucial role as a marshalling yard, particularly for receiving and on-loading ammunition. JIM LAWFORD had joined the railways before the war *(see Chapter 1, Between the Wars)* and gives a picture of the station's considerable expansion:

BROCKENHURST STATION BEFORE THE FIRST WORLD WAR.

When war broke out I was nineteen, but still working on the platform. They extended the marshalling yard and then required extra shunters. I was a shunter throughout the war, becoming head shunter; this meant sorting out the wagons and getting them in the right order for the various engines. Brockenhurst was a busy and important station. Trains came from all over the place, coming direct from Nine Elms, Battersea, Salisbury, Feltham, etc. We used to split them up, for the maximum a steam engine could bring in was 90 wagons, equal to 900 tons. However, as soon as they left here, because of the banks at Sway and Wimborne they were limited to 600 tons. It was an extremely busy yard employing 11 shunters and 2 yard foremen.

I can remember at one time there being over 100 wagons on this side for Brockenhurst and being unable to find a space in the unloading bays. Lots of them were full of bombs, ammunition and stores that were used in the offensive; bombs, etc, going to Stoney Cross, Ibsley, Beaulieu and Homesley airfields.

I went up twice for a medical, passing A1, but was told, "What are you doing here? Get back to work." I was quite pleased naturally, having a young family, but at least my job was of national importance, coming under the essential works order.

Funny thing really for I was nineteen or twenty but people who were a bit older were called up from the railway, but they were not doing the same job as me. However, they never upgraded me. By the time the war ended I was still getting junior porter's wages, but

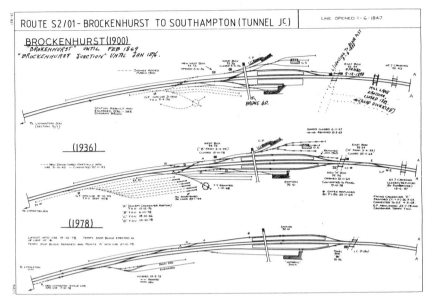

PLAN OF RAIL TRACKS, 1900-1978 TAKEN FROM TRACK LAYOUT DIAGRAMS
BY GA PRYER, PROVIDED BY MR J HONEYBUN.

acting head shunter, the reason being those returning from the war took up their seniority. Wages at that time being – Porter £2, Under Shunter £2 15s, Head Shunter £3 5s, Policeman £4, Guards £3 something. Engine Drivers got the same as Policemen.

We had some fun, I can tell you, during the early part of the war. I was under shunter doing all the chasing about. In our slack spells we would make cigarette lighters out of the brass bicycle pumps, using blow-lamps and soldering gear; if you were lucky and knew someone who worked in Wellworthy's and could get them chromed, you could make yourself an extra shilling or two.

Everyone used the porters' room for their meals or came in for a cup of tea. Any rate Mr Gale from Sway, a head shunter, had his blow-lamp well pumped up with a clear blue flame making one of these lighters. When in came this driver for a yarn. He started telling us about saving up clothing coupons of his and his children to buy his wife a coat: this meant saving 75 of the bloody things. He then looked around, "Can I have a light?", forgetting for the moment where he was, and picking up the blow-lamp and not seeing the blue flame, and so badly burned his moustache. He was more accustomed to the engine tender-lamps with a funnel spout and wick. We did laugh, I can tell you!

132

I left the railways in 1963 of my own accord because I could see what was happening. All the traffic fell off with the arrival of the diesel engines. When they came, 900 tons would come down and 900 tons would go out, no problem.

Hearing that a job was going in the post-office I took it and became a postman. I cannot say that I enjoyed it the same, but at least I didn't get so dirty. I wondered what I had let myself in for, because the railway is a family and the feeling in this was not the same, but they do look after their staff well.

VE DAY (Victory over Europe Day). May 8, 1945

JUNE DRAYSON had returned from the Marden orphanage to Southampton a short while before VE Day. It had been a shock and going from Brockenhurst to Southampton with its devastation "was something!" Her mother had been bombed out twice. The Victory Celebrations which she describes were typical of many towns:

The night peace was announced, I went mad – never seen anything like it! We couldn't move in the streets, lorries piled with people everywhere, windows open with music screaming everywhere – Pomp and Circumstance March – all the ships at anchor hooting. I have never heard such noise! I must say it was glorious, brilliant that night.

While in Brockenhurst itself WALLY KNOTT was among those who helped to build a huge bonfire on Waters Green which hundreds of folk enjoyed. Celebrations were also held in the Morant Hall and what is now the College. Wally helped to decorate both stages with flowers from his garden. And there were Victory Parades which included members from the Home Front Organisations and pupils from the schools. JOHN PURKESS, when asked what he remembered of the events, said with glee, "We were given two – TWO – days off school!"

VJ DAY (Victory over Japan Day). August 15, 1945

Waters Green used to be the place for many village events. There was a football match to celebrate VJ Day; and beforehand a parade with a brass band. "I led it – my horse was terrified," recalls COLIN TOWNSEND-ROSE.

The dark days of war had come to an end and street parties, with the lifting of the blackout, heralded the advent of peace. At last it was all over! We had, it seemed then, not for the first time, witnessed a war to end all wars and a clear bright dawn spread across the troubled face of a weary world.

A WAY AHEAD

Even in May, 1945 Winston Churchill, who had given courage and inspiration to millions, was speaking of his vision for the United Nations which he had helped to create:

"We must seek nothing for ourselves. We must make sure that the World Organisation does not become an idle name, does not become a shield for the strong and a mockery for the weak. It is the victors who must search in their glowing hearts and be worthy by their nobility of the immense forces that they wield."

CHAPTER 4

BROCKENHURST HOTELS

*These hotels are mentioned elsewhere in the anthology. We are very grateful
to them for providing the background information.*

BALMER LAWN HOTEL

Until the 17th century it was called Palmers Lawn. In the First World
War it was used as a Field Hospital *(see Between the Wars chapter)*. In
the Second World War it was commandeered by the army and run
as a Staff College. In 1943 it became the centre for planning the
Normandy invasion. General Eisenhower visited the hotel frequently
and it is said that the orders for the day of the invasion were issued
from the Balmer Lawn. *(I have been unable to verify this – Ed)* After the
war the property was purchased by Lady Honeywood, who ran it as
a hotel.

LAWRENCE S POWELL, *Camp Commandant, HQ Royal Marines
Division, October 1941 to May 1943, writes:*
The recently formed Royal Marine Infantry Division, consisting of
two Royal Marine and one Army Brigade moved its Divisional
Headquarters from South Wales to the Balmer Lawn Hotel. The
troops required to maintain Headquarters, i.e. Defence Platoon,
clerks and drivers were accommodated on heathlands to the west and
north of the hotel, while the ancillary services such as the Royal
Signals, RAOC and REME were located in the surrounding villages.
The General Officer commanding the Division was Major General
(later Lieutenant General) Sir Robert Sturges, who had successfully
carried out the occupation of Madagascar, then in the possession of
the French. He was given the important duty of breaking down the
divisional organisation in favour of individual commanders who
would then be linked with the already existing Army Commandos.
They were to play a vital part in Operation Overlord of 1944.
The Division's stay in the New Forest was a pleasant one, for
despite the necessity to keep itself in trim by day or night exercises,
we were not under any great pressure. Moreover, 'the natives were
friendly'.

135

BALMER LAWN IN EDWARDIAN TIMES. COURTESY OF BRIAN DOWNS.

I also have in my possession an officer's Sam Browne belt of the Great War vintage which, in the course of an exercise near Picket Post, a local farmer gave me, out of the blue. It had been in his farm buildings. As it was made of true leather and was such an improvement on the rather shoddy imitation leather that I'd been compelled to use before, I wore nothing else for the rest of my service.

All who survived the war and are still alive today have lively and happy memories of their stay in the New Forest.

CAREYS MANOR HOTEL

Originally a hunting lodge built for the King.

Most large lodges would have a retainer who managed the property on a permanent basis and John Carey was such a person. The old manor was given to John Carey by Charles II for services rendered during the period 1660-1685.

The Bowden-Smith family took over the ownership of the house in 1790, when Robert Smith, a wine merchant, married Miss Bowden from Cornwall.

The original house was built about 100 yards into the college grounds but was demolished. The present house was built in 1888 and stood in approximately 14 acres of grounds. Within the grounds was the village cricket pitch, and over the years the house had its own tennis courts.

Herman Bowden-Smith built a row of houses within the village which is now known as Careys Cottages. These were given to the village so they could be rented to the poor, with priority given to the retired estate staff. He was the last member of his family to own the house which he sold in 1934, before he went to live in Switzerland. A Dutchman called Mr Builderbeck bought the house and turned it into a hotel. Most of the land was sold off separately to the local council.

During the war the hotel was used to accommodate a number of Welsh Guards.

EVELYN SEATON *was a Bowden-Smith whose family had formerly owned Careys Manor. Although her childhood was spent in Berkshire her interest in Careys Manor intensified when she came to live in Brockenhurst in the later part of the Second World War:*

In 1943 my husband (Group Capt Hodder) had been reported 'missing presumed killed' in a raid over Germany. I arrived in Brockenhurst with two boys aged three years and one year and used to help at the Forces Canteen in Lyndhurst Road. British Army officers were occupying Careys Manor and one of these, a Welshman, used to frequent the canteen. He was very homesick and missing his own two children. So he took a great interest in my sons, helping to bath them and accompanying us on forest walks.

On one of these walks he asked me whether I had seen what many officers had seen at the Manor: a funny old lady who regularly walked up the main stairs, ran her finger along the bannister rail, talked to herself and sniffed incessantly. When she reached the landing she always vanished as abruptly as she had appeared.

I knew that he had described my Great Aunt Charlotte who had died many years before. When she had stayed with us at our Berkshire house, we – young children – used to hide under her desk while she wrote letters. She sniffed continuously and muttered to herself the contents of her letters. Thus she revealed to us what she thought of us and our parents. Sometimes polite, sometimes not!

You will have to ask the hotel staff and guests whether Great Aunt Charlotte still appears.

THE FOREST PARK HOTEL

In the latter half of the 18th century, the Morant family acquired 425 acres of Brockenhurst making them the chief landowners in the area.

In 1879 a vicarage was built on a forest site granted by the Crown and in the gift of John Morant. The site was one of seven on the Forest Park Estate. The Rev George Octavious Wray was the first vicar living there in 1880.

In 1893 two men, Donald W Preston and EEJ Francis, then took ownership, calling the house Little Aimers.

In 1897 the house returned to being a vicarage, the vicar being the Rev Rupert Pain. At the turn of the century a WH Dore bought the house and again called it Little Aimers, but we do not know who lived there as he himself lived in Bournemouth. On his death in 1902 the house was put up for auction as a hotel called the Forest Park Hotel.

During the 1914 – 1918 war the hotel was used as a military hospital returning to its role of hotel after the war.

(Referred to in Between The Wars' chapter – Ed)

The present owner, RE Collins, bought the hotel in March 1968 adding a new wing of bedrooms a few years later, and all its present amenities.

(The above information was provided by Sean Cooney.)

RHINEFIELD HOUSE

Many of those who have been interviewed were at some time employed by the Walker-Munros, owners of Rhinefield House before it became a hotel.

For centuries the New Forest was divided into Areas and Walks – each supervised by a keeper; then a prestigious post, appointed by the Crown. Keepers lived in a series of lodges of which Rhinefield was the first to be built in 1709. During the reign of Charles II (1660-85) the use of the Forest as an exclusive hunting area waned and the office of Keeper of the Walk became a Grace and Favour appointment.

By 1859 Rhinefield, which had been the site of a succession of keepers' lodges, had become the home of a Forest Nurseryman, who was responsible for the creation of the Ornamental Drive and the planting of many fine conifers in the grounds.

In 1877 many of the Crown Lands were 'privatised'. Grace and Favour appointments lapsed and vacant lodges were leased to private individuals. Rhinefield passed to the hands of the Walker family which owned Eastwood Colliery, immortalised in the novels of DH Lawrence. In 1885 the only daughter of the family became engaged to a Lieutenant Munro RN and her father's engagement present was £250,000 with which to build a family home at Rhinefield. After their marriage in 1887 the couple adopted the name Walker-Munro and

1914. FOREST PARK HOTEL, WHEN A MILITARY HOSPITAL.

supervised the construction of an impressive country seat comprising the Great House, a hunting lodge, stables, gardener's bothy and a gate lodge.

There was even enough small change left over to build a modest beach hut, which is best known today as The White House at Milford on Sea!

The Great House contained four suites for the four daughters who were part of the family plan to which Mother Nature was unfortunately not privy, since the lady of the house gave birth to a son in 1889. The mother took little part in her son's early upbringing, which was left largely to servants. After a public school education and service with the army in France in the First World War, Major Ian Walker-Munro emigrated to Kenya to become a farmer with financial assistance from his father. He married in 1919 and had four sons.

Controversy seemed to follow the Walker-Munro family. For example, they styled themselves Lord of the Manor at Rhinefield – a wholly fictitious title which brought them into conflict with another local family, the Morants, who were official Lords of the Manor of Brockenhurst and Rhinefield. Their mutual antipathy even extended to a refusal to worship in the same church and, in 1903, the Walker-Munros decided to build a church of their own – now St Saviour's, by the Watersplash in Brockenhurst. However, Mrs Walker-Munro quarrelled with the incumbent, a relative whom they had themselves installed in the living, and work ceased. The full significance of this only became apparent on the death of her husband in 1923. The church, being unfinished, was not licensed for burials, so, rather than let him lie near the Morants, she buried him in a copse on Ober Farm, which at that time was the Home Farm.

Mrs Walker-Munro was now a very wealthy woman and became the benefactress of many charities, to which she intended to leave her fortune, to the exclusion of her estranged son. However, even this plan misfired. Having revoked one Will and not yet signed its replacement, she died, effectively intestate and the unthinkable happened – the whole estate passed to her son. Frustrated to the end, she joined her husband in the Ober Farm plot in 1934. Rhinefield remained in the possession of the family until after the death of her son in 1950, when crippling death duties forced his widow to dispose of it.

OTHER LARGE HOUSES, which were used for military purposes during the Second World War:

Lawnside, Meerut Road
Nethermoor, Rhinefield Road (Medical units)
Orchard House, Wilverley Road
Whitley Ridge Hotel (Officers' quarters)

The Masonic Hall was called the Kia Ora Hut. During the Second World War it was occupied by Wellworthy Piston Rings, which also took over the rear of Gates Garage.

Old Foresters Hall, behind the Masonic Hall, was used by Redmayne Engineering.

Brockenhurst Railway Station provided a large marshalling yard of great importance for assembling military vehicles and ammunition.

(see Brockenhurst at War, Chapter 3 – Ed)

The above information was provided by Jack Place and John Purkess.

CHAPTER 5

MORE BROCKENHURST BRED

– AND EARLY RESIDENTS –

JUNE DRAYSON (neé Dawn Jennings)
My mother was widowed shortly before the war. She had a family of
four – three girls and a boy – and as she could not cope with all of
us, me and my two sisters, Joyce and Audrey, were placed in an
orphanage in Southampton. When war broke out we were
immediately evacuated, firstly to various homes in Boldre, but soon
a suitable home was found in Brockenhurst and we all came together
again.

In Marden, a gracious old house, thirty-two girls were accommodated under the charge of a lovely young matron, Mrs Pearl
Wilson, a missionary's widow. I was eleven years old at the time. I
was there most of the war and, to us, it was a happy time. We went
to the Village School and remained there till we were fourteen and
then had two years of training at the orphanage. This was right from
scrubbing floors to being a companion to Matron – this made us
ready for domestic service. We also helped in the garden. The home
was self-sufficient.

Troops were billeted, not in Brockenhurst itself, but throughout the
Forest. The troops, besides the British, were mainly American and I
believe French Canadians: and guns were posted in the New Forest.
Matron used to reassure us when we heard their noise and said that
the guns are out there to protect us. The orphanage was huge and
there was a great passage down the middle of the house. Every time
the air-raid sirens went off we all gathered there. We had quite a few
air-raid warnings, but I recall only two hits and not much damage.

We were much involved with 'war activities'. The girls received
ballet, dancing and elocution lessons. When the troops' entertainment came to Brockenhurst the girls always provided 'in-betweens'
– filling in between acts with song and dance. At Christmas time we
always put on a Nativity play for the orphanage and troops. They
used to take us to the pantomime at Christmas. We were taken in
troop carriers under the canvas tarpaulin in the lorries – great fun.
We girls also knitted for the troops – scarves, socks, helmets and

so on. These were distributed by the Women's Voluntary Services.

On the green, where the common is, the troops used to gather for different talks by big-shots, whoever used to come out from the military. I can remember the Americans all being there and packed in; Matron took us out there because it was just across the road from us. We were all introduced to General Eisenhower, who came across and spoke to Matron. We stood out for we were always in uniform. Another time when the British troops, lines and lines of them, were out there it was Field Marshal Montgomery. I shook hands with him too – it was a treat! At one time we were hoping to see Winston Churchill. He did actually come, but for some reason we could not go out there.

When I turned sixteen shortly before the end of the war, I went back to Southampton to help my mother. Southampton, though, was a wreck, but one thing stood out – the Church had been bombed out but the cross stood up on its own: that really made one think. To see that cross in the rubble standing in defiance to all the destruction around!

(Further memories are recounted in the 1940 and
1945 accounts of Brockenhurst at War – Ed)

FRED ENGLAND

I was born in 1923. My father was a blacksmith and worked at the back of the 'Foresters'. Depending on the time of year we went catching minnows in the stream on the way home from school or probably when the weather was sufficient like, we'd meander up around the back and come through looking for hazel nuts or anything that was going. We would invariably come home with wet feet.

I left school in 1937 and went to work at Baker and Spencer's garage, hoping to become a motor mechanic. Another lad and myself alternated, one finished at one o'clock and went back at five o'clock until eight in the evening. That was for a gross 10/- a week. By the time you had taken your overalls out and insurance it didn't leave much to give your mother. You just managed to get your sweets or whatever you wanted on perhaps a fourpenny tip for blowing up somebody's tyres.

What probably spoiled us here for travelling was the good rail and bus services. You had a bus every half-hour until quite late at night. The trains . . . well, when we were young we would ride our bicycles down to the Blacksmith's, leave them there and straight up on the train. If we were going to Southampton – Mum, Dad, younger brother and myself – we would buy a week's supply of butter from Edwin Jones and bits and pieces, go to the cinema, then go and have

fish and chips in a cafe. My mother would say, "Don't get much change out of a pound on these trips to Southampton!" That was probably a third of Dad's weekly wage gone, but we were fairly self-sufficient at home with vegetables and everything else. We didn't have a radio, but that didn't matter so long as you had enough to eat and drink and something warm.

Of course bicycles were part of us, I mean we hardly went anywhere without a bicycle, we would cycle to the pictures, even Southampton. Allen Eede and I would cycle down to Bournemouth just for a swim and that sort of thing and didn't think anything of it.

Baker and Spencer's kept going until 1940, I imagine it was when petrol was zoned. So we closed the garage and then we went our different ways. I went into Wellworthy's in Lymington cutting piston rings from a casting. I didn't like it in there so they offered me a job in the tool room.

One particular night on my way home, as I came across Setley, they were bombing Southampton and the old anti-aircraft nose caps were going through the gorse bushes.

On another occasion I remember John Iddes coming up the path all breathless, saying, "Quick, can we put this in your shed?" He had half an undercarriage leg of a 109 Messerschmitt he'd got from Silver Street where this thing had crashed. As he was leaving with it tucked under his arm, the army arrived and chased him.

Why that shed didn't blow up because of all we'd got in there –

cannon shell, incendiaries – I don't know! We used to take them up to the sandpits this side of Hincheslea and set fire to them there, together with what we used to bring back from the bombing range at Ashley Walk. We would go by bike and come back with all these bits strapped to our bicycles – flare parachutes, bits of the flare, if not whole ones. One night an oil bomb landed just this side of the stream. But there was no explosion as such and probably that oil bomb is in the ground and nobody has discovered it. When you think of the boggy ground and the stream that is around there anything could be down in it!

When I was called up for the RAF I became an engine fitter.

(Fred England's War Service away from
Brockenhurst is recounted in Chapter 7 – Ed)

JOYCE ENGLAND

My main memories of Brockenhurst when I was young, were the weekly dances at the Morant Hall, that was about every Saturday. I have seen great changes as far as housing here. I was in Shirley, Southampton, at the beginning of the War and we lost our home in 1940. We were bombed and my mother and father were very fortunate to come out alive. Our house and the one next door was down and you couldn't live in it no more. Fortunately that night I had not arrived home from work – I worked at Portswood in the library – but Mum and Dad always wanted me to be with them at nights. I couldn't make it home because of the sirens. When I came back home next morning there was a message at an aunt's to tell me not to go home. I thought why's that, why can't I go home? Any rate I did. I found only rubble, I could see the shelter well covered and I was looking round there – couldn't see into the shelter. Fortunately a warden came and said, "Who are you looking for?" I said, "Mr and Mrs Pope." He said, "Don't worry, they are in a hall and all right." Any rate I went to my brother, who had been informed, of course. I stayed with him for three months. Then Mum and Dad came to Brockenhurst to live with a sister in the village and she wanted me to be down here as well. My two brothers were away in the army and navy so I came to Brockenhurst in February 1941 and have been here ever since.

MARGARET EVANS

My father died when I was three years old and later my mother re-married. My step-father was a builder but both my parents taught at the Village Primary School, where I was educated. The School then

144

consisted of just the brick building with five classes and pupils stayed to the age of fourteen unless they went to the County School at the age of ten or eleven through the medium of the Scholarship or the Entrance Exam. The County School was originally housed in the old wooden buildings in Highwood Road, now the site of the Village Hall. A new building for the County School (later to become the Grammar School and now the Tertiary College) was erected in 1938-39 and I moved there for my own sixth-form education. A Portsmouth School was evacuated to Brockenhurst and took over the Highwood Road buildings, although sharing the science laboratories at the County School. After the war, Priestlands School was established in the buildings in Highwood Road.

Had it not been for the War I would not have met my husband Bob, who was in the forces and stationed at Balmer Lawn Hotel where all the preparations for the D-Day landings took place and where Churchill came on occasions. He gave me no indication of the imminence of what was about to happen.

My first wartime memories were of the arrival of evacuees from Portsmouth. The Billeting Officer visited all the homes to say how many evacuees one would have, there being no choice. My mother had three boys billeted on her.

During the war strange things happened in Brockenhurst. I would go to bed at night and wake up in the morning to find all sorts of vehicles including bren gun carriers and tanks had filled the side roads along the Sway Road, Partridge Road, Avenue Road, etc, or conversely I would go to bed with the roads filled with vehicles to find they had all gone by morning. It was quite eerie as one heard no sound of them during the night. Not long before D-Day there were big oil tanks at the bottom of Sway Road with notices up saying "No naked lights, no smoking", but I remember one black American soldier sitting on top with a cigarette in his mouth. There were also notices all round the village saying, "You are forbidden to speak to the troops" in case any let out any secret information. Two elderly ladies approaching some American soldiers sitting on top of the tanks were greeted by them with, "Good morning," to which they replied, "Good morning," only to be told, "You are not supposed to speak to us."

Despite the dark, and hundreds of troops around, we felt perfectly safe wandering the streets. No-one was ever attacked. This is one big difference compared to the fear which exists today. As Brownies we used to walk to the Forest Park Guide Hut alone while our parents had no fear for our safety, even though we were often late back because we played around on the way home.

I feel that Brockenhurst was a much closer-knit village before the war. Not only was it smaller but families tended to stay in the area so that everybody knew one another and everyone shopped locally. In those days you were served by the shopkeepers rather than helping yourself. Many of the shops, though in different hands, have remained the same sort of shop. For instance, the butchers, green-grocers and fish shops, the chemist, the jewellers, the dress shop near the Watersplash, the sweetshop and the other clothes shop have stayed the same type. And, of course, Purkess and Streets have long been established. The Island shop was another grocer – my mother could remember it as a forge – and Gosling's was another butcher. Small shops at Butts Lawn, Avenue Road and Mill Lane have long since gone as has Miss Wingate's School at the top of Avenue Road, though Miss Wingate herself still lives there.

Church congregations were large during the war years and the Church had a strong influence in the village. In fact it is generally recognised that a more united community spirit was prevalent during this period of time. For instance, the occasion when six people from Southampton, whose homes had been bombed, arrived on the doorstep. I was turned out of my bed in order to put them up and neighbours arrived offering part of their meagre rations. Friends and neighbours produced clothing coupons when we were to be married to help us to buy our wedding outfits.

Now there is a more selfish attitude in general. For example, when the school was housed in the old wooden buildings with its leaky roof and other disadvantages, everyone helped one another. Once in the new building at Priestlands, staff adopted a more selfish attitude – "This is my classroom – keep out!" People tend to become self-centred when things are going well.

It is strange that in spite of all the horrible things that happened, my recollection of the war years is that they were happy ones enriched by the good feeling engendered by everyone pulling together and the support they gave one another. My dominant memory is of the camaraderie.

IAIN HAYTER (*Owner of the family garage in Brookley Road*).
The garage was established by my grandfather in 1927. He put in my father to take charge of the taxis and his brother to look after the workshop. The cars were mostly little Morrises and Austins. My father and uncle are dead and I'm the last of the line. I have two daughters, but no sons.

I was born in one of the two white cottages belonging to the garage in 1935. During the war, my parents used the cottage for meetings of the White Rabbit Club, which my mother founded for Service men and women; British, American, Canadian and Free French. As a young child of five or six I often used to wake up in the morning to find a RAF pilot or WAAF sleeping in my bed! I'd never hear a thing.

My grandfather used to live at the top of the stairs; his room was next to mine. He would say, "Boy! Boy! Come and look. There's a dog fight going on." I remember one night a whole lot of shrapnel fell on the roof and our garage. Very exciting. My mother was furious and fetched us both off. I remember the stick of bombs which fell on Brockenhurst and especially the one on Purkess's shop. I wasn't scared. As a child, I thought it great fun, like the soldiers, my brother and I played with. The hardships of our family didn't come home to us. As long as I was fed I didn't mind. One night my mother woke me up. "Look what Hugh's brought you?" I said, "What's that? Oh, a cucumber." I went back to sleep. It was a banana which Hugh Sutherland, a pilot, had brought from Egypt. I'd never seen a banana before.

Most of the early part of the war my father was in the Eastleigh Sanatorium. When he went for his army medical they discovered that he had TB. It was a traumatic time for my mother who had to look after us, visit my father and, with my aunt, run the business. Financially it was very difficult. There was very little petrol to sell and there were just a few taxi jobs.

(see Brockenhurst at War 1943 for details of the White Rabbit Club — Ed)

IVY LEWIS

I have lived in the same house in the village all my life. Father worked on the railway so most of the family travel was by train. I had no bicycle until I was about sixteen. There was little money for things such as Wellington boots and food was very simple. Home grown vegetables, a few biscuits, cocoa and an occasional glass of home-made lemonade was a treat. The cul-de-sac was a safe place for children to play hopscotch, rounders and a kind of cricket with Floss, the dog, fielding in the deep!

There were about two hundred children in the Village Primary School of whom no more than three each year would pass the scholarship exam to the Grammar School in Highwood Road. All the rest stayed at school until they were fourteen. I was lucky to be taught typing and book-keeping and went to work in the Lymington Telephone Exchange.

On September 3 I was on duty and there was an immediate 'Alert', which turned out to be a false alarm. Life continued very much as before. I felt saddened rather than frightened by the onset of war and at the instigation of a colleague gave up having sugar in my tea!

During the Southampton Blitz the Lymington Telephone Exchange was involved with the redirection of calls.

After Dunkirk the troop trains laden with exhausted men were marshalled in the sidings near Tattenham Road and food and tea were given by those who lived near.

I feel that there was much more consideration for other people in those days. Children could play outside safely and had much more freedom. The NHS did not make much difference to us when it was introduced after the war as we already had a form of insurance through the Friendly Society and my father paid a hospital insurance so that if he were injured on the railway he could be taken directly to Boscombe Hospital, which was right by the line.

I was lucky to live in such a friendly village.

MARY LEWIS *now sharing a house with Ivy her sister-in-law.*
I spent my childhood in London and my main early memory is of life during the Blitz.

In 1942 I was conscripted with all the other twenty-one year olds and joined the WRNS. I trained as a Pay Writer working on the ledgers. About six of us went together to the Naval Barracks at Portsmouth. All the ledgers were transferred to Goodings, a country house near Newbury belonging to Mr Ricketts – an oil millionaire. Before we went there we had two or three weeks doing nothing else but tots – adding columns of figures – because the Paymaster Captain at Goodings was complaining that Wrens couldn't add up! I volunteered for service abroad with a friend, but I got rated Leading Wren and sent to Southampton, while she stayed a Wren and got sent to Malta!

The South Western Hotel was HMS *Shrapnel.* I was there on D-Day. At about nine o'clock they were already bringing the wounded back and they were lying on stretchers in the foyer of the hotel. We had a collection and bought some cigarettes for these poor men. I'll never forget that. Only when we read the papers did we realise what really did happen.

CYRIL OTTER
My father was a ticket collector on the railway and we lived in a railway house. I was born in 1922, left school at fourteen, and went to Wellworthy's Stanford Hill Works as office boy. My first job was the licking of the stamps and putting those on. Next year you were promoted probably to taking the tea around, getting the cakes for the girls in the office and gradually you worked yourself up. I eventually

finished up production control manager.

The railway station at Ampress was built during the war when we employed a lot of people from the Isle of Wight. You can stop there now, I believe, if you say to the Guard you want to.

We had a managing director who was well in with Sir Stafford Cripps (Lord Privy Seal). He used to come down to our factory and tell us what to get on with. Lord Beaverbrook (Minister of Supply), he was quite a frequent visitor.

During the war I was treated well. I was playing football and got kicked in the head and had a blood clot and went paralysed for six months. During that time I had my calling-up papers. Well, you can appreciate I wasn't top of the class, so I had to continue on my work at Wellworthy's.

But I did find the soldiers and the troops around here were ever so good and we used to try and do what we could for them. I remember my mother used to say, "Bring your friend up." We used to have the old British Legion in those days along Fibbards Road. We used to go in there, meet them down at the Pub and that. They understood how I felt a bit guilty you know about not being called up but I couldn't do anything about it. I did go for my medical but things didn't turn out.

About the football club that ground used to belong to the old grammar school. That was their sports ground. We put in a bid for it from Mr Morant. He let us have that bit of ground for £800. That was for that ground plus where those council houses on the left-hand side of Horlock Road are and the left-hand side of Fathersfield. About 10 years ago a fellow came over and said, "I will give you £250,000 for it." What would go into the village if we had sold that? That's a prime piece of ground for the village. The kids will enjoy it for years and years. All I hope is that nobody ever takes it or ever thinks of selling it. It is under trustees at the moment – but they do at times find legal loop holes.

In 1955 I became Chairman of the Football Club and remained so until 1984. So I did my stint.

TED PERFECT

I came to Brockenhurst at the age of twenty-one. Because I had lost a leg at the age of twelve, and because of the deep recession in the 1930's, I had to leave my Norfolk home when I was eighteen and go to a training institution for crippled boys in London. Courses were offered there in either tailoring or boot making, but I was directed to the boot workshop. I spent three years there in Dickensian conditions. As I completed my training the superintendent put me in touch with Mr Charlie Knapp, Shoemaker, in Brockenhurst. He himself had earlier trained in the same place. I came to Brockenhurst and lived in lodgings in Park Close with the family of Mr Knapp's brother.

On the day war was declared I heard the news lying in my bath! I certainly did not feel frightened. It takes more than war to frighten a Norfolk man!

As soon as war began I was registered disabled. My wages increased because we had a contract to repair hundreds of pairs of army boots brought in huge sacks every Monday. They were dumped at the little shop in Butts Lawn and collected a week later by lorry. We also used to look after the leather footballs for the Brockenhurst Football Club. They had to be repaired and pumped up. Football became a lifelong interest and I served as Club Treasurer for many years – only giving up at the age of sixty-five. I used to cycle to the local grounds to watch every fixture.

Mona and I were married in 1940, and settled in her old family home as her father had moved over to manage Plumbley's Stores in the new shop built in Butts Lawn. Our first son was born in 1942 and during the air raids, when shrapnel was flying in Park Close, it was difficult to know where to keep the baby safely.

In response to a government appeal Mr Knapp and I joined the Fire Service and were issued with uniforms as part-time firemen. We took turns on alternate nights to do control-room duty between 9 pm and 7 am. At first, contact with the Lyndhurst HQ was by telephone but later, a teleprinter was installed.

Social life centred on the British Legion Club where we played billiards and card games, and organised children's entertainments. One night the building was hit by a bomb, and the old caretaker who slept there woke up to find a set of antlers had been blown off the wall and ended up stuck round his neck!

After the war the shoe trade declined so I worked at Wellworthy's. I remained with the Fire Brigade and rode round on my bike to tidy up after the appliance had gone out. Sometimes it was difficult to convince the 'powers that be' that I had come as quickly as I could. It took some time to get everything together and to get on the bike, and so I challenged the critical officer to improve on my time! He didn't try!

Certainly the old days were better! We kept rabbits and chickens and were never without a meal. Purkess had an allowance of bran for rabbit food in wartime, and we grew lots of green vegetables. There was always someone worse off. Next door lived Mr Clare who had been blinded in the First World War. He worked as a picture framer. While I was struggling home in the blackout holding onto the palings to feel my way, I could hear him hammering away in his workshop. His was always a 'blacked-out' world. Makes you think!

JACK PLACE

I was born in Wallands House. When I left the Village School at fifteen, I was caddy for a year at Brokenhurst Golf Club for 1/6d per round plus 1/- tip. Then on September 26, 1938 I joined the Bournemouth Gas and Water Co, which had just taken over Brockenhurst Gas Co I looked after domestic gas appliances in Brockenhurst and Sway. The gasometers and office were near the bridge in Sway Road.

During the war the air raid siren was where the old Fire Bell is now, by Lloyds Bank. That was our communication with the 'powers that be' to say that Jerry was on his way.

There were lots of ARP wardens, but at the gas company by the railway line we had our own wardens. One of them used to sleep there every night.

At the gasworks we used to have Scannells come and deliver coke for us to sell to the general public. They also used to bring coke to sell to the POW camp at Setley. One day the Italians brought their own lorry into the yard. They started to pile on the coke which had been delivered. Some of them suddenly disappeared into the copse, which then stretched alongside the gas works all the way from Fern Lodge to the bridge, and eventually came back with a rabbit. They built a fire in the middle of our yard, skinned the rabbit, cooked him over the flames and then tore him into pieces, beat the embers off him, shared him out and ate him. Don't know how they caught him, but they certainly ate him!

After the war the Council took over the camp at Setley and converted the Nissen Huts into homes for the homeless. They all had kitchen ranges. Bunny Munden opened up a grocery shop there.

Just before D-Day Brockenhurst was swamped with Canadians and Americans. There was reinforced concrete on all the verges of the road from Holly Bush Farm onwards towards Lymington. Vehicles were parked both sides of the road.

We were all nippers then – about seventeen years old. We used to cycle up Sway Road and, as beer was rationed, the GIs and Canadians would give us jerry cans to take down to the Foresters Arms and get filled up with beer. The soldiers weren't allowed to go. We cycled from Sway Road backwards and forwards. For that our reward was packets of Lucky Strike and Camel cigarettes.

One morning every soldier, vehicle, all equipment had gone. Not even a bit of paper there. It was uncanny. It wasn't a dwindle – just a disappearance.

Once I was stopped by the army at Latchmoor for not having an ID card. The village policeman, PC Sherratt, came round to issue me with a summons. He knocked on the door, gave me the summons, then asked me if I could give him some of my roses! I still had to pay the 10/- fine, which in those days was a week's wage. The policeman said if he, rather than the troops, had caught me he would have let me off!

Another night I was cycling with my mate through Priestlands Place in Lymington on our way to a dance. A copper was waiting for us. He stepped off the pavement and stopped us and said he would summon me for riding without lights. All lights had to be covered with paper and a slit was cut into the paper to let through just enough light to see to ride. My mate who worked at the stores at the bottom of the High Street said to the copper, "If you make a case of this you'll get no more butter." I never heard a thing!

STANLEY WILLIAM PORTER

We lived at the Lodge at Culverley where my father was head gardener to Mr. Montague Ellis, a London solicitor. I went to the Church School, which I left in 1934.

In 1942 I noticed that no less than 600 people were working on war-work in Brockenhurst. Dad was one of the 102 people in the Home Guard, 83 in the WVS and no fewer than 43 people on telephone duty at the Morant Hall. What they all did I don't know! The Home Guard platoon of which Dad was corporal, was guarding Marlpit Oak Bridge, hoping that Hitler would come down that way. It was a proper 'Dad's Army'. In the early days they were drilling with broomsticks. I always remember one incident that was particularly funny, a stick of incendiary bombs dropped in Brockenhurst. No-one knew where, but everybody turned out. I was in the Auxiliary Fire Service in those days. We were on duty alternately at the Fibbards Road Station. This night I was actually off. We were all running, actually running down the Sway Road. A lot of the air raid wardens, Dad's platoon of the Home Guard and we, arrived at the bottom of Partridge Road on the triangular piece to find one solitary incendiary bomb sizzling away doing no harm whatsoever. One of the air-raid wardens had a bucket and he promptly put it over the top of the bomb. He got a blast from my dad and it was the first time I had ever heard him swear. "You silly bugger," he said. "You should have had sand in that bucket!" Considering he had run the best part of half a mile down the road carrying the bucket, he had done fairly well!

We went out round trying to find these particular incendiary bombs that night. I had a pal, Wal Hewitt, who was with me in the Auxiliary Fire Service. Dad thought they had fallen on Culverley but they weren't there at all and we learnt afterwards they were down at the back of Leachy Pond behind Butts Lawn. We went looking and we got down as far as that on a beastly night with the river in full spate and Wal decided he would go over the river. It wasn't necessary because it was all boggy ground over there. All of a sudden Wal was missing and I heard an almighty splash and he was in the middle of the river. This was in midwinter. Anyway we got him out and left the bombs wherever they happened to be!

The Auxiliary Fire Service was quite busy. One of the things I remember was the army magazine at Marchwood being hit and we had to move. Totton went to Marchwood, Lyndhurst went to Totton and Brockenhurst was supposed to go to Lyndhurst, but as things happened we got to the top of Clay Hill and the fire engine wouldn't go any further. It was a very old engine given by Mrs Walker-Munro, donated to the village many years before the war. We had to push it and it started at the bottom of Clay Hill and away we went. In those days the Lyndhurst headquarters were in the main street. We arrived there, but one didn't go into the fire station. That wasn't the done thing. The headquarters of the Fire Brigade was in the Mailmans Arms and that's where they operated from. We had lots of laughs.

One outstanding memory was one night when Jack Dunkinson, Father and I went to Beaulieu to play darts and to everyone's amazement we came back with the Birt Challenge Cup which still exists in the fire station at Hythe. We came back to the British Legion at Brockenhurst and I don't know whether PC Sherratt ever knew it, but we didn't close at 10.30 that night. It was quite amazing the amounts that were drunk.

One of the things a lot of people will remember is the searchlight battery down at Bridge Farm which was fully operational. The Sergeant Major who was there used to shout "Hup" and it could be heard right through the Sway Road.

Brock was a good place to live. Everybody knew one another and I think that was why we never got into mischief. I left Brock in 1941 and went into the RAF.

That's about it! By train two shillings return to Southampton and you could reach London in two hours!

COLIN TOWNSEND-ROSE
I was born at Little Prescotts, Tile Barn Lane; my parents had the house built in 1924. There was a thousand-year-old yew tree but

it is now dying.

A few days before war was declared my mother (who had been a nurse during the First World War) went up to Harrods (people from Brockenhurst did shop there in those days) and stocked up with £120 worth of goods, including a hundredweight of soap. When war was declared, I was eleven. My father, who had been on the North West Frontier during the Great War, told me the news and how serious it was.

Over the years many fortifications were built in the area. Near the railway cottages near the Sway Road there was an enormous tank trap, thirty feet by fifteen feet together with four telephone poles and some old cars ready to obstruct advancing German vehicles! The bridge itself had nine-inch holes drilled at the top into which mines could be dropped. Where Tile Barn Lane enters the A337 there was a machine-gun nest with guns pointing down the Lymington Road. The tumulus on the Sway-Hincheslea Road was an observation post.

We ploughed up three of our eighteen acres and with our bicycles we towed our produce to the WI stall next to the post office, and made about £100 each week for charities. We built a gardener's cottage for £495 and employed a gardener throughout the war. There was no bathroom put in the cottage.

We turned over our lawn to rabbits: a buck and six does, who had three families a year. When they were an appropriate size my father blipped them and made them into rabbit stew. My mother's rabbit in aspic was delicious. It tasted like chicken. My governess looked after the rabbits – seventy-five in total. My father made our gloves out of rabbit fur.

A passing thought – war films show people telephoning and speaking immediately. In fact, you had often to book long-distance calls several hours beforehand. When I was farming in Canada just after the war, desperate to get news of my father, who was critically ill, I was told that there would be a two-day delay.

TERRY WINGATE

My dad was born in Winchester in 1883 and used to visit Brockenhurst from an early age to see his aunt who managed the Rose and Crown Hotel. In 1900 the family moved to Brockenhurst and Grandfather took the licence out for a pub called The Holt, now the Balmer Lawn Hotel. My earliest memories go back before the Second World War to the Guy Fawkes bonfires at North and South Weirs. I was born in 1934.

On the day war broke out I was the recipient of a brand new BSA bicycle, a very high spot in my life. Other memories associated with the war were the blackout, followed by the village air-raid alarm system. This consisted of a Mr Hill, a local grocer, rushing by on his bike blowing a whistle signifying the alarm, followed by Curly Warne ringing his bell for the all-clear – that meant the cattle could resume their ruminating!

Later air-raid sirens were installed. They seemed so sophisticated after the whistle and bell. I was attending the Village School and hating every minute. Imagine our delight when the new fangled siren started bellowing and we were told to pack our things and go straight home. The blitz was the next thing I recall, with the bombing of Southampton; the sky was often red with the town fires. The thump of the bombs, the bark of the Ack-Ack guns and the fingers of the searchlights and streams of tracers often disturbed my slumbers. In Brockenhurst, Dad said that they had bombs in a field at Brookley Farm where there was a herd of cows and they never hurt one. I remember that because I went up there with Dad and saw the small craters about eight yards across. This was towards Hincheslea. Dad also said, "You must watch the horses, for horses have good eyesight and if a horse's head comes up to have a look, they often have their attention focused on something – could be enemy troops."

Gradually I became aware of a build-up of troops, the RA personnel. Hollands Wood was a transit camp. The Balmer Lawn Hotel was then the Duck and Duckling and was the Divisional Headquarters. Sometimes there were lots of troops about – suddenly they were all gone. Very often they left behind considerable stores. Then came our chance. We acquired a variety of things – fleapowder, helmets, ammunition, bits of uniform, smoke canisters, a variety of military bric-a-brac, which we shared out at a place we called 'the basement'. This was just up river from the Balmer Lawn Bridge. The ammo was great. We used to build a fire, pile it all on and crouch behind a bank until it exploded. One day we had a small bomb and did the same with that! Luckily it didn't explode, so we took the blackened object to PC Sherratt and said that we had found it.

Around D-Day I remember lessons being interrupted when the tanks went by. Of course every tank took about 20 seconds to pass. Then we had 40 seconds of lesson followed by another 20 seconds of a tank roaring past!

My dad was in the Home Guard along with Mr Knott. There was a hell of a bang on our front door one morning – it was about 1940. "Quick Wingate, you are to report to Headquarters immediately." Mother says, "It's the invasion, Bert. They are invading." Dad says, "I don't care what they are doing, I am going to have my breakfast." His breakfast consisted of porridge, a whole fry-up, marmalade, the whole damned caboodle! It took about three-quarters of an hour at least. He sat and had his breakfast and wandered over there about an hour later, was greeted with, "Where the hell have you been Wingate?"He said, "I have been having my breakfast" – of course he got a rocket over that.

There were two Fenners in the Home Guard. Sergeant Fenner, who was a First World War man and said you had to kill three Germans before they killed you, and little Fenner, the Station Master, who was a nervous man. One day Sergeant Fenner says, "We are going to throw grenades." And he marched them all up to the bomb pits with their steel hats on. Poor little Fenner was at the back. He kept on saying, "We shouldn't be doing this, it's dangerous." When they got to the bomb pits to throw them, each time one went bang Fenner was crouching down and Spikey Purse would throw dirt on his helmet. He still kept saying, "It's dangerous, they should stop it."

Another night they got up to Hincheslea Bog where a stream comes out. Corporal Knott was in charge of the patrol. When they got to the bank they hesitated and wondered how to get across. So Corporal Knott says, "There is only one way to get across and that's jump it." There's a gasp from the ranks – jump it? Knott says, "Of course you can jump it. Here, hold my rifle." Took a running jump and landed smack in the middle.

Another tale about the Home Guard: Blackmore, the Commanding Officer, gives Dad a 303 rifle and says, "Go to Setley, outside the Oddfellows Pub – now the Filly Inn – and stop everything coming along the road." "Everything?" says Dad. "Everything," he says. "Everything."

So Dad is up there stopping everything. Presently who comes along but Blackmore in his car. (This is, of course, all Dad's recollections.) He says, "Halt! Who goes there?" but, Blackmore in his car still kept coming. Dad repeated, "Halt, who goes there?" but he kept coming. Dad brings up his gun and says, "Halt or I'll fire." Blackmore realises he is going to shoot him, slams on his brakes and says, "You bloody fool." Dad said, "My orders were to stop everybody!" When Blackmore went to drive away, his brakes were jammed!

Another incident that Dad recalled were the two bombs that fell by the side of Church Lane. Dad was on duty with another chap that night up somewhere near the railway gates. They heard these two bombs rolling down and Painter throws himself down into the mud. Dad thought, "Christ, that's bloody muddy down there. I'll stay upright and take my chance. I would rather die clean!"

PART II

THE WAR
BEYOND
BROCKENHURST

CHAPTER 6

CHILDHOOD MEMORIES

Collected by Geraldine Roberts

As I gather the memories of my contemporaries (give or take a few years either way) I ask myself whether there was anything special about growing up during the war. One clear aspect that emerges is how 'normal' strange events seemed because to us it was just the next step in our lives. This acceptance by children is most startlingly shown at the end of this chapter in the interview with Bridget Corrie-Hill, who was a prisoner in Hong Kong. But many of the memories recounted involve evacuees and in several cases, here too, a child certainly had to be resilient to survive.

While many of us were obviously aware of the fluctuating fortunes in the progress of the war, it never occurred, certainly not to me, that it was possible for us to *lose*. I was in church on September 3 and the vicar brought his wireless into the pulpit for us to hear Chamberlain's announcement. Afterwards we bought ice-creams from the 'Stop Me and Buy One' tricycle where they were being sold off at half price; that was one halfpenny for a prism shaped water-ice.

I can remember being frightened by the tip-and-run raids of the Luftwaffe; the drone of wave upon wave of bombers going to raid Coventry or Birmingham, and their return, knowing they would jettison their remaining bombs before leaving our coast. I slept in all sorts of strange places including the dining room, under the kitchen table and under the stairs. It saved my mother from rousing me when the siren went.

Once, when playing tennis at school, we saw one of the German yellow-nosed squadron zoom up the valley on a level low enough for us to see the pilot. Another time, when in a school house near the railway, I recall the extraordinary way time became protracted as I raced – seemingly in slow motion – down the stairs and into the room with the Morrison shelter (a reinforced metal table), yelling at a Junior, who was frozen at the piano, to join the rest of us squashed beneath it.

On the beautiful blue-skyed day of the Battle of Britain, we were celebrating my mother's birthday with a picnic on a ledge under some

Dorset cliffs. Poor Lishie, one of our hens, had been sacrificed, and we were enjoying her tough old legs when the German squadrons started to fly in. It was totally disorientating because, as they surged over, the beat of their engines echoed against the rocks behind us and we were submerged by the sound.

Later, I was in Sussex when the V-1s started, but I realised that they flew in definite corridors and, fortunately, we were safely between two of them.

As I grew into my teens, I followed the progress of the war more seriously. My brother and sister were 'in it' and then the news of casualties among relations and family friends increased awareness. But it was when a close friend at school lost her brother in the submarine HMS *Sickle* that it really came home to me, and it was only much later, with a family of my own, that I appreciated just how agonizing it must have been for the adults.

On the Home Front, food was a great preoccupation, but my mother dealt with that and I just ate the nettle soup, got used to the strange taste of eggs preserved in isinglass, watched the patterns made by the weevils in the flour and, at boarding school, tried to keep my own two ounces of butter to gorge on at the end of the week. The school cook must have been a magician because I can still remember actually enjoying many of our meals. We always had full-grain bread, but the Ministry of Food banned it as being unfit for human consumption. There was such a rumpus from the baker's customers that we were finally 'allowed' to continue eating it. It may seem strange now to think that the Ministry's original action was possible, but white bread was the only 'good' bread before the war.

What else? The rubbery smell of gas masks when we had to practise putting them on quickly and the feeling that one could not breathe properly through the double filter; the importance of not losing my Identity Card (the same number being on my Medical Card to this day); and immediately handing in my Ration Book when staying away. Rationing continued right up to 1954.

By 1945 I was just old enough to volunteer (we were given adult ID cards at sixteen I think) but with the Services already being demobbed, there was little point and so my 'war work' consisted only of brief stints helping out in the WVS canteen and sweeping the floors of the Cottage Hospital. My mother, though, was an ARP warden and my father was in the Home Guard. Yes, there were quite a few 'Dad's Army' moments I believe, such as when the poor rabbits got a salvo meant for some practice targets; and the subtle manoeuvering between private and officer when they moved in the same social circles. But there is no doubt that every single one of them would have fought to the death had the Germans actually invaded.

RICHARD TAYLOR, *the instigator and compiler of this book, was also a child at this time but his concerns lay in a different direction.*

In July, 1940, aged twelve, I was very frightened by the imminent prospect of a German invasion but excited by air-raids over Southampton, which we could watch sixteen miles away. Young boys can be heartless.

On September 3, 1939, John, my brother aged sixteen, Jill, my sister aged fourteen, and I were sitting in our hired caravan at Wootton Bridge playing the usual acrimonious game of Monopoly, when we heard the flat voice of Neville Chamberlain announcing that Britain was at war with Germany; or words to that effect because I was concentrating on acquiring my favourite properties of Trafalgar Square, Fleet Street and The Strand. When my parents returned from getting milk and eggs from the farm, my pessimistic brother – sixteen is often an Age of Pessimism – predicted that by Christmas, Manchester, where we lived, would be destroyed by bombs and in any case we'd be gassed before that. By Christmas the only raids we'd had were those of German planes dropping leaflets on British citizens to demand peace from their government. So I began to think that perhaps my brother wasn't infallible.

Meanwhile, my father, who on the outbreak of war had said, poignantly, "At last I shall be needed," had died. So my mother, her brother who was desperately trying at the age of forty-three to become an RAF pilot, and his wife, all three of them Mancunians, decided to leave Manchester, where my mother's father, until his death in 1939, had lived since 1870. They wanted a large house somewhere in the South. Invasion could happen at any time they felt, so rented property, particularly in the south of England, would be cheap. Cheap because it could be the first area to be overrun by the Nazis – or 'Nasties' as my Richmal Crompton hero, William Brown, called them.

The two families selected an eight bedroomed house, plus two cottages, 30 acres of fields and woodland for £7 per week! The beautiful house, Hazelhurst, on the edge of Sway, was empty except for faded X-ray photographs of what looked like buttons inside a human stomach!

I had books on aircraft recognition, so on our first day at Hazelhurst I knew that the lone plane flying over the hayfield was a German. I was helped by the German markings! We were standing with the charming farmer, George Ingram, when an object dropped from the plane. I, being obsessed by the thought of invasion, shouted, "It's a parachutist!" We dropped to the ground and seconds later heard a mild explosion. A small bomb had landed near the Hare and Hounds two miles away.

This didn't stop me worrying about invasion. The visit of a Home Guard (or LDV) officer to ask permission to store explosive Molotov Cocktails in our garage; then to place a dilapidated farm cart at the bottom of the hill to impede advancing German invaders and to dig an inadequate looking trench for 'our men' to fire on German tanks,

161

convinced me that invasion was imminent. The officer's request confirmed my suspicion that our defences were fragile. It's true that in 1941 barbed wire and scaffolding were constructed along the coast, but I felt that the Germans might find ways of penetrating that obstacle, particularly as the army had considerately made gaps for sea-bathers at Milford. When the threat of invasion was over, I came to realise that this freedom suggested that the army had its priorities right!

ANDREW KILSBY *was ten years old in 1939 and tells of life as an evacuee, first, strangely enough from the point of view of safety, near Brighton.*

Before the war I lived with my family in Walworth, London, about twenty minute walk from Big Ben. I well remember the Munich Crisis. War had been expected and as instructed in the official handout we had packed our cases ready for evacuation. At this time the local open space had a barrage balloon in it. This gave us Londoners a real sense of security, as we had been told these balloons would create a ring around us and stop the bombers getting through. I also remember we had gas masks to carry about which seemed to me a bit of a joke.

Then came the German invasion of Poland. We joined my sisters at their school and were taken to London Bridge station and put on a train. On arrival at Brighton we stood in groups at various corners of the street, while billeting officers would go backwards and forwards saying, "One girl please"or "Two girls". The area had been told that a girls' Grammar School was coming and was ill-prepared to take boys and, as a result, my family group consisting of my sister Mary, myself and brother, was left till last and eventually taken to a naval captain's household, made up of himself, an unmarried daughter and a maid, in the poshest part of Hove. They were exceptionally nice to my sister – but had no time for boys. My brother and I spent most of the day on the beach and were then put to bed with a mug of Bovril and some of the awful dry biscuits we had brought with us in our luggage. My sister dressed and had dinner with the Captain and his daughter. He obviously thought my brother and I needed some training and gave my sister a rope (with a sort of lead in it – some boating thing) to keep us in order.

The Sunday war broke out we were taken to the Parish Church in Hove which was so packed that our school was put in a balcony at the back of the church. Suddenly the siren went and the vicar said he thought the best thing to do was to take cover under the pews. This we attempted to do. There were inches of dust under these rarely used pews, most of which finished up on our knees, socks and clothes.

The Captain's patience with us soon ran out and to our relief we were moved from this opulent part of Hove to Portslade, two minutes from the harbour and gasworks, and billeted with an elderly couple, Mr and Mrs Grainger. We were transported by a teacher in her baby Austin. As we approached 30 mph the car rocked like mad. This particular journey sticks in my mind as I believe it was my baptism into car travel, and I wrote home at once to give my parents the news. The house at Station Road was too small, and my sister was taken elsewhere, but my brother and I stayed there until the fall of France. The Graingers were extraordinarily strict but caring. If we were very good we were allowed, after our bath – a tin bath once a week – to listen to Jack Warner in Garrison Theatre.

We walked about eight miles a day from Portslade to Brighton and back to attend school at a church hall. We usually walked along the sea front and I can remember the songs we sang to help us on our way. One song had the lines:

Go and wash your dirty socks,
Go and wash them clean,
Go and wash your dirty socks,
And show them to the Queen.

It was important to change step at the end of each verse.

An incident which stands out at the Graingers: I had come in late and was to go straight to bed the next day as a punishment for this misdemeanour. I arrived home from school and to my surprise saw a ten-shilling note in the hearth, beginning to curl up and break into flames. I grabbed the note and so saved 'Auntie' Grainger's ten shillings. She was delighted and let me off my punishment. The strangeness of this kind of morality puzzled me then and puzzles me now.

When France fell we moved on to Chertsey in Surrey. The Graingers were in tears to see us go. My brother and I, as usual, were left for ages standing about while enquiries were made. Eventually we were taken to a lodging house run by two ladies. We were taken up to a bedroom in which were two single beds. One of the ladies, Miss Ellis, pointed to one bed and said to us both, "You're to sleep in that." We cried ourselves to sleep, to be awakened by a gentleman arriving in our room at dead of night. He was wearing oily overalls. He washed, put on some best clothes and disappeared. We discovered he was an Irishman named Jack, who did shift work at a local factory and then went off to some social events till the early hours.

It seemed that the two ladies of the house lived for money. After a short time another lodger was taken in. My brother and I were moved onto camp beds in the dress showroom. We slept among the tailor's dummies and coat hangers. Each morning we folded up our beds so that the room was ready for customers. Then the final move. It was felt we were rather lowering the tone of the dress showroom and so were put in the attic. This we shared with a semi-demented maid, Ada, who was worked to death. My brother tried to run away, but having reached the station was turned back.

After many months my mother came to see us. All sorts of goodies were turned on for her visit – marmalade, coffee, biscuits. But after this reception, Mama took us out and said, "By the way, where do you sleep?" We pointed to the tiny window of the attic and told her all, whereupon, we went back, collected our things and returned to London. Before leaving these two ladies I would like to say clearly what actually happened in this house, believe it or believe it not. They did dressmaking, bred cairn terriers, took in lodgers and had a little adopted child named Cyril. They would play cards at night with their lodgers and used our rations to supplement the other 'guests' meals and refreshments.

Why did we not complain? We did, but little was done. The ladies were so clever at putting on a friendly front. Why didn't we write home? We felt our parents in London were having a tough time and at school we were constantly told not to worry them, but to stick things out as there was a war on.

Our return to London was not for long and my brother and I were sent to stay with Aunt Helen and Uncle John who lived at Lulworth in Dorset . . . but when after some time, my uncle was due to leave, we returned home for good.

My father was an Air-Raid Warden. He would be out during the raids but would look in at midnight during the lull. His voice outside the shelter always brought reassurance. My greatest fear was the noise, particularly an anti-aircraft gun that was on the back of a lorry. When that came near the noise was deafening and frightening.

My grandfather lived next door to us. He was lame. It was said that he had fallen from a penny-farthing bike and his leg turned septic. Sometimes he would go for the night to St Peter's crypt which had been turned into an air-raid shelter. One night it received a direct hit. My father searched for hours in the rubble for Grandad. He was rescued by other helpers but died in hospital from injuries.

Another clear memory was when the City of London was set on fire. The firemen were standing about helplessly, their hoses flat as no water was available. They were trying to pump it from the Thames, but this was totally inadequate. The whole spectacle was strange but I had no idea I was witnessing a major event in history.

Later came the V-1s. When the unique hum of the engine stopped

164

you knew it was about to crash. So you listened and waited, usually pretty terrified, hoping it would keep moving. They appeared to drop in groups, depending on the range set and the prevailing weather conditions. So it was horrible. If one dropped near, you awaited the others.

My clearest thought on VE Day was at last I will be able to go to bed and sleep in peace, with no explosions.

SHIRLEY CRAMPTON's *recollections of being an evacuee, further highlights how much the luck of the draw affected the well-being of these children growing up away from home. She remembers well the answer to the question, "Where were you when war broke out?"*

At the age of six and a half and living just 10 miles from the centre of London I had, on that Sunday morning, been allowed to go alone to buy an ice cream from the corner shop. The noise of the wailing siren sent me running back home in one direction as my older sister ran in another to find me.

When it came to evacuation my parents sent me with my sister's school to Silsoe near Bedford. This proved disastrous. I was very lonely with no-one I knew of my own age and where the boys taunted me by pulling my long ringlets. But my stay in Silsoe lasted only three weeks as, while being driven with the family we had been sent to, my attention must have been drawn to something outside the car and I fell out, presumably through leaning on the door handle which one pushed downwards. I remember sitting in the middle of the main road, seeing the car go round the corner and Mr Catlin running back to pick me up. Fortunately no other car came to run me over first! The worst indignity was being tied into the car next morning to be driven home to my parents, especially as I had no thought of repeating the experience. At home I was greeted by what seemed to be a large family party to view the damaged infant, covered in bandages with a broken nose and stitched lip.

Once I had recovered, the Catlin family were not anxious for my return. My own home school was due for evacuation and I was sent with them to Bedford. Another disaster was impending! It was nine months before my parents realised that the Bedford household was not quite like home, at least not like home as we knew it! My bedding was old coats rather than the conventional blankets, and bath night occurred only when my parents were due to visit the next day, which was once a fortnight. When the lady of the house was ill, which seemed quite often, I was kept home from school to shop and clean the house. I became adept at buying fish and chips late at night and pushing my way through the queue to avoid a long wait. On occasions the husband came home drunk. We were sitting at the table one Sunday lunchtime when he arrived home late. On being told that

his dinner was in the oven he picked up the corner of the table-cloth and shot the remains of our meal over us and onto the floor. The only conclusion I can draw from these experiences is that children are very resilient and get on with life as they find it.

It is said, "Third time lucky." It was for me. I forget for how long I was at home before I was sent for the third time as an evacuee with my next school group. Our intended destination I do not know, as at Paddington we were put on the wrong train. But what a fortunate mistake that proved to be! The journey was long and continued until dark and in the blackout. The dimly-lit train stopped for a long while alongside a troop train. Food of some sort was passed from their train to ours. It was late at night when, having journeyed to Kingsbridge station, we arrived by bus at Salcombe in South Devon. I can see the bus station now and remember standing there, with my identification label on, and carrying my gas mask as well as my suitcase. As we were not the expected lot of evacuees, the waiting foster-parents were told to take anyone. Arthur Lapthorn had come to collect two little boys but seeing me standing crying, took me instead. In later years, Arthur often recalled how he had put me on his shoulder and carried me to his home with us both in tears.

Next morning the evacuees assembled in the local park and we were asked which Church we went to. Being unable to remember 'Congregational' at the age of seven, I said that it began with a 'C', which evoked the reply, "Go with Mr Lapthorn to the Church of England and we will write to your parents." Presumably they thought it best that I went with the family and for my two years at Salcombe I did just that, three times each Sunday. I spent the whole of the first Morning Service looking for Mr Lapthorn who had said that I would sit with Gran (his mother) but that I would see him there. However, I never saw him. Had he told me he would be wearing a strange white cover and singing in the choir I might have been able to identify him. He gave me a prayer to say each night with the promise of a shilling if I learnt it by heart. As you may imagine, I learnt it straightaway, but unfortunately he forgot about it. Just a few years ago I mentioned the omission to Arthur, and shortly afterwards I was presented with a copper plaque made specially for me by a friend of his. "This is instead of the shilling you should have had." Unfortunately I cannot now remember the prayer itself!

My time at Salcombe was idyllic. The kindness of the family and the beauty of the hills, sea and countryside all contributed to a time of joy and great pleasure. The Lapthorn family, which included Ian aged five months and Margaret aged three years, was a very loving and a humble one. Hilda, Arthur's wife, was quieter than Arthur and spent all of her time looking after the family. To add a seven-year-old to her own young family must have been quite a task. Margaret still remembers saying, "Have you got your gasmask, Shirley?" as I left for school each day. My bedroom was in the attic and, with no electricity in the upstairs part of the house, I found it rather spooky going up to bed carrying a candle. The Salcombe school had just two rooms and I soon progressed to the top class which went up to the age of eleven, where Miss Fielding was extremely strict. Talking seemed to be completely forbidden and the ruler used for chastisement much in evidence. But what a delight to be in Salcombe; a great yachting centre today and always boats in the estuary then. The sandy beaches were easily reached by ferry, the return fare being one penny, and sometimes I was taken there after school.

My parents came each summer for a holiday. At the end of the second stay they thought to please me with the news that they were taking me home with them. I wanted to stay! I was so happy there!

Hilda died some years ago and Arthur more recently at the age of eighty. He was a delightful character, known and loved by everyone in Salcombe. At his funeral service the church was packed. He had sung there in the choir as a boy from the age of eight and then as a tenor until just before he died.

Like Andrew Kilsby, EVELYN GREER also spent the first part of the war in Brighton. She recalls:

"The day war broke out", as the comedian Rob Wilton used to say, I was in Brighton with the rest of my school. We had been sent from a convent school in the London suburb of Muswell Hill to our sister convent in Brighton because it was thought to be safer. Perhaps it was, but as German planes passed over on their way to London, we had as many air-raids, our first on that day. War was declared while we were at church. The service was finished quickly and we were sent back to the convent. As we arrived we heard the horrible wailing sound of the air-raid siren and we all rushed into the convent quickly. To this day I still hate that sound.

We were kept separate from the 'native' school. I do not remember anything about lessons or food there, but I do recall an entertainment put on by the pupils, in particular one girl who did a very good impression of Shirley Temple.

Many of the nuns were French and it must have been very hard for them during Hitler's invasion of France, especially as they were not allowed to read newspapers. When my father came to visit me, they always inundated him with questions about the news.

The school returned to London at Easter, 1940. Probably it was recognised that we were hardly any better off in Brighton than in London.

My father worked in the city of London and usually travelled part of the way there by bus. He was joined by a colleague who lived a couple of stops further on. Some time in August 1940, he got on the bus as usual but when he came to the stop where his colleague got on, she was not there. The route of the bus passed her house and my father saw it had been bombed. Then he heard other passengers telling how she had been blown across the road by the blast and killed. He decided that I must leave London again.

My aunt and cousin had just gone for safety to a small village in Herefordshire and I was sent to join them. My time in Holme Lacey was one of the most enjoyable and formative of my life. I loved the country and vowed that I would live there when I grew up.

We boarded in a small bungalow with a couple and their grown-up son, a lot of chickens, and some piglets which were being fattened. I loved the animals and enjoyed feeding them, looking after them, collecting eggs, and helping to catch escapee pigs as they dashed wildly down the lane beside the bungalow. I also enjoyed scratching the pigs behind their ears, which they loved, and riding on their backs, which I don't think they did. We also had fun at the farm next-door. Of course, these were probably normal activities for the children of the area, but for a townee like me they were very special.

The village school was typical of village schools around the country. It had a large room where all of us children worked; it had a black boiler which heated the room; it had a wonderful Headmistress. She was interesting, kind and encouraging – a very good teacher and I loved her very much. I remember the poems she read us and the dramatisation of the chapter in *Wind In The Willows* where mole visited his old home at Christmas. I have only to hear that and I am back in that old school room. Through her, and the arrangement of the school, I realised that I was 'good at maths'. I was in the younger

168

class in the room and was supposed to be doing some writing while Miss Workman took the older class for arithmetic. No-one in that class could answer a question which seemed easy to me so I answered it, right, and from then learned with the older group.

There were only three of us in the village who were evacuees and we were a source of interest to the other children. Perhaps our strangeness gave us glamour.

The fields round about were covered in pyramids of stone to prevent German planes landing. The stones were put to good use on one occasion when we saw a rabbit on our walk. The landlady's son made us stand still; he quietly lifted a stone and threw it at the rabbit. We returned home with the dead rabbit and I was full of admiration for Billy's prowess but when I tried to tell people how well he had done, I was hushed up. My townee experience didn't cover poaching.

We returned to London in the spring of 1941. Of course the raids continued but we got used to them. My grandfather couldn't sleep without the sound of them; we children used to go out looking for pieces of shrapnel, the more fantastic the shape, the better.

The worst bombing to me was the time of the doodlebugs. The sound – the stopping – the holding of one's breath with the wish, "Please not here" – the bang – and then, "It's not us this time!" This brought fear, and shame for that fear. When we really were bombed by a doodlebug, we didn't even hear it; we were asleep downstairs. The sound woke us to tiles off the roof, ceilings down, all the windows out and many doors off their hinges, furniture flung all over the place, but none of us was hurt. My grandmother had a lucky escape. Until that night, she had been sleeping under a light bowl hanging from chains but for some reason she had moved. The bowl was lifted off its chains by the blast and smashed to the ground.

There was one injury from the bomb though. My father was in the RAF by then and came on leave the next day, not knowing about our experience. Reaching home and assured of our safety, he went up to his bedroom to get a better look at the debris in the garden. He leant out of the window and put his hands on the window frames – with the jagged glass edges still in the putty.

D-Day was just before my thirteenth birthday and while most people rejoiced at the opening of the Second Front, or worried about loved ones who might be in danger, my reaction to the news was to be upset in case my father would have to go to France before my birthday. Luckily he didn't go until later.

While evacuated I don't remember anything about food rationing although in Holme Lacey I could see that carcases of pigs were hung in a large room in the roof of the bungalow – and we didn't talk about it. Once I was home again I started helping with shopping. My abiding memory is of queues. The worst shop to be registered with was Sainsbury's. Each kind of food had a separate counter. When you had finished queueing at the bacon counter, you queued at the dairy counter, then on to queue for meat and finally grocery. You could do it in whatever order you liked, but it was still queues, queues, queues.

Food in short supply brought extra long queues but great joy. When we got an egg for the first time for months, my grandfather wrote on it "This is an egg. Spelled E G G." We looked at it and touched it and admired it. I suppose, eventually, we ate it.

We had relations who lived in the Midlands. They used to send us food parcels – poor Londoners! It was very kind of them, but also heartbreaking when we opened a parcel with a dozen eggs – all smashed.

Another Sussex resident was RUTH WILLIAMS *but she was there because of her father's work, not as an evacuee.*

I remember the day war was declared for the sirens we heard wailing for the first time and being sent into the garden to play because my parents wanted to listen to someone on the radio at 11.00 am – only years later did I realise who and why.

My sister at that time was eighteen months old while I was four and so whereas most people were provided with gas masks covering just their nose and mouth, she was carefully laid inside one which completely encased her. This was soon outgrown and she was then fitted with a red 'Mickey Mouse' design before progressing to the black version which had to be carried in its canvas covered cardboard box wherever one went.

Another essential impediment of wartime was the tin of 'iron rations'. This took the form of condensed nutritious food, such as chocolate, which was intended to be eaten only in the case of emergency. Mine was kept at school and on changing schools, anticipating the chance of a feast, I never could understand how my tin had come to be quite empty!

These days there is an aversion to the suggestion that everyone should be issued with an identity card but we all had these – and knew our number by heart – as well as wearing identity discs around our necks. And, of course, shopping for food or clothing was impossible without the ration book which was still in use for butter and sugar by the time I went to college in 1952.

We were lucky that my father's work on the development of radar and later on switchgear for the Mulberry Harbour meant that he was able to live at home throughout the war. It also meant that he was able to get petrol for his car, not only to travel to work in Brighton but also to make regular, lengthy journeys. Occasionally our half term holidays coincided with one of his trips to Surrey and so my mother, sister and I, trying to be as inconspicuous as possible in the car, had the rare treat of being able to ride with him part of the way and spend the day picnicking and walking in the country until his return. Night time driving must have been an enormous strain on the driver as headlights were masked, leaving only a very narrow slit of light to show the route.

Living as we did on the coast between Brighton and Worthing, many children in our area were evacuated to other parts of the country or even to Canada and the United States for the duration of the war, but although my parents decided not to send us away, they did ensure that the family would have alternative accommodation during any emergency, by retaining a room on a farm in deepest Sussex throughout the six years. We narrowly escaped having to leave home on one occasion when a bomb fell alongside the church tower at the end of our road. Next morning we awoke to find a barrier across the road and all our neighbours between us and the church moved elsewhere. We suffered only a crack in the bathroom ceiling!

In the early days the sirens frequently warned of air-raids and we took heed by sleeping, or trying to, under the stairs. Winston Churchill wore his siren suit and so did we, over our pyjamas. Later a Morrison table shelter occupied almost the entire dining room floor where we slept, head to toe, night after night, encaged under a low ceiling of steel, my father joining us after his ARP duties were over.

Given the same situation today it would be almost impossible for children to be so comparatively unaffected by such a war. But there was no television then and although we had radio, the *News Chronicle* and the graphic photographs in *Picture Post* magazine to keep us informed, I cannot recall as a child being present at any time when my parents discussed the war or the worries they must have had, nor was I aware of what we might have been missing if there had not been a war on.

RUTH HIRD *(nee Saville) lived just outside Southampton and obtained a scholarship to Brockenhurst County High School (now Brockenhurst College). She now lives in Lymington but recalls her school days.*

In the early years of the war, I was travelling by bus from the outskirts of blitzed Southampton to the relative peace and tranquility of a forest village where other children were evacuated. Some of these 'Pompey boys' boarded the bus daily at Lyndhurst and gypsy children from the encampment at New Park got on to go to other schools in Brockenhurst.

To supplement petrol rationing, sometimes the bus carried a gas converter at the rear and all the passengers had to get off and walk up Clay Hill.

One day, to our amazement and delight, we saw an elephant move out of the forest onto the road! *(Suddenly coming across an elephant on the road is also one of my amazed memories, but this was miles away in Dorset, outside Swanage. How on earth did the circus manage to keep their animals fed? – GR)*

The catchment area for the school was large, covering many of the little Forest villages. The Hampshire accent of the children was often so pronounced as to be unintelligible and so a strict elocution teacher, Miss Aggie Graham, was employed for first formers.

Schooldays were happy under Mr May, who would never allow boys to stand with their hands in their pockets. The staff gave their time generously for games and out of school activities. The front lawns were dug up for growing vegetables for school dinners. These communal meals were rather frugal and Mr May had a near strike one day when we were given boiled rice and concentrated orange juice.

Each Friday evening, the Army Training Corps and the Girls' Training Corps met for drill and instruction. We loved the uniforms but especially the ballroom dancing which followed.

On VE and VJ Days we joined the victory parades to the local churches.

JOY SCHISAN *was in Northampton when war was declared and had been particularly disappointed that August when her first ever school trip to France was cancelled because of the situation. She was very much involved with the Guide movement.*

Evacuation of children had begun during August. As a Girl Guide I was helping with the reception of evacuees. I had to walk to another school about three miles away and was given a list by the billeting officer for checking off names. Poor little children! Some had never slept in beds; gas masks hung round their necks and they looked like rag, tag and bobtail! They only wanted to eat fish and chips and did not appreciate the green vegetables and home made food offered by their hosts.

It was at the evacuation centre that I heard the Neville Chamberlain broadcast. A Boy Scout suddenly stopped playing the piano and everyone listened intently. It was a really sad moment and though we were only children we sensed the solemnity of the adults. I kept wondering how a war could start on such a beautiful day.

Blackout with yards of black cloth had to be improvised and although Northampton had its share of bombs, it got off lightly compared to Coventry only forty miles away. I remember seeing the night sky over there ablaze with flames. All very frightening.

I had a friend in north London and occasionally ventured on a trip to see her. Once I was stranded in a train held up on the outskirts as we watched blazing sugar factories and burning dockland.

I went to the local cinema most weeks and also the repertory theatre. We often saw actors who became stars in the future learning their craft. My cousins were great dancers so we went to the Palais de Danse where there was live music and a bar. There was no shortage of dancing partners amongst the servicemen, but you never knew if you'd see them again.

We had food parcels from Canadian relatives which were a great treat. Rationed food was stretched by the use of liver, hearts, etc, and I'll never forget the taste of dried egg and dried milk.

We had to grow up so quickly and had no 'teenage' experience. As soon as you went to work you were involved in fire watching or ARP. To relieve the boredom we listened to the radio and played darts. We had a radio star in the office. One of the Beverly Sisters worked there and sang in the clubs in the evenings with her sisters. They made their radio debut singing *Three Little Sisters*.

Now living at Waters Green, LESLEY PEDLEY *was on the East Coast when war was declared. As her family was driven home to Doncaster, she can remember her mother's solemn words:*

"Look well at the sea. It may be a long time before you see it again."

I remember the awful, wailing sirens and the lightening of our hearts when the all clear sounded. I can see myself feeling my way out of the gate and hugging the wall as I went to the nearest shop one very dark evening during the blackout. School did not start until mid-October that year because it could not open until there were adequate shelters built for the whole school of one thousand pupils.

One stick of bombs which fell did not explode. They were found to be empty save for a message – "Good luck from Czechoslovakia".

Travelling on the railway was hazardous. All signs were removed and no announcements made. The porters often did not know where the trains were going and gave conflicting information. Many people found themselves at the wrong destination. I got the habit of asking the driver.

We were not evacuated but had two soldiers billeted on us for six months. They spent their time cleaning their rifles and bayonets!

I heartily disliked our gas masks and remember the tears of rage of my small brother who had a special baby one. There was a host of cheap (2/6d lunch) British Restaurants in nearly every town and village. They were very good and used regularly.

On VE Day we had an enormous length of ribbon to which we all attached ourselves and then danced up and down the streets whilst the bells of all the churches rang.

We expected life to improve immediately. It didn't. In fact many things became harder and scarcer and I even had a ration book for my first born in 1953.

BOB GARDAM *spent his early years in Potter's Bar. He too remembers the evacuees – and many things besides.*

In 1939 my mother was a teacher and with others was responsible for supervising the evacuation of children from London. Aged seven, I remember standing on Kings Cross Station with a gas mask round my neck. There were about 400 children, aged four to fifteen, with their parents. I was going to travel with my mother, but these children were saying goodbye to their parents. I remember many of the parents in tears and the kids laughing and joking as they got on the train.

When we got to Ilkley – I remember it was Ilkley because my father was a Yorkshireman and had taught me 'Ilkley Moor Bah'tat' – my mother told me to go and talk to the children sitting on the pavement outside the station. I was told to keep them happy. Soon wonderful people came up and saw the seated children. They went off in two's and three's until there were only two left. I've often wondered why those two were left! There had been marvellous co-operation between parents, children and organisers. I could tell that even then.

On our return journey to Herts we were in one carriage and the rest was occupied by soldiers. The train stopped on the viaduct outside Welwyn Garden City. There was an air-raid on – we could see the searchlights and hear the Ack-Ack guns. Soldiers shouted to us on the train, "Put out that f . . . . . . light!" That word was new to me!

We had a Morrison shelter built *in* a room in our house. Even if the house had a direct hit, you had a good chance of surviving.

You learnt to tell enemy aircraft by the curious droning noise which came and went. We could hear the whistle of a bomb when they were trying to get Potter's Bar tunnel – the longest railway tunnel there was. The Germans blew up a cemetery in Potter's Bar where a Zeppelin had been shot down in the First World War.

After an air-raid we'd spend ages looking for shrapnel on the way to school. If you had found the largest piece you were a hero for that day.

If in the school air-raid shelter you popped your head through the door you got 50 lines! It was in the air-raid shelters that I learned to knit squares for troops' blankets.

Early in the war we were taken to Devon by my parents. While on Paignton beach we saw three 'Spitfires' coming across Torbay. All the holiday makers stood up to cheer and wave. Then we saw black crosses on the wings. The 'Spitfires' were Messerschmitts. We rushed off the beach. Seconds later, the Messerschmitts sprayed the beach with bullets. They went on to bomb the bridge at Teignmouth.

In 1943 I was sent to my uncle and aunt on their farm, which was

next to RAF Conington, used by the US Airforce. They used to entertain the officers, who became very good friends. I can still see my aunt in tears when she heard that one of the Liberators hadn't returned. This happened often.

My cousins and I used to cycle round the perimeter of the base and count the planes going out. When we heard them returning we rushed back to count them coming back. Sometimes someone would shout, "Quick! Look that one's got no undercarriage." When a Flying Fortress or Libertor landed safely we all used to cheer.

There was a camp for POWs just down the road. We kids were little horrors. We used to throw stones at the white spot on their backs. They left a beautiful model of Salzburg four times the size of a house. Eventually it was just ploughed up by the farmer.

We lived near Hatfield. On the day of the Arnhem invasion you couldn't see the sky for planes and gliders. I sat in a deckchair in our garden watching them for about three hours.

GEOFFREY HAWKES, *whose home is in Pilley, recalls a specific event.*

It took place in the fields below Bishopstoke in the summer of 1942. I must have been thirteen and my brother, David, eleven. We were swimming with some other boys in a part of the River Itchen called locally 'The Sheepwash'. The river bends there in a long deep curve and in those days there were a few willow trees in a group some way from the river bank where we left our clothes and put on our 'bathers'. It was a bright day, warmish, with no cloud cover and we'd been swimming and drying off in the sun for maybe an hour or so when we heard the rattle of machine-gun fire coming across the fields from the Eastleigh direction. We didn't take much notice, for gun practice was common enough from the Home Guard and a local detachment of soldiers, but when the anti-aircraft guns opened up we knew something was 'up'. It turned out to be a German fighter-bomber, a Heinkel as far as I can remember, which had decided to attack the railway sidings. Looking up we saw its markings, the black cross on its wings, and as it turned we could plainly see its pilot, in my imagination at least, looking our way. There were puffs of smoke from the Ack-Ack and we knew shrapnel would follow: all the village boys collected shrapnel from the streets after air-raids (and swapped it for other more desirable souvenirs, bits of shot-down aircraft fuselage in particular), so we bolted off for the shelter of the willows. In spite of the anti-aircraft fire now coming thick and fast from the batteries protecting the railway works and marshalling yards, the Heinkel turned again for a second run, opening up with its machine guns. In the roots of the willow trees I did my best to cover my younger brother with my own body: a vague feeling of 'doing my bit' and of being a hero (at least to myself) ran through me. We were all fed a diet of 'England expects . . .' through radio and comics. I remember seeing the pilot again, the aircraft must have been very low, and of thinking he could shoot us up, but probably wouldn't since he had better things to do and then the Heinkel was gone.

I can't remember if we boys went on with our swim. We probably didn't. News like that was too hot to keep to ourselves, but I don't suppose we told our parents: boys in those days seldom told their grown-ups anything!

In 1939, JOHN BLOOMFIELD *was a nine year old on holiday in East Anglia, when he noticed some newspaper placards saying* POLAND INVADED.

I remember my mother scoffing at two elderly ladies who were buying up all the tinned food they could possibly buy in a little grocer's shop in Mundesley.

Another recollection is of my father's brand new car, the Riley 1½ litre, which had cost £349. We were evacuated to friends in Exmouth and my father was quite proud of the fact that he had driven all that way, because all the road signs had been taken up as it was thought if enemy parachutists landed they wouldn't know where to go. Later, with the problems of petrol rationing he did not know whether to put it on chocks 'for the duration' or sell it. It went for a knockdown price because nobody bought cars in those days. I think it nearly broke his heart.

It was not long before the family returned to East Anglia and I went to school at North Walsham which was inside a 15 mile security zone because of the aerodromes in the vicinity.

Some random memories:

Food wasn't too bad because we were in a rural area. We certainly were short of butter and bacon and maybe meat, but bread (of a varied darkish colour) I don't recall being short of, and of course there was no such thing as sliced bread in those days.

There was no petrol for the school lawnmowers, so the boarders had to form a chain gang as it were to pull this big heavy lawnmower to keep the cricket pitch going, and we also had to tend the allotments which produced our vegetables.

As the war progressed in 1941-1942, every morning our Headmaster would read out the list of those who had been killed. At first the names did not mean too much but gradually the people who were missing were boys you had watched batting for the 1st XI, or who had played a particularly good game of soccer. And towards the end there were people who were only a couple of forms ahead of you and within six months to a year of joining up had been killed. Our Headmaster was a caring man and it's only now I begin to realise the feeling he must have had in reading out the Roll of Honour.

All around Norfolk there was a big area of wetland where General Patten's dummy tanks were set out. All the instructions for an army were daily sent out with the express object of them being picked up by the Germans, in order to confuse their Intelligence regarding D-Day.

As we recall our childhood impressions of wartime in Britain, others were experiencing even harsher realities in enemy occupied countries. One such was BRIDGET CORRIE-HILL *who has lived looking out across North Weirs for the past thirty years, a somewhat more peaceful view than the ones she must have seen as a child. Her contribution speaks for itself.*

In 1939 my family was on leave from Hong Kong, where my father was a solicitor. We were in France and it was nine months before my mother, my younger brother and I were to find a ship going East; it seemed a safe option as there was no fighting there, at the time.

It all started about two or three weeks before Christmas 1941. The day the balloon went up, my brother had a cold and my mother decided that neither of us would go to school – we didn't know why. My mother worked for the Free French, being fluent in French and Japanese. Listening in on the telephone – we only discovered this later, even my father did not know – someone had said that the Japanese had bombed the airport.

The people of Hong Kong had been expecting an air-raid practice that day so had not taken the sirens seriously at first. The raid was quite unexpected. Hong Kong didn't take the Japanese threat seriously.

Father was working in the town as a Food Controller and we saw little of him. My mother received a message from the organisation she worked for, to go with us children to the top of the Peak, after dark.

I'll never forget that night. She put all the clothes she could possibly get on us, we had on several layers, and carried what we could. We walked down the drive of the house, where there was a sentry on duty and the whole place was blacked-out. Suddenly this apparition stuck his bayonet into us and shouted, "STOP! Who goes there? Friend or foe?" As a little child, aged nine, who had led a comfortable life, I felt I wasn't going to breathe again, it was so frightening.

We went on up tiny paths to the top, shells going over all the time, until we arrived at the house. Several families were congregated there. It was pretty awful – word was coming through that the Japanese were in the town and coming up the mountain: that they were murdering ... raping young girls ... all very traumatic. The Chinese had mostly disappeared.

We were told to go to the Naval Hospital nearby, but there was no organisation there, just little family groups trying to find shelter, and the wounded were coming in, lying everywhere.

We stayed there a few days before trying to return to our home. On the way down we were dive-bombed. My mother said, "Lie on the ground" and she lay on top of us both. The bullets were literally all round us! We were very lucky to have escaped, for the Japanese were trying to kill, maim, do whatever they could to destroy those they could get their hands on. We were staying at a neighbour's house, when the news came through that Hong Kong had surrendered – it was Christmas Day.

All Europeans were told to congregate on the Football Pitch in the town, and were then dispersed to the local brothels (the 'ladies' having been removed), where we were locked in. The conditions were extremely sordid. The only air we could get was to go on the roof. It was very unhygenic, rats everywhere. We were there for about a fortnight before being taken to a compound by the Island's prison on a peninsula, called Stanley.

To get there we were put on launches, so overloaded and top heavy that every time the boat leant over, some of the passengers had to shift from one side to the other, just to keep it upright.

The Canadians and others had gone on fighting on the peninsula, because they had not believed the news of the surrender, and the battlefield had not been cleared! It was horrific. As children you accept these things and we just thought – there is a dead body and look at all the blood. Amazing what you do accept, but I can remember my mother saying, "Don't leave me; don't look; shut your eyes." Say that to a child of seven or nine, and they look. My father had been kept on by the Japanese controlling food and didn't join us till later. The prison warders had been turned out of their flats and we were lucky to get one of their rooms, 12 ft square, to ourselves – and here we stayed for three and a half years.

There was a school attached to the warders' accommodation, where teachers who had been interned taught as best they could – no books, no pencils, no paper and the children sitting on the floor. I was very bad at absorbing by listening, because I was thinking, "How am I going to get my hands through the fence to get the guavas growing outside the perimeter?" I was hungry and then you don't think of educating yourself; you think of survival . . .

We were permanently hungry and were not above trying to get hold of someone else's rations, if possible. Mother sold all her jewellery, a bit at a time, for things like codliver oil and calcium, which she was able to persuade the guards to get for her; at least during the first year. At one point the *godowns* (warehouses) were opened up; the internees were so desperate they just looted. Mother found a big, old-fashioned pram, filled it with food, put us on top and wheeled it calmly back to camp. The Japanese gave out rations of poor quality rice and Chinese vegetables.

Regarding relationships in such a situation, there were naturally fights over food and other things; but also close friendships built up. I grew up very quickly because you 'see' and 'hear' and 'spy' on people. There was no privacy for adults.

The internees had an elected group to run the camp and keep it clean and disease free as possible. Everyone had a job – my father's was to collect the rubbish for incinerating.

At the beginning the Hong Kong Japanese civilians were put in charge of the camp. The Resident was the men's barber and he asked if there was anything we wanted from our house. Before the invasion we had been preparing for evacuation to Canada and had packed everything possible in trunks. It was a couple of these my mother asked for. To her dismay they were not the ones full of warm clothes and blankets that came, but evening dresses and books! However, this proved a Godsend. The books formed the camp library and the dresses were used for costumes for plays.

Gradually the civilian guards were replaced by the Military; there was roll call morning and evening and a curfew and no lights allowed. If anyone was missing the whole camp was penalised and not allowed out for several days. If a guard found anyone trying to escape they were beaten publicly. They used very long, thick bamboo poles and two or three guards would beat one person – down they would go – and made to stand up again; a ten minute break and it would start all over again till they had practically broken every bone in their bodies and they were in a terrible state. Incredibly they survived. The man who later became my step-father was beaten because he tried to acquire extra food and medicine through the perimeter fence from a guard.

We children would entertain ourselves with games and were allowed to go down to a little beach and play among the rock pools. In some ways we had a great deal of freedom, the run of the camp, an area of about two-and-a-half square miles, and within its boundaries we were safe. We had no toys, no sweets, no books – nothing, yet we were happy and played well together. In many ways it was harder for the grown-ups. My father found it very difficult, though he was able to help with some marital legal problems. Mother was a natural fighter and found various ways of coping. I spent time looking after babies, as a lot were born in the camp.

There was one guard my mother was able to negotiate with. He came in one night soon after the atom bomb had been dropped. He woke my mother and said something terrible had happened . . . the bomb had been dropped . . . people had been killed, their eyes had fallen out and their hair burnt. We didn't know what he was talking about! Soon after that, for about a week, the Allies flew over dropping pamphlets telling the internees to stay calm and to be careful not to show any signs of being jubilant, to act with self-control and keep an eye on what the Japanese were doing.

I have no feelings towards the present generation of Japanese, though I feel that, as a race, they have an acceptance of cruelty different from that in the West. The military especially, would prefer to die rather than lose face by being captured, so they despised the Westerners for allowing themselves to be imprisoned.

We were liberated by the Australian Navy. They did not give us food – that would have been dangerous – but gave us things like toothpaste. We had been cleaning our teeth with sawdust ash, using our fingers. It was a happy time – also sad because we were all dispersing.

When we returned to England we had to face the brusque efficiency of the transit camp and the non-comprehension from relatives. It was a very strange time, those three-and-a-half years, which is very clear in my mind. I can see it and feel it, and almost re-live it and yet it is so far away . . . 50 years.

CHAPTER 7

FROM WEST TO EAST
– *The Services and Life Elsewhere* –

Compiled by Bé Cooper

Many of the residents of Brockenhurst – those who were born here and lived all their lives in this delightful village, those who lived here during the war and those who came here since the war, attracted them to the New Forest area for their retirement – have memories of the war away from the local area, in parts of Britain, Europe, Africa and the East. This chapter is devoted to these memories.

These are reminiscences of older people. In most cases I have not attempted to alter the spoken words to the correct written word or prose. The same applies to the written word of our contributors' individual styles. Also it is *Their* memories – historically correct or not after 50 years – *Their* personal reaction to a circumstance or happening at the time. It was fascinating to hear how cheerfully some hardships were coped with, not just at present, 50 years after the event, but also at the time. Regretfully I have had to shorten some contributions.

The following have contributed to various sections of this chapter –
SHEENA ARCHDALE – a Girl Guide in Scotland
MARY BATES – served with the WRNS (Wrens)
CHRISTINA BEEVERS – Queen Alexandra's Imperial Nursing Services (a QA)
CAPT TIM BEEVERS – served with the Parachute Brigade
JOHN BLOOMFIELD – a scholar
JACK BRINDLEY – served in the RAF
MOLLY BRINDLEY – joined the Women's Land Army (WLA)
TED BROWN – served in the Royal Indian Army Service Corps
DOROTHY CLARK – was with the American Red Cross and later served in the Fannies

ARCHIE CLEVELAND – served with the Royal Navy
EDNA CLEVELAND – joined the WLA and thereafter the Wrens
BE COOPER-VOSSE – a teenager at the Cape, South Africa
LES COOPER – a driver in the Signals
DR VIVIENNE CROXFORD – was with the Womens Voluntary Service
     (WVS) and a doctor in Scotland
EILEEN DORÀN – was working for GEC in London
BILL DUNKINSON – a naval Chief Petty Officer
MAJ MICHAEL EMANUEL – served in the RA, heavy AA division
BOGDAN ENGEL – Virtuti Militari, KW, DFM: a fighter pilot with the
     Polish Air Force in Britain
FRED ENGLAND – served with the RAF
EILEEN GABONY – was employed by the Ministry of Supply
JOHN GABONY – was called up to the Royal Engineers
JACK HANSON – *see Chapter 3*
EILEEN HARRISON – was called up to the NAAFI
GEORGE JOHNSON – *see Chapter 2*
LES JOHNSON (the late) – was in the Royal Engineers
RUUD LEM – a child near Nijmegen in Holland
FRANK LEWIN – served in the Royal Navy
JOAN LLOYD – a girl whose father was Resident Magistrate on Ascension
     Island
JOYCE MARCHANT – a food chemist with Lyons Food Laboratories
VERNON MARCHANT – joined the Armaments Department of the Royal
     Aircraft Establishment (RAE)
TOM MARDON – drafted to the 79th Armoured Division School for
     Instructors
AILEEN MILLS – living in retirement in Brockenhurst
NORMAN MONTAGUE – called up to the Army Ordnance Corps and
     served at Bletchley Park
PATIENCE NICHOLSON – (died November 1993) was a Red Cross
     Volunteer
BASIL O'DONNELL – 'went into gliders'
FRANCES PEYTON JONES – served with the Wrens
LT COL RICHARD POWER – RE – Indian Army Engineering Unit
MRS PRICE
TONY PURKIS – served with the Army Catering Corps (ACC)
RON REEVES – volunteered for the Hampshire Regiment
PETER REEVES – attached to the Parachute Regiment
VERA RIDLEY-MARTIN – was a VAD. She also worked in the publicity
     department of the British Embassy abroad.
DANIEL ROBERTS – a member of the French Resistance
LT COL KEN F SCOTT, MC* – RE
MAJ KENNETH N SLADE, TD – RA

ELAINE TAYLOR – was working for the Air Ministry in London
PETER TAYLOR – Royal Artillery, Surrey & Sussex Yeomanry
CAPT ARF (TOMMY) THOMPSON, DFC – RAF, fighter pilot
CAPT JKM TOD – RN
SQDN LDR JW (BUNNY) WARREN, MBE – RAF
CAPT JOE WILLIAMS, DSO, RD – RNR
RUTH WILLIAMS – a child living in southern England
MAJ GEN JOHN C WOOLLETT, CBE, MC – late RE
WENDY WOOLLETT – served with the Wrens

WOMEN AT WAR

Nurses, the first women to come in contact with the men coming from the fighting fronts, were regarded as the angels who helped repair both limb and spirits in the dark days when understanding, consoling and comforting were needed. They themselves often experienced adverse situations as CHRISTINA BEEVERS tells. As a QA she embarked at Greenock, on a dreary cold morning in mid-December, on a troopship, the P&O liner *Strathallan*, and sailed in convoy for North Africa. This, however, took considerably longer and was more adventurous than expected –

From the start the weather was rough and no one could do justice to the good food on board. Through the Bay of Biscay we had five days of a most fierce storm sending the lounge furniture, which had been tied down but had broken loose, crashing against the wall and injuring several passengers. Then the weather became calmer, warmer and balmier and we thought 'this is life'.

A not very loud crash in the middle of a calm night woke us. At once we knew what had happened – we had been torpedoed. The most eerie thing was the silence; the ship went completely still and dark. Each day, while at sea, we had had boat drill thus we knew what to do in an emergency. The four of us in our cabin donned our greatcoats and shoes, carried our helmets and emergency rations, and by the light of someone's torch went to our stations. Here we joined our places in line to climb over the rails into our life-boat.

Many life-boats were joining us in the water and the aim was to get away from the side of the ship as soon as possible. There was some panic among the foreign crew who clambered overboard and into boats not allotted to them, causing them to capsize – rafts were thrown to those in the water. Our helmets proved very useful for bailing out and also for being sick into! Where possible we picked up people from rafts, and we sang, doing our best to comfort all.

183

After some time a destroyer came into sight, looking for survivors. To our great relief we were 'pulled' on board and revived with hot drinks and a meal. It was midday when we reached Oran and boarded a train for Algiers; a very slow, rickety and crowded one. All the wooden seats were occupied by Arab women and their children, several carrying baskets with fresh produce including live chickens. At the many stops along the way there was much coming and going, and noise; I ate endless tangerines, bartered for at the stops.

From Algiers we were taken, by truck, to El Biar where we were installed in the local orphanage. Next day was Christmas Day – our lunch consisted of M & V (tinned meat and vegetables), hard biscuits and mugs of tea already mixed with sugar! No choice. During the next few days we were kitted out with soldiers' battledress and boots: my friend being last in the queue had to accept size 7 boots instead of the required size 6.

The Colonel, medical and administrative staff had gone ahead and acquired a large building at Ben-ak-Noun, on the hill above Algiers, which served well as our hospital – the 95th British General.

The rainy season was with us and tents were being erected, with great speed for us in the compound near the hospital. Protesting strongly about the mud and slush in our new sleeping quarters, we were for once grateful for our boots. By now we had some tented 30-bed wards. One night as the patients slept, the top and best blanket from each bed was stolen. The Military Police visited the local Arab houses; sure enough, the women were happily decked out in them. Actually, we liked the Arabs, they had a great sense of humour but they stole anything they could lay their hands on.

Shortly afterwards a NAAFI shop opened in Algiers where we could get fitted out with our proper uniforms. This was a boost for morale – life was looking up for us Sisters; by now I was working in the Officers' Ward where I had my eye on a very handsome young man!

At home, the late PATIENCE NICHOLSON recalls going on night-duty as a Red Cross Volunteer, during the Battle of Britain –

I was living with my in-laws in Wimbledon while my husband was at sea. During the day I worked on a farm pulling potatoes, a back-aching job. I had done a year, as a probationer, at Great Ormond and thus joined the Red Cross as a volunteer. My duties were in a hospital, St Theresa, run by nuns for the incurably ill.

From my in-laws, near the Common, I had quite a long walk to where I was on duty. I was walking along quite happily when a large number of planes came over; they were so low I seemed to be able to touch them. I thought to myself – what are you doing out here, alone. But I had to be on duty by 7 pm. I walked on, no one about, and then I thought I must get under something, the bombing is terrific! I got under – I went back later to see it – a tiny laurel bush no more than four feet high! No real protection but, with my hands over my head and saying a prayer, I felt safe. When it was quiet, I got up and walked on. I had done what I had been told to do: get your head under protection whenever there was a raid, whether it is an umbrella or a tree, no matter how useless, even a tray would do – a psychological reaction.

I arrived on duty and apologised for being ten minutes late, and carried on with the work. Next day I went up to London; I did not recognise it. It was bombed flat and looked like the White Cliffs of Dover, white chalk everywhere in the ozone – all this going on while I was under the laurel bush!

The NAAFI was a very important service for backing the fighting forces and supplying so many of the necessities and little, needed comforts. ELLEN HARRISON speaks of her contribution to these needs. She was born and educated in Brockenhurst and after leaving school she was employed at Babcock's Drapery in Lymington and thereafter at Plummer Roddis in Bournemouth. For a short while she worked as a volunteer helping to make breakfast for the men arriving back from Dunkirk. They were quite worn out and fell on the floor fast asleep. She was then called up to the NAAFI –

We had a smart uniform in barathea, and khaki overalls for work. After working for a month in a bar, I went on a course at Woking. I then took over a bigger branch with fourteen hundred men. Yes, we had our adventures – the vanmen! You had to watch them. Feeling that cigarettes were disappearing, I asked the district manager to come at the same time as the van delivery. From my office window we saw him put cigarettes under his coat on the front seat! I don't think he was selling them, just for himself and his friends, no doubt. But, there was no vandalism in those days and I was never scared, even when I had the keys from the NAAFI safe. The men appreciated what we did for them.

Although only a school girl at the time SHEENA ARCHDALE recalls donning her Girl Guide uniform also to serve the men, this time with 'char and wad' –

Eight o'clock on a freezing morning in Scotland I pedalled furiously to the local depot – an idealistic adolescent longing to do my bit, by invitation, at the mobile canteen. It was the next best thing to a set of call-up papers. Though there was only one other girl (the driver) in the dingy club room, and the buns racked on the baker's trays felt leaden as I buttered them – this was real adventure to me!

Outside stood the van and it didn't take me long to master the mysteries of the hatch opening and loading. Off to the airfield we went, and waved through the barrier as though Royalty. Into the camp kitchen to face the first round of cockney banter and cheeky chat, as hearty chaps hoisted a huge urn of boiling water into place. Then down the runway we went, to park under the propellers and we were surrounded immediately by a hungry group of oily-fingered mechanics calling for 'char and wad'.

Perhaps it was as well that this naive school girl didn't understand what these Londoners were saying. I now wonder why my mother ever let me go. Perhaps useful training for future responsibilities. Thank you, YMCA!

Home needs also had to be catered for. As Patience Nicholson mentions 'pulling potatoes' before doing night-duty, so many joined the Land Army, helping to feed Britain and the troops. EDNA CLEVELAND was nineteen years of age when she volunteered for the Womens Land Army –

I was sent to the Vale of Evesham; there with 70 other women I lived in a hostel – a derelict manor house in Charlton. Every day we were taken by lorry to the market garden. Much of the work was weeding vegetables by hand; it was back-breaking work. We worked from six in the morning to six at night. At midday we'd go off to the nearby village to buy food. Often it was just dry bread which we had for lunch. Many of the other land workers were refugees living in Shrewsbury: women of all sorts, shapes and sizes, all speaking different languages. Our WLA uniform was breeches, green shirt and pullover, a heavy raincoat and a sort of pork-pie hat.

We had a wonderful time, but the food at the hostel was terrible: perhaps because the superintendent was pinching the money provided for our keep (she was dismissed later). I remember one sandwich which had only cold cabbage and onion in it. While there I lost over a stone, and when I got food poisoning the doctor ordered me home. It was sad because it was a wonderful time.

MOLLY BRINDLEY seems to have had a more comfortable deal during her days with the WLA –

In the early summer of 1940 I joined the Auxiliary Land Army as a holiday job. I had finished a first year at Woolwich Polytechnic. The work was hop- and potato-picking in Herefordshire. It was a glorious summer, but soon the war started in earnest and the Battle of Britain began with raids on the cities. Eventually my parents advised me to stay in the country. So I joined the regular WLA, and was sent to a market garden just outside Hereford where I lived with my boss (Mr M) and his wife. I was treated as one of the family. There was good food and I was comfortable and happy.

My working day was from 6 am to 5 pm, five and a half days a week with 'odd jobs' on Sundays. I started on 16 shillings (80 pence) a week plus board. We were woken at 5.30 am with a cup of tea and a biscuit, and worked for two hours before breakfast. The dinner break was from 12.30 pm to 2 pm with time enough for a cat-nap; then after 5 pm there was a bath and a good supper. Evenings were usually spent round a fire chatting before an early bed, but sometimes there was a dance at the village hall or at a nearby RAF camp and I did a little amateur dramatics.

Working under Mr M were a foreman, a young local lad and an old lady from over the road. As time went on I was joined by more Land Girls, till there were four of us.

My working hours were mostly spent 'on my head', planting, short-hoeing, picking tomatoes or sprouts, cutting lettuces or cabbages. It was a relief to be put onto jobs like packing vegetables into crates or tomatoes into 'chips' – I could stand upright. Best of all was driving the old car round the nursery collecting vegetables for the packing shed, or using the rotavator. There was one very boring job; twice a day someone had to hand-pump water from the well to a header-tank for household use. We took it in turns.

There were winter jobs such as cleaning out greenhouses with a hose and formaldehyde solution, mending crates, glass-cutting to repair cloches and sawing logs for the house; also seed sowing and pricking out. An unpleasant job was pumping out the cess pit; Mr M gave us a supply of cigarettes and cider for this, but whether as an antiseptic or reward we were never sure!

My years in the Land Army were very happy. I was lucky to be working for a good boss under comfortable conditions. Everyone in the village was friendly, and we were welcomed into the houses of the farm-workers, the squire and the doctor alike. Many social barriers were broken down during the war.

The Women's Royal Naval Services (Wrens) were based both at home and abroad. EDNA CLEVELAND, after her spell with the Land Army, was called up at the age of twenty-one. The recruiting officer discovered she had a twin brother in the Navy and suggested she joined the Wrens to be near him. She was posted to Southampton and for a year she saw a great deal of him. She continues –

I first met Archie (my husband) when he was posted to Southampton on compassionate leave when his father became seriously ill. He was doing sentry duty at Elmfield Flats where I was billeted. He said he fell for me because I was the only Wren who cleaned the backs of her shoes! We used to go to his home in Brockenhurst – on the Burley Road. After 12 months we got married.

I enjoyed the Wrens, although not so much as the Land Army. But you have to make the most of it, don't you? I'm still in touch with my old Wren friends and with one from the Land Army days.

I was cooking for the Wrens. Before I went in I didn't know how to boil a pan of water. Eventually, I passed a cookery exam and became a Leading Wren. I was posted to the Royal Pier at Southampton. At the end of the Pier I cooked for the Boat Crew Girls. They ferried sailors between shore and their ships or landing crafts. After this I was posted to the Royal Hotel. Our waking call was the Guildhall clock playing 'O God Our Help in Ages Past'. Every time I hear it I am reminded of those days. On D-Day I was still at the hotel; we weren't allowed out; the night before there was a sense of excitement. I remember seeing the planes towing gliders going over.

We were told that some D-Day planning happened in the hotel. Mountbatten and Churchill were there some time before, although we did not see them, we were told not to make a noise. On D-Day we saw soldiers and sailors setting off. Yes, many were nervous, but everyone had got to the stage when they said, "Let's get on and get it over with".

FRANCIE PEYTON JONES began her days with the Wrens at a home base before being posted to the East. She recalls them as very happy ones –

After a very sheltered up-bringing, suddenly meeting and working with men, women and girls of all ages and backgrounds was exciting. I was particularly entranced with a Wren who, in peacetime had had a circus act. She still kept a python, curled up in a basket under her bunk until it was banned by the Administration Officer. Everyone seemed to be one's friend; we were all 'in it together', fighting in ways, however small, to rid the world of what we saw as a cruel and evil power. This sense of purpose gave us an exhiliration in our work, even when it was dull, and it often was. Being a plotter on the South Coast, work had its moments of excitement, plotting U-boat attacks on our convoys, and being an integral part of the team working to scatter and destroy them.

Plotting for the D-Day landings was quite an experience, the amount of shipping was so great.

On June 6 we awoke to the announcement on radio of the start of the invasion and we were filled with mixed feelings of excitement and dread; feared that casualties would be very high. Etched in my photographic memory is a picture of the waves of massed gliders flying overhead on their way to Normandy.

A Wren who was soon to follow these D-Day troops to Normandy was WENDY WOOLLETT (Braithwaite) who gives a vivid account of France as she found it after years of Occupation –

France – la belle France – lay before us, her Normandy shores smiling in the sunshine. Ships everywhere, and then the most wonderful sight – a harbour greeted us, with DUKWS, landing craft, merchant ships, all as busy as bees loading and unloading supplies. When our LCT came alongside one of the pierheads, a great shout of surprise welcomed us – the second party of Wrens to arrive. The hot August sun beat down on us, all struggling with our baggage, but the Marines had the hardest task heaving us and our cases on to the *Mulberry*. Eventually we bumped along in our lorry, along the pontoons of the great harbour to the mainland. We finished our adventurous journey, by arriving at a white farmhouse which had originally been used by the Todt Organisation. However, everything had been distempered by our guardian angels – the Marines – and

189

they had fixed up electric light with a dynamo outside. We had only the canvas furniture we had brought with us, and when we had made our camp beds, we relaxed in comfort for the first time for many hours.

Compot rations which conjure up unforgettable moments (the tea was worst, or maybe that indigestible stew), were the order of the day, eaten off tin plates on trestle tables, and you were lucky if you had a camp stool to sit on. However, we had not come out to grumble at living conditions. The real thrill was seeing those D-Day beaches, and reading the notices outside the pill-box: 'times of DUKWS going to Gooseberry are as follows . . .' We thought we must be back on the old farm again. The sight of hundreds of those wonderful little vehicles, snorting in and out of the water, carrying thousands of tons of stores from the ships to our forces ashore was unbelievable.

We did our work, chiefly clerical, in a large house that had belonged to a pro-Nazi Frenchman, and had been used by the Germans – there was a large eagle painted on the wall. We could watch the ant-like activity on the beaches and the steady stream of convoys to the front line. In those days the Navy was still shelling Le Havre; the windows used to rattle ominously on these occasions. I had the honour of being shorthand writer at a Conference about the taking of Le Havre, Dieppe and Boulogne. The Navy was to use her big guns in the sea attack, and the Army to close in behind on land. The faithful *Mulberry* was of tremendous value, and the ports soon surrendered.

France was much the same on the surface. The blue overalls of the workmen, the cobbled streets, the same smells, but underneath – how much she had suffered or collaborated, no one knew. But, the endless destruction of war was everywhere – the ruined churches, the shattered homes.

Then came a ride to Rouen in a troop-carrier. Normandy in September – her orchards rich with fruit, her lanes overgrown with nut-trees and large fields full of crops – was a beautiful sight. We crossed over the famous Pegasus Bridge: where the airborne landings had been made, there were still ghostly wrecks of the gliders littering the fields. One interesting fact was that our bombing of Rouen docks and ammunition dump speeded up the German retreat beyond doubt, as some SS troops told a French woman that they were going to defend Rouen to the last stone. Apparently they changed their minds when the ammo dump went up.

There were many enterprising shops amongst the ruins. Cigarettes or chocolate were of far more value than francs and lots of mutual bargains were struck. Nearly all the cafés were out of bounds as food and drink were still scarce for the French.

Mention must be made of our office here – the Technical Office. The telephone was the greatest bone of contention . . . can one ever forget the young Scotsman, purple in the face, shouting, "I want Adventure, I want Adventure" (HMS *Adventure* was a Base ship), or Monsieur X's secretary whose voice echoed round the room, even on a telephone. My typewriter was the bane of their lives, as you had to have deathly silence to hear anything – cross Channel or local calls alike.

Perhaps I should explain that some of the French imagined that when *les Alliés* arrived all the necessities of life would come, like manna from Heaven. They did not realise that we had to drive *les sales Boches* right back into Germany first, and that the armies' needs had to come first.

Came the day I managed to go to Paris, where I had been a student at the Sorbonne eight years before. It was too wonderful meeting my old friends, many now married with children. Yes, Jerry had looted everything and now all transport had broken down completely, no fuel, no electricity, no gas, but we huddled over a tiny fire and the water was always cold. Paris still lived, not an existence, but a LIFE. The women were still as smart as ever and the shops had some fascinating clothes and knick-knacks. The quality was not the same, but that was a fleeting impression from my bicycle ride.

As needs in Europe became less demanding after D-Day invasions, FRANCIE PEYTON JONES sailed for India and arrived in Colombo on VE Day, the harbour being full of ships, all blaring their sirens in joyful cacophony –

I did not see as much of Ceylon as I would have liked, as in off-time there was a general feeling that part of the Wren's job was to help entertain the men who were in port, after their long hours of active service at sea. Our off-duty lives, therefore, were a whirl of social activities.

One of the most vivid recollections was volunteering to look after men returning, by sea to the UK, from the Japanese POW camps. Colombo was their first port of call and their sudden freedom made them very disoriented. One whom I took shopping, was very distressed because he could not remember the colour of his wife's eyes so how could he choose the right coloured material to give her a present?

VJ Day came and went in a flurry of celebrations. There was a marvellous firework display over the sea and the inevitable Victory Parade, the March Past and salute taken by Lord Mountbatten. We were up at dawn and stood literally hours before it started and, by that time, the sun had risen and we were exhausted and felt like pats of melted butter.

Invaluable contributions were made by women in non-combatant roles. JOYCE MARCHANT, a food chemist, talks about her contributions towards 'feeding the Nation' –

In January 1941 I began work at Lyons Food Laboratories in Hammersmith. My pay was £200 a year. In those days Lyons' factories at Cadby Hall and Greenford supplied food to their Corner Houses in London and to teashops and ordinary shops country-wide.

A Ministry of Food had been formed to control the rationing and distribution of food, nearly all of which was in short supply. Much of the work in the laboratory was concerned with finding substitutes to overcome shortages, partly caused by fewer imports from overseas.

Miles of Swiss rolls were made at Greenford and the laboratory worked on substitutes for flour and sugar; take some potato and treat it with malt extract – by using this product the production line never stopped. Egg was also required and dried egg from China arrived – sacks and sacks, all of which we had to test and taste. In the early days a lot of it was disgusting and had to be thrown away.

Meat pies were made in Cadby Hall and were popular as an alternative meal when the ration book only allowed half a pound of butcher's meat per week. Substitutes were found to add to pie meat, particularly a dried yeast with a meaty taste (and a high nutritional value).

We also produced 'milk'. Take some soya flour and maize oil, emulsify, and what more could you want in war time? It kept the teashops going in custard, and milk for tea and coffee. Ice cream too had to change its formula. Again this 'milk' was substituted for cream, and I believe a seaweed extract was added to gel the stuff. Hydrolised potato (the starch in the potato being converted to sugar with hydrochloric acid) was another ingredient of ice cream.

We in the laboratory had a taste of real pre-war ice cream when a special batch was made for one of the directors who was seriously ill: sadly he died before eating the ice cream. It would have been illegal to sell it, so we demolished it; it was quite a treat.

What about Lyons fruit pies – still around I think. You take a mangel-wurzel, break it down a bit to sugary pulp, add an appropriate flavouring essence from the essence laboratory – and who would know that they were not eating a genuine delicious apple pie?

Citrus fruits – an important source of vitamin C – soon hardly existed in the shops, and potatoes and cabbage became important as a wartime source of the vitamin. It was found that the teashops, where many people took their mid-day meal, prepared and cooked vegetables at about 9.30 am, then keeping them hot for service from noon onwards. We took samples of cooked cabbage at intervals during the morning and found that well before lunch-time no vitamins remained. The teashops were asked to change their ways and cook in successive batches throughout the lunch period.

Towards the end of the war my employer was the Admiralty, again concerned with food but in the naval victualling yards. We looked for weevils in flour stores, for suspect rum (which involved frequent tasting!) and so on. If this seems a flippant account, because I have omitted the horrors of the war, there certainly were some of these all too near at times.

Also employed by one of the controlling ministries was EILEEN GABONY who joined a small government department when she left school. Three or four weeks later war was declared. She continues –

We immediately became the Ministry of Supply and, the first effect I remember was when workmen came around and altered all the wooden notices on the loo doors which said 'Ladies' and 'Gentlemen' to 'Women' and 'Men'. Oh dear, war was declared and we were no longer to be known as ladies!

We were there for a short period before all being evacuated to Warwick Castle: there were peacocks on the lawns! An interesting period with some funny incidents. All the typists worked in the Main Hall of the Castle. The men – I remember four of the senior staff sharing Lord Warwick's bedroom as a workplace and when they had to dictate, they went into the bathroom!

Eight of us young girls were billeted in a large house where they received £1 a week and a blanket for each of us; not surprisingly the food was absolutely appalling. In those days we worked very hard, only getting one Saturday per fortnight off. The Civil Service pay was extremely low, but we did get free passes. Some evening classes, like choirs, were started for us young girls on our own. Some of the men, however, had been able to bring their families.

The Ministry of Supply, Raw Materials Department was very interesting. Directly war was declared every raw material came under the Government and thus we had iron and steel control, a wool control, a rubber control and so on; all industry was turned over to the Government. After a year, I was only young and very homesick, I applied to go back to London.

I went back to the Ministry in Shell Mex House in The Strand and spent the rest of the war in London, as PA to the Assistant Secretary (the Secretary was the stepson of Sir William Beveridge, famous for his proposals for the Welfare State) of the Allied Supplies Executive co-ordinating Allied supplies. I had a most interesting job. I saw the Government papers on supplies to Russia and other Allies. There was a Russian Trade Delegation in Hampstead that dealt with many of Russia's requests.

On September 4, 1941, M Maisky, the Soviet Ambassador to London, presented a personal message from Stalin to the Prime Minister, Winston Churchill. In this message Stalin complained that Germany was transferring all her forces to the East, and of the great loss of men, arms and ammunition. He requested the establishment of a second front somewhere in the Balkans or France.

Churchill replied that at this stage that was quite impossible, but that orders would be given to supply the Persian railways with more rolling stock, increasing the present two trains a day to twelve per day to and from Russia with supplies.

Madame Maisky, a most forceful lady, dealt with Red Cross supplies to Russia. Those that we could not cope with were supported by the United States. The Lend-Lease Agreement was really something! Whatever we asked for, the Americans supplied. That went for Russia as well. Briefly, the Lend-Lease Agreement was a mutual aid bill to prevent large scale war-debt difficulties. The United States procured and supplied material to the Allies which was off-set by Britain and the Allies furnishing the US forces abroad with supplies and facilities. People knocked the Americans later on, but we had a great deal to be grateful for.

Also working in London but with the Air Ministry, was ELAINE TAYLOR. She was in London for the whole war and gives insight into how they coped over the years –

Looking back my main impression was how quickly abnormal life became normal. The black-out, one of the most depressing features, was soon coped with. First ordinary bulbs were replaced with low wattage blue ones – indescribably gloomy – thus my mother followed the neighbours by lining the curtains.

Another irritating feature was the removal of all street signs and other indicators which might tell you where you were. It was fine when you were in your own neighbourhood but occasionally one had to take a train journey somewhere at night. One would peer from a dimly lit carriage to an equally dimly lit station but there was nothing to indicate where one might be, and if one enquired one was liable to be taken for a spy! Posters everywhere were asking, 'Is your journey really necessary?' and yet, despite all this, on the occasions one had to travel, its seemed the whole of England was on the move.

After the first week or so of air raids, shelters seemed a waste of time! It was different in our own homes at night where we used to sleep under a grand piano. After the Blitz came the VIs and V2s. However, we walked about London at night and went to the theatres – travelling from the West End to my north London suburb between ten and eleven at night. There was also a great feeling of friendship that grew among the people.

In 1944 my mother and I were holidaying in the Cotswolds; the whole place was full of American troops. My cousin, staying in the next village, cycled over one morning in great excitement to tell us the invasion of Europe had started. We then realised that all the Americans had gone. That night as our bombers went over they turned on their navigational lights. Nobody who did not live through those days can imagine the impact the sight of those red and green lights had on those on the ground.

Finally on May 8, 1945 we were able to celebrate VE night. Londoners flocked to the Palace to cheer the Royal Family and Winston Churchill and stayed out all night just feeling so thankful – an enormous party with people singing and cheering; but there was still work to do, a terrible war was still raging in the Far East.

EILEEN DORAN was twenty at the outbreak of war and living in London. Like Elaine Taylor, her office was in Kingsway. She worked for GEC and tells of how she coped with the Blitz –

We once tried a public shelter but found it so uncongenial that we left before the all-clear and scurried home through a hail of anti-aircraft shrapnel.

Following the first heavy raid on the City I reached Ludgate Circus on my way to work to encounter a scene straight out of *Dante's Inferno*. The skyline had disintegrated; buildings were smoking skeletons or heaps of rubble; St Bride's church had disappeared and weary firemen and emergency services were everywhere. Crossing the Circus to get to my office involved picking a way through a tangled mass of fire hoses. Our building was damaged but still standing and it was a case of all hands to restoring order.

By December 1940 I was married. My husband had volunteered for the Fleet Air Arm and was awaiting call-up. We joined a team operating a trailer-pump for the auxiliary Fire Service, and my husband took on the fire-watching rota at work. We did not have raids every night, much depended on the weather, and there was still scope for evening entertainment.

On a never-to-be-forgotten occasion we were awakened by the sound of bombs falling close enough to rattle the furniture, the building was shaking alarmingly and so were we. We grabbed our emergency clothing and dived downstairs to relative safety of our friends' hallway on the ground floor. At that moment something crashed through the roof of their spare bedroom. We were horrified to discover a sinister object with fins protruding from the wreckage. The officiating warden judged it to be a delayed-action bomb and ordered a general exodus. I had a new winter coat that had cost me valuable clothing coupons, and I was unwilling to sacrifice it. In great trepidation I retrieved it, expecting every moment to be my last. On closer inspection of the 'bomb' it was found to be a harmless empty canister which had contained incendiary bombs – we all breathed again! After this there was no question of us sleeping in our own beds, we shared our neighbours' Morrison shelter in their living room.

MRS PRICE having moved to Merseyside, across the river from Liverpool was, however, not as lucky. She recalls a terrifying experience –

March 13, 1942, no I am not superstitious, it happened. Liverpool had been bombed and a few bombs left were jettisoned. I was alone in the large house; I heard the first bomb and thought that was near. The next I did not hear – it collapsed the side of the house I was in. I just heard timber and rubble coming down on me. I was pinned down – it was horrid. I lost consciousness. Then suddenly I heard men's voices calling, "Anybody there? Anybody there?" I had my ribs and collar bone broken, why I was not killed I do not know for I was buried for two days and five hours; my son has the certificate they gave me.

I kept saying "ooch" while the rescuers were busy – I must have given a little smile for one said, "After all that she can still laugh!" – No I was not laughing, it hurt terribly. I was in hospital for a very long time.

A very different contribution was made by VIVIENNE CROXFORD. Dr Croxford, retired from practice, has lived in Brockenhurst for some eight years. Now she and her friend, Rosemary Sheldon breed and show miniature long-haired dachshunds. Their pets are trained and visit various retirement homes and hospitals for 'Pets As Therapy' (PAT), to give comfort to the lonely and ill.

At the onset of war, in 1939, she was living in Dundee, overlooking the mouth of the River Tay –

I shared a home with a retired nurse from the First World War; Territorial Army and Queen Alexandra's Imperial Nursing Service, so we had a First Aid post in our sitting room, and we grew vegetables on what was our front lawn.

I belonged to the WVS and did Civil Defence work as an ambulance driver while completing my Medical Degree. I was then training in the Dundee Royal Infirmary. Here special wards were reserved for servicemen evacuated from the Normandy beaches. They were mainly limbless, as few others could travel that distance on the trains; others went to the Gleneagle's Hospital. I was on the maternity ward and not allowed contact with them.

Nightly there were raids by German planes trying to hit the Tay

Bridge and Leuchars aerodrome (one of the German pilots had trained at Leuchars) but all the planes were housed underground. We even had a day raid when the Hun flew low and fired at people in the street in Broughty Ferry.

VJ Day, in 1945, I spent trying to resuscitate a nine-year-old boy in Arbroath Infirmary (where I was now resident Medical Officer). He had stepped on a mine on the beach and blown himself up, scalped, and his eyes out, both arms partly amputated but, fully conscious and could recognise Sister's voice because he had been in the children's ward previously for tonsillectomy.

Polish forces (medically grade 2) guarded the miles of shoreline, the Royal Navy Air Stations, Condor and Peewit bases in the area. Injured Germans who had been shot down over the Tay and taken as prisoners, were brought into Arbroath Infirmary under guard, until fit to be transferred – they were very violent! All head injuries were transferred to King's Seat in Aberdeen.

In Arbroath we supplemented our rations with 'Arbroath Smokies' – smoked on rods in a hole in the sand, covered with sacking.

DOROTHY CLARK, now aged eighty, was born in India and returned at the age of eighteen to have secretarial training. During the first few years of the war she was nursing her desperately ill husband. In 1940 they moved to Shropshire for his convalescence but this was where he died. Returning to London she replied to an advertisement placed by the American Red Cross in Grosvenor Square, for British staff –

I applied and became Assistant to the Field Director. Amazing. One of my duties was to deal with complaints from American servicemen. Astonishing how many complained in the middle of the war. One complained that his wife was mentally/maritally ill-adjusted to his absence. He was given two weeks leave. Another said his fiancée was imminently expecting twins. She was in America and I had to ensure that lines were kept free so that they could marry over the phone and avoid 'bastards'. Unfortunately they were born before she got through. Interesting work, but I wanted to help more.

A friend asked me if I would like to go to Egypt, as a civilian. Within 24 hours I was being interviewed by a major who said, "I suppose you can't do anything?" I replied that I had secretarial training.

Within three weeks I was on a trooper with 4,000 troops and 200 women sailing for Egypt. As we (troops and women) marched on, the catering staff marched off saying that there were too many to cook for. We had tea and bread all the next day, but eventually we took off. On that day, a message was broadcast from the Captain to say that all lady passengers must report below to dance with the 4,000 men! We did and it took a long time for our feet to recover.

197

When we arrived by train at Cairo from Port Said, I was amazed by the unbelievable luxury. My job was to be PA to the General in charge of decoding German messages. There were one hundred little English girls, on houseboats, doing this. I was PA to General Stoll and later Brigadier Barker Benfield.

I remember an occasion when King Farouk went without escort, to a night club outside Cairo. He got rather drunk; on his return he drove into a ditch. A passing British Army truck saw someone lying there. The King shouted out, "Take me to my Palace, I'm King Farouk." "Oh yes, I'm Winston Churchill," replied the driver The next morning Farouk was in an Army hospital, in the ward of other ranks, and the officials were panic stricken at losing their King.

I also remember writing what I thought was a lyrical account of a visit to Luxor to my mother. She replied, "Lovely to get your letter, your father and I were sitting under the kitchen table while flying bombs went over. When I read your letter I'm afraid I burst into tears". That was the end of my attempt at journalism!

Soon I felt guilty living in so much luxury, and I applied to go to Italy and I became a Lieutenant in the Fannies; becoming PA to Lord Harcourt with Force 266, first at Bari. While there we got a message from Randolph Churchill and Evelyn Waugh who had their plane shot down in Yugoslavia. The fire burnt not only much of the plane, but their trousers. Their message was 'For God's sake send us some trousers on a special mission'.

At the end of the war I went to Venice, from Sienna , to where I had been posted, and watched Field Marshall Kesselring being tried for War Crimes in the Doge's Palace. It was that visit which led me to meet my second husband. He, a barrister, had been observing Maxwell Fyfe at the Nurembourg Trials of War Criminals, and was extremely interested in my account of the Venice Trial. That was the beginning of a romance which led very happily to marriage, and a wonderful life together. The last years were at Lincoln's Inn where we lived after he had retired as an Old Bailey judge. It was after he died, some five years ago, that I came to live at Forest Oaks, Brockenhurst.

VERA RIDLEY-MARTIN joined her husband in Egypt, arriving at Port Sudan shortly after the outbreak of war, in 1939 *(see Naval Section)* –

I went on a cypher course in Khartoum, and then a VAD (Voluntary Aid Detachment) course. I feel sure that the presence of girls (even in modest overalls and closely covered hair) was more therapeutic for the bedridden soldiers than all their pills and potions.

When my husband was posted to Cairo I was lucky to get a job in the publicity section of the British Embassy working as an archivist.

These were good days working with so many interesting and delightful people.

After nearly two years and two really bad doses of 'flu I ended up in the Anglo American hospital with pneumonia. Treatment with the M & B drug proved ineffective. My husband was summoned from his work in Jerusalem, and drove across the Sinai desert on his motor bike!

When I recovered I flew to Jerusalem and stayed at Nahariya for nearly a year before returning to Cairo to work at General Headquarters and later Headquarters British Troops Egypt.

TRAINING AND HOME DEFENCE

KENNETH SLADE was commissioned into the Territorial Army, Royal Artillery, in 1935. He recalls his time defending our coastal areas against enemy aircraft –

In 1938 we were called up for the September crisis and deployed our anti-aircraft guns around a home for mentally handicapped people outside Bristol. When the crisis subsided we were not returned to civilian life, but remained active in the army, and my anti-aircraft battery was posted to the defence of Weymouth and Portland Bill harbours. We sat there during the whole of the Blitz. On one occasion we received a message, through to the gun position, to say we were to expect an invasion of 400 plus German aircraft. During the raid, seven remaining British fighters out of a squadron of twelve crashed into these 400 incoming German aircraft; planes and parachutes dropping out of the sky from both, ours and the enemy.

We continued operations during the Battle of Britain and at one stage I watched, from my gun-site, a German plane being chased down by two British fighters over Chesil Beach. It crashed, I got into my car and happened to be the first on the scene. I picked up a German Count: he was the pilot who had been thrown out when his plane hit the water just off the beach. I took his small mauser revolver from him, which incidentally my wife kept in her purse for the rest of the war; and he was collected by Royal Air Force personnel. I saw him later in hospital in Southampton, but have no idea what happened to him thereafter.

We were then transferred, as a unit, to Plymouth and suffered five nights of non-stop raids. The towns of Devonport and Plymouth were completely shattered and after firing our guns all night, we supplied a volunteer force to help clear up the streets of these towns. Also, we took a few of our chaps down to help with the blazing oil tanks of the Royal Navy at Devonport. As we were trying to lay down hoses to cool the next tank, the German bombs continued to drop on

the already blazing ones – not a very pleasant evening.
(Further contributions in this chapter.)

Along the Hampshire coast MICHAEL EMANUEL was also manning an anti-aircraft battery –

In 1940 I was with a heavy anti-aircraft battery stationed at Marchwood. The gun-site was immediately opposite the Southampton Old Docks. To the south was Southampton Water, with the Esso Refinery on the right, and the Isle of Wight just visible in the distance.

Since Dunkirk we had been warned to be on the alert for sudden air raids. Little had happened, however, during the early part of the summer apart from the appearance of two German reconnaissance planes.

Following the engagement of one of these planes, the RAF at Tangmere had complained that our anti-aircraft had continued to fire when one of their fighters had been in a position to attack. We complained, that on several occasions the RAF planes had not given the correct signals to indicate they were friendly aircraft. As a result AA Command and the RAF agreed that some of the fighter pilots from Tangmere should visit our units with a view to discussing each other's problems.

Not long after that three Spitfire pilots came over to Marchwood. I was surprised at how young they were – I was twenty-five at the time. They discussed the attacking of enemy aircraft as if they were talking about an exciting, but important motor race. Their cheerfulness and youthful enthusiasm made us static gunners feel rather dull by comparison.

Then one beautiful sunny day the Battle of Britain began. There was just a warning that a large number of enemy aircraft was approaching the South Coast. This was followed by more detailed and frequent reports, such as 150 planes approaching the Isle of Wight. At this stage it was very still and quiet. Then a humming noise was heard in the distance, then a rumbling which gradually developed into a roar accompanied by bursts of machine gun fire.

Then we saw them – a tight packed formation of enemy bombers flying steadily up over Southampton Water. I felt that the estimate of '150 plus planes' was no exaggeration. Above were the dog-fights of the fighters manoeuvring and diving like a group of angry mosquitoes. Some planes exploded, some dived smoking to the ground. Here and there parachutes were coming down. The anti-aircraft batteries were already firing and as soon as the planes came within range, we joined in.

The bombers surged on at quite a low height, by which time the noise had become a deafening, exploding roar. They went in over the docks and Southampton releasing their bombs –

As we were firing as much as possible, I had no thoughts of what might be happening elsewhere, but, after what seemed quite a short time, the bombers re-formed and flew back from where they had come with the fighter dog-fights still going on above them.

We were quite elated being in action after months of waiting but, there was an underlying feeling of tension. We were a local Territorial Battery and many of us, including myself, had families, relations and friends living in Southampton which was now covered by smoke from burning buildings. I also thought about the young Spitfire pilots, and wondered whether they had survived.

New armaments had to be developed to help combat the tip and run and other air attacks. Before the war VERNON MARCHANT was working as a refinery engineer in Bahrain. He was invalided home, and back in England in August 1939 soon joined the Armaments Department of the Royal Aircraft Establishment (RAE) at Farnborough. Having a degree in engineering and science, he was engaged on the design and development of small mechanisms relating to aircraft bombs –

In the early summer of 1940 the RAE experienced what must have been one of the first real air raids of the war. It took place during the day. The sirens went off and we all trooped to the shelters, which were not much more than small Nissen huts half-buried with a few feet of soil. A single aircraft dropped a stick of small bombs, perhaps about half a dozen twenty-pounders, which made craters along the edge of the airfield. There was no serious damage, but a useful experience to warn us of what was to come.

After a year I was asked if I would like to be transferred to the Ministry of Aircraft Production in London. Since it involved promotion, I accepted.

My new office was in Thames House, Millbank, and with two colleagues rented a furnished flat in Tufton Court, between Millbank and Parliament Square. This was extremely handy for the office and for the air raid shelters there; only five minutes walk, but no more than two minutes hard running when the bombs began to fall.

The Thames House shelters had bunk beds for the staff in the sub-basement, three floors below ground. It was extremely basic, but at least it was possible to have a night's sleep relatively undisturbed by incessant noise. We also imagined that it was safe, though I had doubts about this when I discovered that the shelters were well below the level of the Thames, which was only just across the road.

One night I saw the lovely old church of St John's, Smith Square, crashing down in flames; on another morning I walked across Parliament Square and saw the shambles where the House of

Commons had received a direct hit. Parliament moved to Church House, Westminster, close to Tufton Court.

Thames House survived almost unscathed. Only my office had all the windows broken, the black-out curtain torn and some secret papers were blown away down the Embankment. But, we had our share of casualties. The head of my department, the Director of Armament Development, Air Commodore Huskinson was looking out of his window one night watching an air raid: a bomb went off near by and blinded him in both eyes. He never recovered his sight.

I did a certain amount of flying as an observer on bomb trials, and visited a number of RAF stations. Most of these visits were for no more than two or three days, but one, to RAF Middle Wallop, Hampshire lasted some weeks. At that time this was an operational fighter station and as well as a normal squadron it housed a newly-formed squadron of Douglas DB 7's which had been specially modified to drop Long Aerial Mines. This was a nasty new weapon intended to intercept German bombers, but it was nearly as dangerous to our forces as to the enemy. I was by way of being a technical expert on these things and the complicated mechanism for dropping them, and my job was to see that their introduction to service use went smoothly. I was successful to the extent that no one on the station was actually blown up by them, but neither were any enemy aircraft. For tactical reasons they proved to be impractical, and they were soon withdrawn.

My main memory of life on an operational RAF station was how agreeable it was compared with civilian life in London. For the operational crews, life was always hazardous and often short. It was a privilege to work beside them and live with them, as I did, in the Officers' Mess. But they were indeed few, only a small minority of the thousands on the station. The rest worked hard, but for the officers, at least, it was living in a luxury hotel. There were batmen and mess waiters, and barmen and car drivers. And there was food, of a variety, quality and quantity that was quite unbelievable in ordinary civilian life.

Another RAF station which I visited fairly frequently in connection with bombing trials, was the Marine Aircraft Experimental Establishment, then based in the former clubhouse of the Royal Northern Yacht Club at Helensburgh. This was a very agreeable place, especially as some of the club staff were still there working in the mess. I particularly remember the porridge and the whisky!

In London working hours were long and our office was open seven days a week including Christmas Day, with a rota system allowing for one day's rest in seven.

In 1942 I moved into digs and thereby obtained, what might be described as, one of the fringe benefits of being a bachelor in war-time London. In these digs there resided about a dozen girls and only one other man. I need only mention that one of the girls later became my wife, Joyce (a food chemist with Lyon's Laboratories). We were married in 1945.   *(see Women at War)*.

Besides new armament, repair of the damaged and crippled aircraft that returned home or crashed during a dog-fight, was an essential part of the backing-up of the air force. BUNNY WARREN returning from Iraq, was posted to Ibsley in Hampshire of which he recalls –

Here we were engaged in repairing the aircraft damaged in cross-Channel raids. When news of a crashed aircraft was received a unit was sent out, with an officer to assess the damage together with a recovery team with specialised equipment. A low loader and crane were used to move the wreckage. If it were possible to repair it at Ibsley it was brought into the cleverly camouflaged workshops there, and was soon flying again. Although we could often see towns blazing in the distance (Southampton and Bournemouth) we had no direct attack ourselves.

I was then posted to South Cerney, where, in spite of the constraints of duty rotas, there was an exciting social life focusing on the dance halls of Bath and Cheltenham.

Of service to the airfields as well was FRED ENGLAND who, when called up to the RAF was an engine fitter but had instruction on all firearms plus hand-grenades, cup dischargers and the like. After 16 weeks' technical training he became a flight mechanic –

Once you had done your work as a flight mechanic you went on an 18 week course to become a fitter. Eventually I went to Gravely in Huntingdonshire. We were on Mark I Halifaxes which weren't too bad provided they got off the ground. But nine times out of ten they were taking more fuel than bombs – they were poor old things; the later Mark III Halifax was a different aircraft.

Within a few months we went to Norfolk and formed a new squadron with Lancasters. I was happy then and I was actually working on the aircraft full-time, whereas previously I was doing all sorts of odd jobs. Then as a bonus we had a squadron of Mosquitoes: we usually did one Lancaster a day or two Mosquitoes. There was quite a lot of work involved, each engine had a 35-gallon oil tank: 30 gallons of oil to be changed, scavenge filters to be taken out, cleaned and inspected, also sparking plugs to be checked.

After VE Day volunteers were asked for to go into the Fleet-Air-Arm. Our little mob volunteered with the idea of going on an aircraft carrier to the Far East, but due to the atom bomb, got no further than Scotland.

It was on Salisbury Plain – a vast military training area where TIM

BEEVERS found himself in the summer of 1942 as a twenty-two-year-old Platoon Commander of No. 1 Platoon, A Company, of the 1st Parachute Battalion 1st Brigade etc. He tells of his training –

We trained on Salisbury Plain, learning to be infantry soldiers, as well as being commandos dropped by air, only without the transport and heavy equipment of an infantry soldier. So we had to carry more, and be more self-reliant than the normal infantry soldier. This meant carrying more ammunition, and this is notoriously heavy. If you have seen pictures of World War II parachute soldiers marching across an airfield before embarking on an aeroplane in full battle-order, under the added burden of a sizeable parachute, you may remember that their step was far from sprightly. There were no friendly helicopters at hand in those days, and 'Christmas Tree Order' meant that we carried everything, down to the last pound of plastic explosive (or if you were in a mortar platoon, down to the last ten-pound shell or thirty-pound base-plate).

My platoon, who called themselves the Free Welsh, mostly stocky, square-shouldered Welshmen had excellent stamina, could carry a heavy battle-order, and were cheerful when conditions were adverse. We thought of our unit with pride, bolstered by the fact that we all wore parachute wings and our fairly recently acquired red berets.

Salisbury Plain was full of American parachute troops (101 Division). We began to jump out of Dakotas, instead of the old Whitleys, and our first encounter with two cigar-smoking pilots aged (it appeared) about sixteen, who assured us they had had several hours training in Texas, came as a considerable shock.

Late in the summer we began to train even harder, and with a special emphasis on long-distance exercises, marching up and down very steep hills with full equipment. The American airborne troops had to do this too, and we liked to think they suffered more than us in their 'smart soft brown boots'. We didn't know what all this marching was about. It seemed a strange way to train for the short, sharp, commando-type raids which parachute troops expected in those days.

On November 8 came the first of a number of landings by a large Anglo-American force along the French North Africa coast, from Casablanca to Algiers. Some days before this date we had warning of a move from Bulford, but instead of going into battle in a civilised way in an aeroplane, we found ourselves getting into a train (an operation we were not very good at in the dark) and going to Glasgow where we embarked, in the dark, on a large cruise ship. Our 'Christmas Tree Order' had increased enormously, and continued to do so throughout the voyage.

No-one knew where we were going, but by the time we reached

Gibraltar we knew about the landings, and knew we were going ashore at Algiers, where the landings had met some opposition from the French. When we finally saw Algiers, it appeared as an amazingly beautiful white city in the brilliant sunlight.

The engagement in North Africa is continued in another part of this chapter. But before this engagement took place many troops had embarked for France and in May 1940 British and Allied troops were evacuated from Dunkirk and re-deployed. JOHN WOOLLETT leads up to this event and tells of their return to home territory –

In 1938 I was stationed at Aldershot, as a Section Commander (Lieutenant) in the 23rd Field Company, part of 1st Division Engineers. In August 1939 the Regular Army was brought up to full strength by calling up the regular reservists, and the Company consisted of three Sections of 60 men, 4 lorries, 3 small trucks and 2 motorcycles.

On September 3, I heard war had been declared, and walked out to where my Section Sergeant was supervising the loading of equipment and told him. He looked up at the sky and said, "I wonder when we can expect the first load", and the air raid alarm promptly sounded! However, there was no attack. This illustrates how conscious we were of the air threat. A day or two later we moved out of our barracks into the countryside and the barracks were taken over by the Territorial Army and the Emergency Reserve troops. My section moved into a farm near Guildford, where the troops occupied the barns and I had a bed in the house. The farmer and his family were very kind and helpful, in spite of the inconvenience we must have caused them. After a few days we embarked for France, where the same pattern of accommodation in farmhouse and barns continued.

On May 10, 1940, when the Germans invaded the low Countries, the ensuing battles and the withdrawal to Dunkirk are not part of this story, but we finally embarked in the destroyer HMS *Winchelsea* on June 1 having sustained a number of casualties and having to abandon our transport and equipment. As we approached England I recall feeling sad and ashamed at our defeat, but when we arrived at Dover there were people cheering us on the quay, and WVS ladies handing out cake and tea, and cards to send home. It was a tremendous boost to morale and I remember feeling very proud of our country and determined for the future.

Trains left Dover at regular intervals taking soldiers to various camps from where they were sorted out and despatched to the places where their units were re-forming. We re-formed in Leeds and were billeted in private homes, where again people were most supportive and welcoming, and made it clear that they were proud to be able to help the war effort in this way.

We then moved to the Lincolnshire coast, just north of the Wash, to prepare the coast defences against invasion. The whole coastal area had been evacuated except for the farms in which we were again billeted. No-one except service personnel and those working on the farms was allowed in the evacuated area.

Shortly afterwards I volunteered to join a Commando unit that was to train for raids on the enemy held coast. These units were raised wholly from volunteers, and No 6 Commando formed up in Scarborough where we sent the new arrivals out with the Coastal Patrol and, if they were sea-sick they were returned to their units.

JOHN BLOOMFIELD as a scholar at North Walsham, Norfolk remembers these 'no-go' coastal defence areas –

Our school was within the 15-mile security zone and, because of that, we had permits which allowed us to visit or move freely within the security zone of the coast. I had a friend at Stiffkey on the coast. The marshes and the whole coast were heavily defended but the locals knew where the mines were, and we just used to walk through them.

The East Anglian countryside was littered with wrecks of planes, both Allied and German and our Sunday walks from school would often take us to a downed fighter or Messerschmitt. They were guarded, but wreckage was scattered over a large area so we always went home with some sort of souvenir.

In the autumn of 1943 JOHN WOOLLETT moved to Aldeburgh, in Suffolk, which had been completely evacuated –

Here we trained with Armoured Engineer tanks to breach the coast defences. The area west of Aldeburgh and south towards Orford, bounded by the rivers Deben and Alde had been closed off and all the villages evacuated. Here copies of the enemy coast defences had been constructed and we were able to practise breaking through them. There was tight security and any unauthorised person found in the area was liable to be interned for the remainder of the war. One result of this was no poaching, and game multiplied in the area quite unaffected by our explosions. We were able to get some good shooting with cartridges scrounged from our RAF friends, who were issued with them for rear-gunners to practice with.

Finally we moved to another evacuated coast town, Worthing. After a few days were moved to Lee-on-Solent and embarked for Normandy in July.

There were numerous RAF station in this East Anglia area. TOMMY THOMPSON, a fighter pilot from 1940-43 was stationed at one of these. He recalls this amusing incident –

Whilst serving with 249 Squadron at North Weald, Epping, during the Battle of Britain in 1940 we had a group of labourers on the airfield who filled in bomb holes and sandbags and generally made themselves useful.

I was chatting with one of these labourers at our dispersal point one day and somehow the topic of conversation turned to money. He told me he was paid his basic wage, plus danger money for working on an airfield, plus 'bussing' money for being brought in from some 20 miles away each day. This all amounted to about £13 a week. A considerable sum in those days. He then asked me how much I got a week. I replied that as a Pilot Officer I got just £5 a week. "That's about right then," he said. "'Cos, every time the alarm goes off, you get in yer aeroplane and buggers off out of it."

I have often wondered where he thought we went!

No 249 Squadron was the second highest scoring Squadron in the Battle of Britain. The Polish Fighter Squadron was the highest. TOMMY THOMPSON continues –

249 Squadron also boasted the ONLY Fighter VC of the war. Flight Lieutenant 'Nick' Nicholson who won his VC when he was shot down in flames over Southampton in September 1940. There is a Memorial Plaque to his memory – he was killed later in the war – just off Millbrook Road, where he landed by parachute.

The diaries kept by BOGDAN ENGEL, a Polish pilot during the war were made available by his wife, Vera Engel. They lived in Auckland Place, Brockenhurst until his death in 1993. The following extracts are abridged from these diaries –

I was a pilot attached to 3 PL Squadron based in Poland. On August 28, 1939, I learned that I was to be transferred to a different squadron. Although confined to our barracks, we were permitted to go each evening to our families and friends.

Each night meant saying goodbye, not knowing if it might be our last visit. On August 31, I had a feeling that this actually was my last one at home. Having bade my family a fond farewell I went on to visit friends who had been very good to me. Mrs Kujawa gave me a small packet to keep always as a souvenir. Back at camp I untied the parcel to find a small picture of the Virgin Mary with Jesus and a note saying: 'I am giving this to you. As a mother, I hope it will guide you to safety and happiness and keep you from all dangers, both in the air and on land, and hope that one day it will bring you safely back to us.'

My feelings from the previous evening had been correct. At 15.00 hrs we were to take off for Deblin, near Warsaw. The date was September 1, 1939, the day on which Hitler invaded Poland. Without warning several places were attacked from the air, causing much damage. The Germans did not bother about military targets, but

207

bombed towns and villages indiscriminately. The same day we observed Nazi planes on reconnaissance flying over Deblin. We knew our turn was coming. It was not far away, unforgettable hell started! The next day, late at night we were transported to Warsaw where we were greeted by yet another raid just before we reached the capital.

Next morning I was directed to a plane I was to deliver to the 6th Squadron near the town of Wegrowo. With my rear gunner, we inspected the plane which was minus an instrument panel and short on petrol. I took a chance and flew out with maps only for directional guidance. Near Katuszyn the engine began to cough for want of petrol. I decided I would force-land and luckily found a field of freshly cut wheat.

Suddenly I noticed that from all directions farm workers were rushing towards us with their farm tools raised in defence, thinking that we were Germans! Without fear, I opened the cockpit, took out my revolver, stepped on to the wing of the plane and called out "God be praised", to which they all responded, "Now and forever".

The following morning a crew from another aerodrome woke us to say they had been sent to collect the German aircraft. They seemed very disappointed to learn it was our plane. Later they brought us petrol and by midday we were ready to take off. On eventual arrival back at my own base, and having reported to the Commander, I found my friends amazed to see me again as I had been 'missing for three days!' Soon we had to leave Warsaw in flames, crossing by the Poniatowski Bridge towards the south of Poland. It was September 18 before we finally reached the Roumanian border, having travelled in hazardous conditions for four days, covering about 200 km each day, with the Germans hard on our heels.

We crossed the border at 1.30 pm. There a shock awaited us. In Roumania we had anticipated that we would collect new equipment to continue the fight against Germany. Instead we were surrounded by Roumanian soldiers, disarmed and sent to an internment camp near Bucharest. Some stayed there, the rest were separated into pairs and housed in various farm houses. The farmer we stayed with was good to us.

Plans began to form for escape: a new Polish Air Force was being formed in France. The day arrived for me to escape – it was Sunday October 30, everything was ready. That evening I used the pretence that it was my birthday and took the farmer, his wife and some friends to celebrate. After a merry evening, they were soon asleep on returning to the farmhouse. At 11 pm I heard the knock on my window and got up; I was fully dressed as a civilian. It was raining heavily. We removed our shoes and socks, pulled our trousers above the knee, and went on our way. We had to walk 18 km through the night to the nearest railway station. Eventually, after devious routes, we arrived at Marseilles, by ship. From there we went by train to Lyon and on to Bron, a special depot for Polish Airmen serving in France.

Before long the German forces were on our heels once more. The German offensive was on and the French forces were in full retreat. We tried to get to the west coast but the German Panzer divisions cut us off. We took the southerly direction. Again by devious ways we finally arrived in Liverpool, it was July 12, 1940. From here we were sent to Blackpool, a holding unit for the Polish Air Force.

My training in England was very short as I was already a fully trained pilot. After three days on a Magister and then a twin-engined Anson, I was soon on to the Wellington bomber and night flying. We all worked very hard knowing that we were doing this to save our fatherland, Poland. The visit of King George VI and Queen Elizabeth to our station marked the day I began my duties as operational pilot: my heart beat pitter-patter with excitement.

I shall try to describe a few of the trips which left outstanding memories in my mind.

August 7, 1941 – Essen

On approaching the target area I heard the rear gunner reporting, "Something wrong with the turret. It will not budge. Also the guns have dropped. I cannot operate them." I was really disturbed. "OK understood. Keep a sharp lookout, especially on the back," I instructed. Essen was a place where one expected very strong defences. We began our run towards the target when I heard the rear gunner shout, "109 from port". I grabbed the controls and let the aircraft go in a steep turn towards the Hun fighter in order to be away from his line of fire. We dropped from 21,000 feet to 17,000 feet and lost him. Not for long though.

We came to level flying, making another run and another shout, "Same again from starboard." So into a steep turn, and down again we went, dropping this time to 14,000 feet. Although we had a full load on, good 'Ole Wimpy' behaved very well. We flew for a few minutes before we attempted another run. Bomb doors open – bombs gone – when I heard another shout, "110 from the front!" I thought, "This is our lot!" My front gunner opened fire, squeezing the triggers seven times. We saw the Hun going down in a turn. On our way home we had a jolly good laugh, but it was too close for comfort.

Next day I was notified in our Daily Orders that I had been awarded the KW (Polish DFC).

Twenty-second sortie – over Hamburg

I always allowed the second pilot to take over the controls from home until near the target, when I took over to complete the mission. A new second pilot and rear gunner were in my crew, they got the taste of German ack-ack as well as the strength of the British coastal defences. As we ran into Hull in very bad weather, we were met by very fierce ack-ack fire as we were flying in a prohibited area. We immediately fired our colours of the day which saved us from serious trouble. The searchlights helped us out of the balloon area. there was an important message waiting on my return. I had been awarded the Virtuti Militari (equivalent to the Victoria Cross).

The Thirtieth sortie – Essen once again

I was notified that this trip would be my last. I had cheated them so many times before, God help me in this case, to do it once more and I shall be happy. The target was Essen, right in the middle of the Ruhr, on the night of April 10, 1942. Once more into the lion's den.

Before take off I had a funny feeling, maybe a premonition, that something would happen on this trip. I kept it to myself.

As we approached the target area the guns, light, medium and heavies were pounding away with full force. I heard the navigator say, "Open bomb doors." I answered, "OK, open." At the moment I turned the handle to operate the bomb doors, I switched hell on. Hundreds of searchlights popped up on us and the ack-ack went mad.

I took evasive action but whichever way I turned, they had me. Wriggling like a snake, trying to get out of their clutches, it was in vain. Sweat began running down my face and in a few moments I was wet through with perspiration. I was scared stiff.

The navigator shouted, "Bombs gone." I closed the doors and continued changing my position all the time to avoid being a sitting duck, and after a while we managed to get out of this hell.

My wireless operator came to my seat. When I looked at him I nearly had a fit. His face was black. He had been about to drop a flare from the side chute when the hit had occurred. The explosion had caught the canister, the casing had burst into small fragments, but fortunately for him although singed he wasn't even scratched.

On landing we found 28 holes in the aircraft, some of them as big as footballs.

A few months later I was congratulated by Air Vice Marshal Harris of No 1 Bomber Command, for non-immediate award of DFM, who said, "The award is well deserved and I am glad your effort has been recognised in this way." The date, September 7, 1942.

There were many who quietly supported the forces as Tommy Thompson mentions the group of men filling bomb holes, so there were engineers providing lighting; chefs producing that essential, good meal; signallers transmitting messages and numerous other tasks which had to be performed. Some of them tell of their contribution or memories of those days, 50 years ago.

The late LES JOHNSON was born in Brockenhurst (see Chapter 2) and lived here all his life. He was in his early twenties when war was declared, and volunteered for the Royal Engineers, training as an engineer –

I was put in charge of internal combustion engines – our job was to supply electricity (from the engines) and light for camps. For four years I travelled up and down Britain providing lighting for new camps: no excuses for not doing the job within ten minutes!

We ran cables straight off the engines in the Bedford trucks and put light bulbs on the cables. We always wore wellington boots as insulation. Although it was only 110 volts it was enough to give you a nasty jolt. It was a job I quite enjoyed. For our engines we used aviation petrol, not the pink petrol always issued to cars.

Another engineer, but working on a very different aspect was NORMAN MONTAGUE who had joined British Tabulating Machine Company in February 1939. Because of his engineering training he was selected to go, in 1941, to the ultra secret Bletchley Park, to assist in the decoding of intercepted German messages. He tells us his story thus –

In 1940, I was called up to the Army Ordnance Corps with the twenty-one-year-olds, and spent 18 months at various training establishments: basics at Woolwich, then transferred to Park Royal, London and then to Tidworth, Wiltshire to join the 21st Army Tank Brigade. Then it was Colchester to set up workshops for the servicing of Matilda tanks and on to Bury in Lancashire.

One morning, in August 1941, I was called into my senior officer, who gave me a rail warrant and told me to leave immediately for Bletchley Park in Buckinghamshire. I was given no explanation for this.

On arrival at Bletchley, I was sent in to be interviewed by Commander Travis who explained that I was at the Government Codes and Cypher School. He showed me a machine which he said was the German 'Enigma' machine, that was used to encode and decode the German messages. The problem was to find the initial key setting of the Enigma. He told me that Bletchley Park employed the best linguists and mathematicians in the country to work on the problem. Apparently, my experience with British Tabulating Machines meant that I could be useful to what was being done there. I signed the Official Secrets Act and began work. My wife moved to Bletchley, but she was never to know what occupied my days, or the part I was playing in the war.

211

THE LATE LESLIE JOHNSON IN 1942.

BTM had been given the task of building machines to search for the wheel settings. These were very large machines, their code name was 'Bombs' and they were set up using a series of wheels and plugs; the information was supplied by expert cryptographers from another department, and these were called 'Menus'. The Bombs would be set in motion ·until they stopped, the indicator wheel letters would be sent to the experts who would test them against the message and if proved to be correct, we would receive an instruction to say, Message cracked, strip machine and plug machine on a new Menu. The machines were kept running 24 hours a day, 365 days a year. My job, together with others was to service and repair the machines. Initially this was done by 12 ex-BTM engineers. As we expanded the number of Bombs, more staffing was needed. Men were drawn from the RAF as engineers and operators from the Wrens.

A number of new branches were opened at Adstock and Gayhurst in Bucks, Stanmore and Eastcote in Middlesex. The spread of branches was made to offset the chances of a branch being knocked out by enemy action.

The only branch to receive a visit from the enemy, was a near miss at Stanmore. I came out of our building at 3 am one morning and could hear two V1 doodlebug flying bombs, heading from the east in our direction. I waited for their engines to cut out, followed by the explosions. As this did not happen I realised they were gliding. One exploded in a lake near Elstree Studios, the other continued in flight and I saw it bank in our direction. There was an emergency water tank close by, so with one eye on the bomb, I ran round the water tank and threw myself to the ground until it exploded. By good fortune it had exploded between our building and a group of houses, causing only very slight damage. I was covered in dirt and water!

The highlight of my time at Bletchley Park was when Winston Churchill and his Commander-in-Chief visited the Park in 1942. He came into our hut, No 11; I had the task of showing him the Bombs, and how they worked. Afterwards, all the departments gathered on the front lawn, at his request, and he thanked us all for the contributions we were making to the war effort. He said, "There are so many chicks laying eggs without crowing."

The messages came, not only from German U-boats and behind the enemy lines, but transmission intercepted world-wide also included coded messages received from Resistance Movements. Les Cooper mentions this, but even after 50 years he remarks, as Norman Montague did, "one talks little about it".

LES COOPER was twenty-seven when war was declared and working in Wellworthy, on pistons – he hated it and in 1940 volunteered for the Signals –

Although I had worked with motor cars for years I had to be a cook! Plus square-bashing. The Motor Cyclist magazine had asked for Army volunteers to enlist as despatch drivers; I volunteered but only drove a motor-cycle once before becoming a driver in the Signals.

My unit trained many people to go behind the lines as wireless operators. I drove them, many were foreigners who had escaped from occupied countries. Also we were converting Packard (American cars) engines into wireless vans for transmitting and receiving messages. We weren't supposed to talk about it.

JOHN GABONY, another member of the Royal Engineers who was involved with transport, but of a very different type. After a spell in Africa and then as defending officer at court martials, he was posted to the Directorate of Transportation, War Office, working on the construction and operation of the artificial harbours for the D-Day invasion −

The Mulberry harbours were used in the Second Front off the beaches of Normandy. As all the major ports were in enemy hands, these Mulberry ports were essential for landing heavy equipment. The components were designed and constructed along the south and east coasts of England: difficult to keep it a secret! They were towed across the Channel. A ring of still water was provided by their big concrete caissons (watertight chambers used in construction work under water as a foundation) and ships that were scuttled around. This provided an artificial port for pierheads and jetties to land the heavy material of the war. Ships either went alongside or goods were put in lighters. The American port was destroyed by bad weather, but today one can still see the remains of the British port at Arromanches, on the French coast. This survived all storms and became the main base for the invasion forces.

Wendy Woollett, who was with the second party of Wrens to land on French soil after D-Day, mentions how they were landed at a Mulberry port.   (see Women at War).

RUTH WILLIAMS as a young child recalls her father's involvement with the Mulberry harbour −

We were lucky that his work on the development of radar, and later on switchgear for the Mulberry meant that he was able to live at home throughout the war. It also meant that he was able to get petrol for his car, not only to travel to work in Brighton but also to make regular, lengthy journeys to meetings at Southwick House on Portsdown Hill and to Haslemere. Occasionally our half-term holidays coincided with one of his trips to Surrey and so my mother, sister and I, trying to be as inconspicuous as possible in the car, had a rare treat of being able to ride with him part of the way and spend the day picknicking and walking in the country.

So far we have had memories from many an essential service rendered during the war but none of these would be possible without the most essential of all – the feeding of all to keep the spirits going!

TONY PURKIS *(see Chapter 2)* recalls his days at Brockenhurst Park and later in the Army –

When the war broke out all the servants came in to hear Mr Chamberlain announce the war on the wireless, while I was preparing the Sunday luncheon. Six weeks later I went to Southampton to join up. I was rejected, at first, because of poor eyesight. However, there was a job at an AA battery in Marchwood, on Southampton Water – situated in a sea of mud! I cooked for the artillery battery there and soon in the Officers' Mess. I kept niggling about it and when the Catering Officer came around I was told to report to Westminster Tech to train as an army caterer. Sir Isadore Salman (owner of Lyons Corner Houses) had been given the task of re-organising army catering: thus the Army Catering Corps (ACC) was founded. The RSM turned out to be Francis Cracknell of Brockenhurst. This helped my army career. I soon became a Sergeant Instructor. I had to train recruits which I didn't like, and said so.

So the army, in revenge, sent me to Glasgow to take charge of catering for the Highland Light Infantry.

In May 1940 I was at Dunkirk and we got out of France in a French fishing boat. On our return we landed at Steyning, Sussex. No-one wanted to know us, so I went home for a fortnight.

D-Day saw me back in France. *(see this chapter).*

TOM MARDON was born in Liverpool in 1915 but his father died when he was four months old, and his mother returned to Hampshire, near Andover and later to Brockenhurst. He tells of his war service –

In 1939 I volunteered for the navy, but on June 25, 1940 I was called up to the army! I joined the Hampshires at first and should have gone into the Eighth Army but the army doctor diagnosed varicose veins. He said, "You can't go to the desert with them, you'll bleed to death!" After the operation I was drafted to Monty's 79th Armoured Division School for Instructors, where I trained to handle amphibious tanks, becoming a sergeant instructor.

These tanks were ordinary tanks but with built-up canvas sides. If you put a stone in, it would sink in water; if you lengthened the sides it would float. The steering was done by moving the propellors with the Duplex Drive. The Germans did not have amphibious tanks – they were the invention of an Austrian refugee in England – brilliant! We also tested tanks against rough seas. We only lost one – at Studland, where it sank. It was all very hush-hush. A British Tank-Landing-Craft (TLC) carried five tanks, whereas the American TLC

215

carried eighteen. On nearing shore we let the doors down. When the nose of the tank came up, the Tank Commander knew to let his propellers down as it slid onto the water, to get away from the ship. It sounds tricky but I've done it thousands of times. After D-Day we trained men to get these tanks over rivers. Eventually we were sent to Eindhoven. *(see elsewhere in this chapter.)*

*

Shirley Bateman, a Brockenhurst resident, met many of the 'gentlemen' of 93 Coy Pioneer Corps in Southampton, commanded by her father. It consisted of escaped German Jews – including many brilliant musicians – who risked death for themselves and their families to fight Hitler. One drew him.

In spite of the nightly raids on London and elsewhere the British did not give in. Instead of bemoaning their lot all joined and worked together. A 'secret weapon' of the people was their sense of humour which carried them through many a dark day.

THE NAVY AND SEA RELATED INCIDENTS

Britain's main fleet was anchored at Scapa Flow, in the Orkney Islands, when war was declared. Defences here were very unsatisfactory and on October 14 a German submarine, U47, penetrated these and sank HMS *Royal Oak* at her moorings. (R Chalk from Brockenhurst was one of those killed).

KEN TOD, a retired Royal Navy captain recalls part of his war service there. He was posted to Scapa Flow from the RN Dockyards at Chatham. He recounts –

216

I was then appointed to HMS *Sheffield* and spent some time searching Scotland for her. I found her at Rosyth, and sailed to Scapa Flow where the Home Fleet was assembled among the wrecks of the 1918 German Fleet, scuttled by their own crews . . . We were joined by a draft of midshipmen from Dartmouth. They had received a telegram on Friday to join *Sheffield* on Monday, but found it not possible by train, so settled back for a last weekend at home; that is all but one. He went to London and hired a taxi which, surprisingly, made it to Thurso by Sunday evening only to find there was no ferry till Monday! The Admiralty refunded less than half his expenses.

At Scapa there were many air raid alarms. One of these caught the Captain in a motor boat in the middle of the Flow. He and his crew scrambled onto the upturned hull of one of the capsized German battleships; this refuge tickled his sense of humour!

Seagoing was uneventful but always tense, as everyone slept on deck near their action stations, and with the ship totally shut down to show no chinks of light; as a result the atmosphere got pretty thick. At the time of the German invasion of Norway in April, 1940, we took soldiers on board for Namsos, north of Trondheim. Then back home for another lot for Molde. Then back to Rosyth for, we thought, more soldiers but no, we returned to Molde for the evacuation. We found Andalsnes, at the head of the fjord in flames after an air raid. The stops in Norway had to be at night and as short as possible, so as not to be caught by bombers. We had newspapers on board and hoped they were not seen by the soldiers, weary and dispirited, as they were full of gung-ho journalists' guesses about our success in Norway.

After the Norwegian campaign, German troops had swept south: after a valiant fight put up by our forces, the British Expeditionary Forces (BEF) would have to be evacuated from the coast of France, by sea, and as many as possible small craft had been assembled by the Admiralty.

MRS PRICE who had by that time followed her naval husband to Merseyside remembers being told by her father that their yacht *Chanticleer* made fourteen trips across the English Channel, from Ramsgate to Dunkirk. She had a flat bottom and was therefore most useful on the beaches –

About 200 British naval vessels and over 600 small craft were engaged in the evacuation of Dunkirk. These, however, were not the last of the British troops to leave the French shores.

JOHN GABONY was not yet twenty when war was declared – he had been called up to the Royal Engineers the week before and was billeted at a school in Twickenham from where he embarked for France. He recalls his first crossing to French shores and his return after Dunkirk –

On landing in France we embarked on a twenty-six hour journey in an unheated train with no provisions – our unit was destined to take over the port of Brest. When we woke in the morning, we collected hot water from the engine of the train for shaving, and we stopped at one or two stations en route, where the ladies of the French Red Cross brought us sandwiches. It was a long, phoney and rather boring spell before the Blitzkreig.

After Dunkirk, we were the last British troops to leave the French shores. We were packed into the hold of a cargo vessel with nothing to sit on except the bare decks. The crew then began to pull the covers over the hold! We called up to say that if anything happened to the vessel we were 'sealed up' inside. The officer in command, eventually, ordered the covers to be removed. We spent a night crossing the Channel and landed at Devonport the following day, en route for Tavistock. On arrival back in Britain, we were rather surprised to see the artillery still carrying out peacetime drills!

Britain soon took control of the seas between the Shetlands and Iceland, and the northern stretches of the Norwegian Arctic Sea. This becoming a most important convoy route during the coming years.

Returning to the North Atlantic, JOE WILLIAMS describes an incident on one of his escort duties in the area –

The narrative which follows is entirely based upon the memory of an eighty-two-year-old man. I have no recourse to Admiralty records, the keeping of diaries was discouraged in those days and we certainly never wrote anything on operations other than Official Reports.

In April 1941 a Flower Class Corvette under my command (as Lieutenant) slipped her moorings in Gibraltar harbour and proceeded into the North Atlantic to rendezvous with a large convoy (about 50 ships) from South Africa and Sierra Leone, bound for the UK. Convoys on this route made a wide detour to the westward, into the Atlantic, then steered a northerly course between longitudes 25° and 35°W until reaching about latitude 55°N and then headed eastward to the UK making around the north of Ireland and thence dispersing to their final destination ports.

After meeting our homeward-bound convoy I took up station on the port beam, about a mile or two distant from the nearest merchant ship. When between three and four hundred miles from the north of Ireland, at about 10 am a German Focke Wulf four-engined Condor came over the convoy and dropped two bombs on the nearest ship to us; one bomb made a direct hit on the merchant vessel, penetrating her No 2 hold, immediately forward of the bridge. The 3rd Officer and helmsman were killed instantly. Although many merchant ships and the naval escorting vessels opened fire, the Condor escaped at great speed. The bridge and engine room were put out of action; the vessel stopped and the Captain, crew and passengers abandoned ship.

There were only four passengers and about fifty crew on board. Two or three lifeboats cleared the burning vessel, I proceeded towards them and took them on board. There was a lady amongst the passengers, who was about eight months pregnant. We carried no doctor, nor was there one on the bombed ship; but we did have a sick bay attendant (but with no midwifery experience – nor had any of us). However, we made all the survivors as comfortable as possible, and the lady passenger was put to bed in my cabin.

The Senior Officer Escort (SOE) told me to proceed with utmost despatch to Lough Foyle (Londonderry) where a tug would take off the survivors, land them at Moville and thence to hospital in Londonderry. We immediately worked up to full speed and proceeded eastward to the northern Irish coast. Two of the crew taken on board had died, and these were laid to rest at sea in accordance with the customary procedure. The 2nd Officer who was on deck at the time of the attack was severely wounded. We made him as comfortable as possible on the Ward Room settee, but he died during the night. His body was landed at Lough Foyle: he had had his skull fractured.

Shortly after we had left the convoy, we saw the bombed merchant vessel settling down by the bow and she sank within a few minutes. I remember going to talk to the lady passenger (I have forgotten her name) and re-assuring her that by early morning she would be in hospital.

Then, about four or five hours after leaving the convoy, I received a Wireless Telegraphy (W/T) message prefixed MOST IMMEDIATE instructing me to proceed to Falmouth to discharge the survivors. This message was made in an obsolete compromised code and by a certain abbreviated word I new that it was a feint, and most likely meant to be known to the enemy. So, no action was taken by me and I continued on my way in accordance with my original instructions. Thanks to a calm sea, a light following breeze and a competent engineering staff, we made a record speed. At this stage I had an idea – why not make the approach to Lough Foyle by the less obvious, close inshore route, on the land side of the laid minefields. We altered course slightly to the southward and headed straight for Arran Island (off the Donegal coast). It was dark when we picked up Arran and went very close inshore, almost rock-scraping: past Owey Island; Gola Island; very close to Bloody Foreland; through Tory Sound; south of Inishbofin; rounded Horn Head, Fanad Head, Malin Head and thence down to Inishowen Head and so into Lough Foyle. After transferring our survivors to the tug we proceeded up the River Foyle and an hour and a half later we arrived in Londonderry. I went ashore and made my report to the Naval Officer in charge.

When in Londonderry I was informed that a U-boat had been sunk in the vicinity of the normal approach to Lough Foyle, quite a few miles north of our inshore route. I was ordered to return to sea and pick up the convoy which I had left. So back we went and about two days later returned to Londonderry with the convoy. While having a few days rest in port we learnt that the 'phoney signal' which I had received telling me to go to Falmouth had, indeed, been picked up by the German U-boat command who acted upon it and despatched a U-boat under the command of Ober Leutnant Werthe, to patrol the approaches to Falmouth. This U-boat was detected by two destroyers sent out from Plymouth and was attacked while at periscope depth, she surfaced, survivors were taken off and the U-boat sunk. Two or three weeks later I went to the City Hospital, Londonderry to visit our lady survivor and was greeted by the lady holding a five-day-old boy: mother and child were fit, well and happy.

Sometimes contact with the enemy did, many years later, end happily as Joe Williams tells of his second meeting after the first 'contact' on this escort duty in the Atlantic –

In 1951 I was in command of a Shaw Savill Line ship proceeding to Hamburg. On approaching the dock I embarked a Docking Pilot. After the docking was completed I asked the pilot to my cabin for the customary whisky. While signing his papers, I noticed the name Werthe, and asked him a question or two. He told me that he had been in command of U212 which was sunk in the English Channel, near Falmouth. I told him of my connection with this incident, and we both sincerely congratulated ourselves on meeting now, instead of in 1941. We became friends, I enjoyed a dinner and most pleasant evening at his home, and later, my wife and I were able to return his hospitality at our home.

ARCHIE CLEVELAND also spent time on Northern Patrol. From an early age he helped his father look after stock. He says –

I always had a hankering to go to sea. In 1939 I joined the Royal Navy. After training at Skegness, I was posted to HMS *Laconia* (a former liner). Our first job was to take £3 million of gold from Devonport to Halifax, Nova Scotia. For the next two years we were on Northern Patrol and during this time I trained as an ack-ack Gunner and became an Able Seaman.

After leave in London we were back on patrol, this time escorting Lend-Lease ships from the States. On one occasion we left America with 72 ships and arrived at Liverpool with only two: a lot were sunk and the rest scattered and didn't manage to re-group. We were often bombed, and didn't have any defence against the German bombers who stayed out of reach of our ack-ack guns. Sometimes we were dive-bombed by Stukas – one was too clever and was shot down. The crew of two Germans was picked up by a French ship before we got there. I, myself, saw the French sailors strip the clothes off the Germans and throw them into the sea. We never ill-treated German prisoners. Once we brought some back to Belfast, when they went down the gangplank they turned round and said 'thank you'.

On another occasion we took convoys to Russia, but we were never allowed to land. Of course, I was often scared – God yes! If anyone in convoys says they weren't scared, don't believe them. I was never sunk and came back without a scratch.

Another mariner who recalls escort duty in the North Atlantic is FRANK LEWIN, who brought his young wife to Lyndhurst during the early years of the war while his ship was in for a refit in Southampton. Eventually Mrs Lewin found a base in Brockenhurst with a Mrs Anson, who took her under her wing and detailed the advantages of village life. This was a great delight to her, having come from the northern suburbs of Liverpool. The stay was only short but they eventually returned to visit his niece and her husband who had bought a house in Brockenhurst. Frank Lewin continues –

In 1942 I was sent to HMS *Palomares*, an auxilliary AA cruiser, armoured with six-inch guns on the sides and four-inch guns over the deck. We sailed from Belfast under sealed orders and finished up at Seydisfjord, Iceland; there to form part of the close escort for PQ17, the disastrous convoy to Russia, about which so much has been written.

After the threat of attack by German ships, the convoy was ordered to scatter. We obeyed orders; later we tried to find as many surviving ships as we could. We took some into Matochklin Strait, Novaya Zembla and slowly mustered the sad remains of our convoy. We then had a very hotly contested passage to the Dvina River, Archangel and lost more ships. By the time we got in we had just about exhausted all our ammunition, so we were stuck there for weeks until HMS *Marne* and *Martin* brought us supplies, together with a field-hospital designed to care for the thousand or more casualties from PQ17, and earlier convoys. These were being treated in appalling conditions in a Russian hospital. We, apparently, were given a choice; give the hospital to the Russians, or take it home; if landed it would have disappeared towards Moscow. I believe it came home again.

So we spent six or seven weeks at Archangel. Our Gunnery Officer was arrested. He took a regular country walk near our berth and our allies could not understand why he walked the same route every day! One man was shot in the town by a policeman for disobeying the standing order to go straight to the nearest shelter. He had stopped to try to extinguish an incendiary bomb! We were glad to get away and leave our gallant allies to their peculiar ways.

EILEEN GABONY, as a young woman and before she married, was PA to the Assistant Secretary of the Allied Supplies committee – co-ordinating allied supplies. She speaks of her interesting job and the PQ convoys –

. . . seeing all the Government papers on supplies to Russia and the other allies. The PQ convoys to North Russia ran regularly once or twice per month using Archangel or Murmansk as their destination. I particularly remember the ill-fated convoy PQ17; we had all the details of that dreadful convoy, when so many ships went down, and the survivors that returned to Glasgow.

Earlier FRANK LEWIN had been in the South Atlantic after he was appointed to HMS *Marsdale*, designated an Ocean Boarding Vessel. The job was to try to keep tabs on merchant shipping in mid and south Atlantic, checking 'navicerts' – which certified that the cargo carried would not be used for blockade running or enemy use – and investigating suspicious ships –

We patrolled for long periods – boredom interspersed with alarms about raiders and U-boats. Then the excitement of boarding, being dropped from about six feet in a Montague whaler, perhaps at three in the morning to row to some ship to be examined. Our ship never stopped, that could be dangerous, so she steamed in a circle. We would row downwind to the suspect, board, seize the bridge and engine room and start the examination. Usually we would find everyone friendly and innocent. When that was verified we would set off for our own ship, again rowing downwind and laden with the latest newspapers and magazines, gifts from the merchantmen. Our ship would slow down and come alongside us. We would hook on and as the ship worked up to normal speed, we would be lifted up to deck level. We would repeat this five or six times a week for about a month, then a day bunkering and storing in Gibraltar. After three patrols we would go to some convenient port for four or five days and a boiler clean. The port could be Halifax, Novia Scotia and here we stepped out of war completely for a spell; blissful memory!

KEN TOD also visited Gibraltar –

We were sent to Gibraltar to join Force H for an active time escorting convoys in the Atlantic and, more explosively, the Malta convoys. Force H consisted of a battle-cruiser HMS *Renown*, cruiser HMS *Sheffield*, aircraft carrier HMS *Ark Royal* and a flotilla of destroyers.

When things were normal, which they seldom were, we had three weeks at sea, then three days in Gibraltar. On return to harbour we worked into the night making good, machinery defects. One watch went on shore leave each evening and, of course, went to the beer bars. On one occasion a 'beer ship' had been sunk and the bars sold the sailors something called Malaga wine with disastrous results! As often happened, there was a call to sea during the night and it was not possible to wake the watch ashore and the remainder on board were not enough to steam the ship and man the guns. Shore leave, thereafter, was restricted according to the beer supply!

Another memory is of HMS *Hood* arriving having been fitted with someone's brainwave – an apparatus that fired off projectiles skywards which opened up releasing parachutes trailing wires with a charge on the end to entrap attacking aircraft. *Hood* chose to test these while in Gibraltar harbour. The local garrison had been told that a German attack could begin with a drop of paratroops. They heard an explosion and suddenly the sky was full of parachutes – just what had been expected. The whole garrison of 10,000 men stood to arms until they found there were no men at the end of the wires!

One of the first Early Warning Radars was on the top of the Rock of Gibraltar; a man was posted up there to report any blip appearing on the screen. Days passed with nothing to report until he phoned for an electrician saying the set had gone wrong; the whole screen is covered with blips. In fact, it was working perfectly and recording the approaches of a French air raid attack in revenge for the British attack on their fleet in North Africa, to prevent it being taken by the Germans. There was another brush with the French when one of their merchant ships was trying to smuggle arms through the Straits to Germany, *Sheffield* and some destroyers were sent to intercept. The ship made for a north African port, we followed and a destroyer went alongside, but came under fire from the shore batteries. We all withdrew at full speed pursued by angry French bombers. At Gibraltar we were refused permission to enter until the raid was over. So, *Sheffield* provided wonderful entertainment for the people on shore by zig-zagging under a smoke screen in the Bay until the French ran out of bombs.

VERA RIDLEY-MARTIN was on one of the first ships to visit Gibraltar, after the declaration of war, waiting for a convoy to be assembled –

I was on board SS *Kemandine*, when war was declared; returning from leave, and bound for Port Sudan. Our husbands had already sailed on the SS *Montcalm* – a much larger and faster ship.

The first day out we were summoned to boat drill. Being young and light-hearted I went to my boat station and thought I must look for a nice strong, hefty-looking sailor to position myself next to, so that if we were torpedoed he would be at hand to help me! To my horror I looked and realised that the men on the ship were a frail lot. Then

I looked at the non-crew – mostly young mothers with babies and toddlers! No lusty young matelot to help me! As one of the younger people on board I would have to help the young mothers with their babies.

Next day we assembled in the saloon and heard Neville Chamberlain make the fateful announcement that we were at war with Germany. The ship immediately took a zig-zag course. One morning I woke to unaccustomed stillness: no creaking of the bulkheads, no sound of the engines. We had broken down and became a sitting duck for 48 hours. Later we heard that two ships had been sunk in the area where we should have been, but for the breakdown. A chilling thought!

Slowly, we zig-zagged to Gibraltar, where a convoy could be made up. While waiting we went ashore each day. At long last a scruffy collection of small merchant ships were assembled with *Kemandine* as flagship, and guarded by Tribal Class destroyer HMS *Cossack*. She was a beauty to behold as she darted about amongst the ships; like a sheepdog rounding up a straggling flock.

At Port Sudan the quayside was lined with husbands with pockets full of cash to pay our expenses!

Off to the Mediterranean, but in a troopship was JOHN GABONY –

We embarked on the Dutch troopship, *Marnix van St Aldegonde*, at Glasgow and sailed in convoy north of Ireland, into the Atlantic and past Gibraltar, north African beaches towards Malta. This was a decoy; we turned round at night and headed for the beaches of Algiers. We had been at sea for eleven days with some rather good food! We were ferried to other ships that had all our equipment and then on to landing-craft and, on to the beaches. Our landing was to coincide with the Eighth Army approach, in 1942.

An amusing incident happened there – in transferring from one craft to another we had to climb a long rope ladder dropped over the side of the vessel. I was behind one of my men who, suddenly, froze halfway up and would not move, so I had to push him all the way up; one could not look down, the drop was terrific.

After a spell in north Africa, having been mentioned in despatches, he had a serious motorcyle accident and was returned home in a hospital ship. In November 1942 the *Marnix* was torpedoed by German aircraft near Algiers; she was carrying some 3,000 troops who were safely landed at Philippeville.

FRANK LEWIN's ship had damages repaired in a refit in Tilbury, and then returned to the Mediterranean for the landings at Sicily and Salerno. During his time at sea Frank Lewin was mentioned in despatches. He remarks –

Anzio saw our luck run out and we had barely arrived before a mine floated into our stern and blew about forty feet of the submerged section to pieces, fortunately without casualties. It took quite a bit of hard work to keep her afloat long enough to be towed to Naples for temporary repairs. We arrived in the middle of the Mount Vesuvius eruption! We had seen enough fireworks but, this was a show spectacular enough to hold our attention.

Eventually, we were towed home for another refit – this time to Liverpool. Then we set out for Malaysia, the war in Europe having now ended, and the Red Sea was open. We had a bad fuel leak and a very nasty fire in the engine room. I received some nasty burns and took no further part in war affairs other than being a pampered patient in a succession of hospitals.

However, before Suez was opened and the war in Europe was still on, all ships had to sail the long way round the southern tip of Africa. PETER TAYLOR, as a member of the Royal Artillery, Surrey and Sussex Yeomanry, sailed to Egypt via this route, which took seven weeks, to Suez. He tells of this voyage –

Due to not being loaded in time we missed our convoy at Liverpool, so had no escort until we reached Freetown, West Africa. On the way to Freetown torpedoes were fired at us twice, but we had heard nothing as we were playing Bingo down below.

At Freetown we caught up with the convoy and were greeted with "nice to see you, thought you had bought it!" From there we sailed in convoy, round the Cape of Good Hope and on to Suez and to desert warfare – that is another story.

Sailing in a troopship, in convoy, was invariably a long, slow and rather tedious period. TED BROWN, who retired to Brockenhurst some ten years ago after a spell in India and then the City, writes –

I joined up – as we used to say – at the end of 1940 as a cadet destined for the Indian Army because I had passed my Certificates A and B at school, and thus I was in the Officers' Training Corps. I reported to Aldershot on a very cold day and that cold continued for many a day.

Eventually the move was on. Confined to barracks, all very hush-hush. On the day of the move we paraded with full equipment, and strapped to our pack were our topis. Even the dimmest spy could see that we were off East: fortunately there were no spies present – we were not sunk en route to India.

We boarded the ship at Gourock – what a shock! Instead of a towering liner – an old tub, *The Highland Chieftain*, a converted meat ship normally on the South American run. The ship's holds had been converted into mess decks. We slept, one on the mess table and two above in hammocks. Hammocks are good when the sea is rough, but all was rather chaotic. We headed north almost to Iceland. Our armament was four Lewis guns mounted on the top deck. They were never used in anger. I spent time in the bow of the ship, two hours on and four off. We were supposed to be looking for something – I never knew what it was; possibly some sort of fish – tinned or otherwise!

As soon as the alarm bells sounded I had to make my way down to the engine room to close the watertight doors. The alarms rang a few times, whether in danger or practice was not very clear, nothing happened. I only reached the engine room after everyone was sitting by his lifeboat! It was like trying to get into Highbury Stadium when a match had just finished.

By degrees, as we turned south, the weather improved and became warmer. First, we could sit on deck in our greatcoats. Next, we could dispense with our coats and strip down to our khaki shirts and finally shorts. Very smart our shorts – they reached halfway down the leg for nightwear, but were turned up during the day, and were fastened with buttons on the side: army cotton was of poor quality and the buttons were soon lost. The purpose of this invention was to guard against mosquitos. She was not deterred as she – only the female goes for blood – could bite through socks with the greatest of ease.

We all did service as mess stewards. From time to time I had to go to the galley and collect food for the table. I was on duty while in Freetown, in the galley I was given an enormous *dechi* (pan) of potatoes which the cook, an enormous negro was stirring, sweat pouring off his forehead into the potatoes – possibly there was a shortage of salt on board!

Most of the senior officers on board were retired Indian Army officers called back to the Colours. All of them had loved life in India. They recounted tales of the North West Frontier, mess dinners, polo and other Indian delights. As cadets we had to study – not too hard; the sun was hot and the beer plentiful. We bashed away at Urdu, a mixture of Hindi and Persian, used in the Indian Army. Tactics followed – the North West Frontier type – of little use in the Burma jungle where I went early in 1942.

The convoy of ships, some 50 or 60 of us, ploughed on, the maximum speed was that of the slowest vessel, only eight or nine knots: round the Cape we sailed and into Durban. Here we transshipped to the *Windsor Castle* and on to India, not in convoy and at a faster speed.

In 1942 KENNETH SLADE was also bound for India. No, he was not one of Ted Brown's retired Indian Army officers returning there. He had been commissioned into the Territorial Army in 1935. After some years on anti-aircraft duties on the south coast of England he was destined for India. He recalls a serious, but in retrospect, amusing incident that happened en route to the East –

We embarked in Glasgow, we knew not where, as a complete anti-aircraft regiment. I was in command of a battery at this time, with the rank of major. Shortly before sailing a number of rather stern-looking nurses boarded the ship. However, once at sea they became lovelier by the day. One of my young fellow officers was very taken by a young nurse. When we and the nurses were invited to a small gathering they decided to enjoy each others company, and walk the decks. They headed for the sharp end of the ship, strictly out-of-bounds for the troops; he pressed her so tight against the railings that she fell overboard! A cry of "man overboard" resulted in the ship's floodlights being put on – this was very strictly against all safety rules. With good fortune the young lady was picked up by the vessel behind us, and to everyone's relief she was not harmed.

We were at sea for nine weeks until we arrived two days short of Singapore, when it fell. The skipper of the convoy about turned the whole convoy and came back into Bombay.

(*Service in India is elsewhere in this chapter.*)

FRANCIE PEYTON JONES, serving in the Wrens and having been involved with plotting the D-Day landings was, thereafter, drafted to Ceylon, and makes this remark about her voyage –

I was lucky to be drafted to Ceylon but remember little of interest on the outward voyage, except for sleeping with one's bell-bottoms under one's pillow and ready for instant wear. We were banned from going on deck after dark, supposedly to protect us from the too intimate attentions of our fellow soldiers and sailors! However, there was a lot of organised entertainment and fun to be had, and several ship-board romances ending in rather hasty marriages, on arrival.

Little did she know of Kenneth Slade's experience but, maybe her commanding officer had a notion of the possible!

JOAN LLOYD came first to Sway and then Boldre when her husband left the RAF and entered into business in the area. Like Ted Brown's voyage in the *Windsor Castle*, the *Arundel Castle* also made excellent speed, quite a change from most, tediously long voyages –

In September 1938 my mother joined my father for his last year as Manager of the Cable & Wireless Station and Resident Magistrate on Ascension Island.

As the political situation was unstable she decided not to leave me at boarding school in London but, to take me with her. Although my education may have suffered, I had the experience of a wonderful year on Ascension.

My father was due to come home in December 1939. My mother recorded in her diary that at 7.30 am on the 15th we boarded the *Arundel Castle*, coming from Cape Town, to England. There was only

227

one other First Class passenger and a few young men in Tourist Class returning home to join the forces. We were instructed to carry our life-belts at all times. It was like a phantom ship, and most of the spare cabins appeared to be stacked with cartons of food.

The story went round that Lord Haw-Haw (William Joyce who broadcast for Germany – he had a British passport and was hanged for treason in 1945) had promised our ship to Hitler for Christmas. I should add that we were not in convoy as it was considered that we were fast enough to out-manoeuvre a U-boat.

We were due back to dock at Southampton on the 24th but we were enveloped in thick fog, and had to anchor off the Isle of Wight until the next day. It was a great relief to land on Christmas Day, in spite of the snow and very little in the way of winter clothing.

Many convoys called at the Cape, first taking troops from east to west and later from west to east. BÉ COOPER-VOSSE was a teenager at the Cape and recalls a 'character' living there at the time –

Those who came ashore and particularly seamen of the Royal Navy might remember Able-Seaman Just Nuisance, a true friend of the sailors. Briefly the story of his life – Nuisance was born on April 1, 1937. His owner was manager of the United Services Institute in Simonstown. Here Nuisance came in contact with, and developed a life-long fondness of seamen. He boarded the ships regularly and was fed on them. He also travelled on the trains to Cape Town with his pals, always occupying a bench to relax on.

This in the beginning, caused a great deal of problem being thrown off the train by guards, only to jump in again by a door left open, or if the worst came to the worst, wait for the next train to pull in. All this was 'cured' when the Commanding Officer at Simonstown decided to officially enlist Nuisance into the Royal Navy.

Filling in his Certificate of Service a few problems arose. Nuisance needed a Christian name, 'Just' was inserted: occupation 'bone-crusher': religious denomination 'Canine Divinity League – Scrounger' and as he had been an 'unofficial rating' for about eighteen months he received promotion to Able-Seaman. He also received his Identity Disk, a South African Railway free-pass and a cap with a linen chin-strap. The Commanding Officer exempted him from wearing it at all times, except on official duties. *(Details of his enlistment are from his biography by Terence Sisson, one of his minders).*

By now readers will be wondering what creature this new Able-Seaman was. He was a very large, almost human Great Dane. He escorted sailors to and fro from various bases, travelled with them on the train and in service lorries and cars, went to the pub with his pals for he loved his beer, flew with his Fleet-Air-Arm minder, attended fund-raising functions with his Commanding Officer and guided

many an over-indulged sailor to the train or Seamen's Institute for the night. He had his own bed allocated at the various bases and branches of the Institutes and, woe betide anyone who accidentally occupied his bed – they were soon turfed out!

I recall during these years a parade of the Dutch Royal Navy through Cape Town. Just Nuisance presented himself and fell in alongside the Commanding Officer at the head of the parade (I cannot recall whether he was wearing his cap that day) and escorted the parade through town. Thereafter he went about his own business, no doubt visiting a bar or two on the way, for he knew where he would receive a pint or two!

Nuisance died, aged seven, from paralysis of the sciatic nerve after spending some time in a naval hospital. He was buried, with full naval honours, at a naval camp near Simonstown. A life-size bronze statue of Able-Seaman Just Nuisance RN was erected, some years after his death, on the terrace overlooking Simonstown harbour.

Homeward-bound (but not past the Cape) after VJ Day, the Wrens stationed at Colombo found themselves boarding the *Athlone Castle* FRANCIE PEYTON JONES writes –

. . . 300 of us packed into four-tiered bunks in the ship's swimming pool, with just enough room to walk between the tiers. Washing facilities were equally scant, but I personally thoroughly enjoyed the voyage home. The important thing was to meet and ensnare a major or above, somewhere, somehow . . . He could then invite you to the boat deck, out of the cramped conditions, and from then on a relatively comfortable voyage was secured. Arrival at Southampton was an anti-climax indeed after the social whirl of the voyage, everyone in the streets looked so incredibly old!

INDIVIDUAL TALES FROM ABROAD

RUUD LEM – **A Narrow Escape**

Ruud Lem, a businessman, was born in 1938 in Nijmegen, Nederland and moved with his family to Brockenhurst in 1978.

War is called the game of the Devil and brings pain and misery to people. Though sometimes idealised, there are great risks and mistakes happen. One such took place in Nijmegen in the Netherlands on February 22, 1944; I could have been a victim...

I was born at Nijmegen in December 1938. My family lived in the centre of the town in Molenstraat. Arnhem is just 18km away and both towns are near the German border. I was five years old and not aware of all that was happening around me. I went regularly, with my eldest sister, Marian, to the nursery-school run by RC Sisters.

After lunch, on a clear day, we went back to school when the alarms sounded. We were on the corner of Molenstraat opposite St Canisius Church. People rushed towards air raid shelters, but a shopkeeper told us to go back home. Mr van Woerkom, the grocer, actually saved our lives.

At home the sound of aeroplanes was loud and we could hear bombs falling. Later we heard that one quarter of the town was burning or destroyed, including our school and the church.

The irony of it all was that the aeroplanes dropping the bombs, were Americans! They mistakenly had dropped their cruel load on our town instead of Kleer, across the German border, 20km away. They are similarly set on a river, both on hilly positions with a castle and many church spires; from the sky they were almost identical. This navigational error cost Nijmegen dearly and was a terrible experience for the Dutch people, in general, and Nijmegen in particular. The Germans tried to exploit this by saying, "This is what one can expect from the Allies – your so-called friends".

However, the inhabitants of the town, though grieving their lost relatives, did not lose confidence in the Allies, who had to come one day. They resisted the Occupation even more...

BILL DUNKINSON – **Crossing the Channel.**

Bill Dunkinson is a member of a family who have lived in Brockenhurst since 1700. *(see Chapter 3)*

By D-Day, as Chief Petty Officer, I was in charge of the engine room on a Landing Ship Tank 180 (LST) of 600 tons. It had a crew of 80 men and we used to average about 11 knots. We towed the Rhino ferry, which was part of Mulberry harbour to Gold Beach, Arromanches. About six days after D-Day we took over a load of American troops who had to disembark 50 yards from the shore. Most of them were shot in the water, by the enemy, and never made it.

On the return trips from Arromanches to Gosport we took on the wounded. On our first trip we had Canadians from the 3rd Canadian Division, many of whom had been stationed around Brockenhurst before crossing the Channel. We carried well over 200 men on our three decks. There was a surgeon and sick-bay attendants with us, looking after them. On that voyage two Canadians died and we buried them at sea. On another occasion we brought back Lord Lovat, DSO, MC (he commanded the 1st Special Service Brigade Commandos). Sometimes we brought over Germans captured in France.

Altogether we did 37 trips to and from France always returning with wounded.

TONY PURKIS – In France.

Tony Purkis was born in Brockenhurst. Before the war he was employed by the Morant family at Brockenhurst Park. (see Chapter 2)

D-Day + 1 we went over to France with the 51st Highland Division. We were heavily shelled, I was terrified. The American skipper of the landing craft could not get close inshore, so he dropped the front of the craft and with all our equipment and rifles aloft, we marched through four foot deep water, and then three miles inland.

My duties were still feeding the men *(see Training and Defence)*. After two weeks the 10th Battalion HLI landed and I joined up with them. All our supplies, equipment and clothes had got lost at Tilbury. We lived off the land and the French were very good to us but they were scared the Germans might throw us back into the sea and would then take revenge on them.

A memory – dehydrated yeast! After three or four weeks a local padre came along and asked if there was anything we wanted. I had collected several hundredweight of flour by now which I had put on three ton lorries at Tilbury – God knows why! The padre said he would look for some yeast. I didn't find out for ages that he'd walked twenty miles there and back to a local brewery to bring it to us. We cut dustbins in half and baked bread for the battalion – every man got two slices and the rest we gave to the French people. We were mentioned in despatches.

We were then sent to Cherbourg to form the spearhead. We cooked in the open fields and always dug slit trenches nearby. A man with a whistle warned us when there was a mortar attack; I was first into the trench and the others followed me. We had a direct hit on the trench – I was the only survivor. I had a shrapnel wound in my arm. Later I had my watch returned to me. It had stopped when the shrapnel struck it, saving my life. A watch, taken from a dead German, had stopped shrapnel passing into my lung!

LES JOHNSON – **To France and the Lowlands.**

The late Les Johnson was born in Brockenhurst. *(see Chapter 2)*

The day before D-Day we were sent down from Scotland to Rowlands Castle, near Southampton. We waited in the woods, ready to leave for France. A warship with huge guns escorted us as we sailed, with hundreds of other troops, as well as our Bedford trucks and their generating equipment (for supplying lighting to camps), across the Channel. As we neared the coast of France little landing boats came to take us onto the beach. I remember counting 13 of us on one of these boats and thought that was unlucky, but I was wrong because we all got back safely.

On the beach we were being fired on from both directions, the Germans were shelling us on one side and our troops firing on the other – it's queer, we weren't terrified, we were too interested in getting to where we had to go.

Our first job was to make a road above the beach. That night we pulled into a little paddock by the road. We set up camp and got the lights on straight away, putting the engine into a little shed. We then went into a nearby trench dug by the Pioneers. During the night I woke and said, "That engine sounds queer, but I am not going to look at it now". A few hours later we saw that a shell had blown the roof off the shed. We might have been there.

One evening we got a message to say that bombing of nearby Caen would start. I saw a British bomber circling over, dropping flares: the whole sky was lit up. Soon about 2,000 of our bombers came over. We by-passed the destroyed Caen and just kept going for days. During this time we saw many gliders being towed overhead.

The next thing I remember is the battle of the Falaise Gap where the Germans were trapped – it was the worst devastation I have ever seen, miles of it. I picked up some German electric cable which came in useful.

Eventually we got to Belgium where we stopped near a First World War cemetery, my father was buried there but, as I got to the gates I was re-called to continue our advance. I never saw my father's grave.

On into Holland where the Germans were in the woods. A farmer was carting a load of hay when I noticed it moving. I went up to him with my rifle and shouted at him and from the haystack tumbled two Germans, with their hands up.

When we got to Düsseldorf there was a terrific lot of fighting and you daren't leave your trucks because the German boys stole everything they could. When we were near Berlin we got orders to retreat. The Russians advancing from the other side had to enter first.

BASIL O'DONNELL – In a glider to Germany.

Basil O'Donnell was born in Brockenhurst in 1909.   *(see Chapter 2)*
I was in various regiments including the 12th Devon Airborne and also did some parachuting but was considered too old (being thirty when war was declared), so I went into gliders.

In 1945 we were stationed in a secure camp at Dunmow, Essex. On the day of our departure we did a five mile route march and on leaving the base the civilians had placards outside, wishing us luck.

It was a beautiful day when we crossed the Channel in those flimsy Horsa gliders, it made you wonder whether you would make it to the other side. Some planes were towing two gliders: I also saw a few go down into the sea.

We were fighting in a small town in NW Germany called Hamminkin when I was wounded in the right knee by shrapnel; the Regiment lost around three-quarters of its men in this action. Eventually I had to be flown home and transferred to Nottingham Hospital. I was there for eleven months and then demobbed.

RUUD LEM – When gliders filled the skies.

Can it be that someone very young can remember a Second World War incident? If important enough it may leave a deep mark, as in my case, and I will never forget those moments!

In 1943 my father, a barrister, was wanted by the Germans as a hostage for the bridge over the river Waal, at Nijmegen. The Germans feared the Underground Movement might blow it up in order to cut off German supplies coming from Arnhem.

Our family took refuge at our summer house in the hills, at Mook; father cycling the 14km to Nijmegen. Our house, on top of the hill, enjoyed a panorama over the valley of the river Maas, to the west.

On Sunday, September 17, 1944, the skies filled with thousands of aircraft, all coming from the west. A beautiful day turned into an unforgettable day as the skies darkened. Not only the big bombers made a deep impression, but the gliders being towed by long ropes – all the way across the Channel to Holland! Operation 'Market Garden' had started!

Why should those gliders leave an impression on a young boy? Firstly, they were almost silent, coming down gradually lower and lower and one could see, from our elevated position, the faces of the crew. I looked in amazement until my parents drew me inside, as this was not without danger – the Germans, in the woods behind the house were shooting. The long awaited Liberation! Not that I, aged six, understood it all . . . the aeroplanes, the gliders or the parachutes that filled the western skies.

During the fighting we lived in the cellar – 4 x 3 metres – under the house; cooking was done on a small wax-light, it took ages to warm. Suddenly there were people in the house and coming closer to the cellar. The first boot came down followed by the nose of a gun, suddenly my mother yelled, "Tommies . . ." But a dark brown, loud voice only said, "No, American . . ."

TOM MARDON – Crossing the Rhine

As an instructor trained to handle amphibious tanks he was sent to Eindhoven, Holland to get the tanks across the Rhine.

It wasn't easy, the river current flowed at five knots and the tank speed was only four. So we manoeuvred the tanks above the prepared landing place, faced the current and then drifted down – a tricky business. As the Germans were lower down the Rhine, we were issued with jack knives; if the engine failed, our orders were to rip the canvas and sink the tank.

Then I was attached to the Bedfordshire and Hertfordshire Regiment, whose tanks all had trained commanders except me. I was asked to take over a tank; when I got this tank over the crew said, "We haven't any confidence in our sergeant, what about you taking command?" My orders were to get across the river and return by the nearest bridge as soon as possible, thus I had to refuse.

I can't say I was scared; keyed up, yes. A job had to be done. I shall always remember the first soldiers to cross the Rhine. Watching the Highland Infantry marching and wading behind the six Pipers – unforgettable. The Scots were usually the first to lead the attack.

DANIEL ROBERTS – A Maquisard remembers the war.

Daniel Roberts was born in France and spent part of his youth there. He settled in Brockenhurst on retirement, with his wife Geraldine.

(see Chapter 6)

When the war broke out and the Germans laughed at the Maginot Line, my father, an English artist, went on working in his Montmartre studio until 'things' became somewhat uncomfortable.

He bought a car and travelled south. He reached Bordeaux just as the last ship was about to sail for England.

His family, wife, myself aged seventeen and a young sister, were on holiday in Chamonix. We were advised to travel to the Spanish border, but Mother thought it too hazardous for my sister. So we stayed on and were soon occupied by the Italians, *les Pioulets*, as they were called in the local dialect. They were rather comical with the long feather on their hats.

Once, smuggling an Egyptian diplomat over the border to Switzerland in winter mist, we were suddenly confronted by two Italian Bersagliers pointing their guns at our entrails. *Papirs*, they demanded. So I waved my pink birth certificate, which they obviously could not read. They gave a smart salute, and disappeared.

For the descent I had chosen a route I knew in summer, but which was now a murderous ice gully.

I started a cautious slalom, caught an edge, and found myself sliding faster and faster towards unfriendly Swiss granite. By moving my body, I managed to guide that frightening fall between rocks, ending by hitting the other side of the valley and breaking both skis (with modern skis, it would have been both legs). I looked up for my client, but could not see him. Ah, he was still at the top, frozen with fear. "I am OK," he called. "I have skied for my University." Ha, ha . . .

A cold half-hour later I greeted him with a collection of adjectives I managed not to utter. "Right," I said, "now we must reach Martigny without being caught." And, as we started off, two Swiss border guards appeared from behind a serac.

"Bonjour messieurs," they said with a friendly smile. "Could we

see your passports, please." Out came my Somerset House birth
certificate, but to no avail. "Passports, please," they repeated. But we
had none.

They shook their shoulders, and one started to laugh. "That gully,"
he said, "has only been skied once, by a couple of mad Englishmen!
Now, please follow us."

We stopped at a small inn for a cup of real coffee (not the roasted
acorn brew we had been having). Bliss! Then down to Martigny
where we were given a bedroom, and locked in for the night. A little
later, the door opened and a comely girl walked in with an enormous
omelette and more coffee. But then, as we were getting ready for
sleep, a 'Hallo, Hallo' type of officer burst in, insisting on searching
our rucksacks. Seizing the manuscript of a children's book I was
writing, he brandished it with delight. "Ah! This so-called book of
yours must hide a code! We'll hand you to the police in the
morning."

In Bern, I was taken to the British Embassy and questioned on the
Italian occupation of Chamonix (so much for Swiss neutrality!). I
knew little of interest and, ungratefully, was handed back to the
Swiss and their 'concentration camp'.

That short stay in the camp was something I am glad to have
experienced. We were of several nationalities, waiting to be
repatriated against our will, but the waiting was not as boring as it
could have been. There was a group of despondent-looking Russians
who would suddenly burst out into beautiful singing. I made friends
with a young Frenchman escaped from Germany. But something
began to worry us. We were given rich food, something I had not had
for months. The result was a bad liver-attack. Cheekily, I complained
that their food made me ill. Glad to get rid of me, I think, the doc in
charge despatched me to hospital.

The young nurses were delightful and I soon recovered, but
pressed the thermometer to the central heating, just enough to stay
there a while. It was not long though before the trick was discovered,
and a smiling and charming official suggested that the best thing for
types like me was to be chucked back over the border. "However,"
he said, "if you wish to stay here and go to university, it could be
arranged."

I found that amazingly generous, and was sorely tempted, but my
place was with my friends in Chamonix. The Germans would soon
replace the *Pioulets*, and there would be work to do. "I understand,"
he said with a friendly smile. "Tonight, I'll show you where to cross
the border."

So I was put on the train, locked in the loo, and deposited on a wild
stretch of country where a stream was the only sign of the

Swiss/French border. But I was not alone. A truly gorgeous young English woman had joined us.

The Swiss told us to follow him. The moon was bright and we had to be careful. Crawling in wet grass, we reached the stream. Our friend looked at his watch. Quite soon we heard someone whistling a tune; a German quietly patrolling in the moonlight. We waited until he was out of earshot, whispered goodbye to our friend, and waded onto French soil: a large expanse of pasture with a few chalets and cowsheds. One still had its light on. We knocked and asked for a place to sleep. The man pointed to an empty cowshed and, without a word, went to bed. Lucky man . . .

The shed floor was bare concrete. So we lay on our hard couch, and soon broke all barriers, holding each other tightly, turning round when the exposed side was cold. At one time my companion started giggling and rubbed her legs against mine. "What on earth have you got there?" she asked. (I was wearing the old-fashioned *fusseaux* – ski trousers hooked under-foot). "Cigarettes," I replied, "strapped to my legs with elastic bands."

She had a lovely laugh. At dawn, she made her way to her own *Maquis*, and I to Chamonix. The *Pioulets* had been replaced by the Germans!

> *(The word "maquis" originates from the Corsican scrubland where smugglers used to hide. It was adopted by the French Resistance.)*

Life became grim in more ways than one. The chief of the Secret Army (the man who had asked me to take the Egyptian to Switzerland), was taken by the Germans and sent to Germany to be used as a guinea-pig, and given several kinds of injections. When he was released, this tall, good-looking and gentle man was a wreck. He died within a few weeks.

One day, the Mayor asked my mother if she still had English papers. She had. "You are mad," he said, "burn them. I'll forge you some French ones." As for me, being just seventeen, I was meant to be sent to Germany for forced labour. But their medical check showed I only had one kidney. They released me, not without some signs of disgust . . .

At first, my only activity was to pinch timber from Government forests (we would have frozen otherwise), and I had to do a bit of black-market dealing in order to feed my mother and sister. I smoked in those days, mostly bought fag-ends for my pipe.

One day I was having a hair-cut, when, to my surprise the barber mentioned six names, six of my friends! "They are all your mates, are they not?" he asked. "Yes, they are."

"We would like you to organise a team for the *Ravito* (Italian for food supplies). This will mean cycling down to a place at the dead of night, without lights, of course. Go and see how many are willing. The Maquis won't always be in the same place, and soon it will be on skis." When we reached them, the Maquis greeted us without much enthusiasm. "What! Leeks and spuds again!"

When winter came we moved on skis, high up in the hills. Carrying heavy loads on our backs could be uncomfortable, especially when falling head first in deep snow, with heavy rucksacks hitting us on the neck. By and by, the Germans sensing their defeat, became more nasty. Our radio operator, a lovely twenty-four year old woman, was caught and questioned. She would not talk, so she was thrown alternately in tubs of icy and scalding water. She soon died.

The Germans had settled in the Hotel Majestic. One day the Maquis surrounded the hotel, and our chief demanded to talk to the officer in charge. "You are surrounded by over a hundred Maquisards. If you do not surrender you can stay there and starve," they were told. They all came out with their hands up, and were packed into lorries to various types of prison (like churches). What they did not know was that the 'hundred Maquisards' did not number more than thirty...

There was no longer much for our little group to do, so I volunteered to join a Red Cross unit, going with our chief, Dr Gerbier, to where there was still some fighting.

Going to the front in our Red Cross van took us on a narrow road. We came to a blockage, close to a hump-back bridge, and had to get out to remove barbed-wire. As we worked we saw a German officer on the other side. He raised his arms, as if to surrender, but stayed where he was. Our doctor took out his revolver and stepped onto the bridge to capture him. When he reached the hump the German threw himself on the ground and shouted, "Fire!". Two machine-guns reduced our doctor to a sieve, and we dived into the shallow, muddy stream, crawling on our tummies, with bullets whistling close over our heads.

Pretty soon, all the Germans were herded into the nearby church, insulted with great gusto by one of our men – an Alsatian...

By and by I found myself in London, in time for the 'doodle-bugs'.

TIM BEEVERS – **The Red Devils in North Africa.**
Tim Beevers, born in 1919, served with the Parachute Regiment (see Training and Defence). On retirement he and his wife, Christina (see Women at War), settled in Brockenhurst.

"O the great days, in the distance enchanted
Days of fresh air, in the rain and the sun . . ."
These two lines begin verse three of the Harrow School song, 'Forty Years On.' Today it is fifty years on, since as a young man of twenty-two I set out on a war time convoy, forming part of the Anglo-American invasion of French North Africa.

This short description of my life fifty years ago, and the war in North Africa, will be no exception to the rule that time and distance spread enchantment over memories. We had our experiences of mutilation and devastation, but with a difference. Often they were accompanied by such individual bravery, that the sight of it has left a permanent mark on those who were present.

After training on Salisbury Plain, described in another section of this chapter, and landing at Algiers, the scene soon changed abruptly. A move of three or four hundred miles eastwards along the coast-line to Tunisia – to Souk-el-Arba, Medjez-el-Bab and Béjà.

The next day we went on board our Dakotas and flew along the coast. The Platoon Commander of No 1 Platoon had now added a dozen or so almost incomprehensible maps of mountainous terrain to his over-loaded battle order. We were going ahead to prepare the way for ground forces to capture Tunis and eject the Germans from Tunisia. After a false start, we made a successful drop on the airfield at Souk-el-Arba on November 16, and moved on as quickly as possible to Béjà, where we met Germans in position. We were well ahead of the ground troops, and the tanks of 'Blade Force' hastening towards Tunisia. When the tanks arrived, No 1 Pl was guarding a steep valley through which they had to pass. I remember stopping the first tank to see if they had any pipe-tobacco on board. The head that appeared through the turret belonged to a friend in the Derbyshire Yeomanry. How small the world is.

On November 28 a British Infantry Brigade and part of the US 1st Armoured Division got to within 12 miles of Tunis, but no further. The Germans had brought in massive reinforcements, and the rains had made it impossible to operate our temporary makeshift airfields.

In December and January the Battalion fought as ad hoc infantry. We spent a lot of our time on night patrols trying to find out exactly where the enemy was. What I remember most vividly about those patrols was trying to keep quiet, and listening. We had to keep clear of Arab settlements because every Arab hut had dogs which barked. I remember overhearing some Welsh voices saying they preferred to go on a patrol with their Platoon Commander because he was very careful, not so slap-happy as some of the other officers. Actually I think he was merely a deal less brave. However, 'some of the officers' lost their lives and their Platoon Commander is still here to tell the tale. On one skirmish I remember that my braces broke, at the same time as I was running along with a Bren gun and intermittently trying to fire it. I saw all the grass beside me being cut down by an invisible scythe. I didn't realise what was happening until a chap behind said, "That was a bit close!"

When we got back to base from a patrol we used to get de-briefed, and eat and, sometimes, we got a rum ration, which knocked you out, if you were tired. Amazing how we always got fed.

We couldn't always cook in our mess-tins, because of making smoke which attracted aircraft. My batman was hit by a bullet from a German plane, and we learned a little more about 'dispersal'. I was able to give an injection from the little tube of morphine with which we were provided.

In those days in the hilly country of Tunisia we had a strange climate to contend with. Mostly we spent the night in the open, it was extremely cold, but all soldiers are good at acquiring items which increase their comfort, or finding places where they can get shelter. By day it either poured with rain, which filled the dried up wadis, and penetrated our camouflage jackets, or it was a glorious cloudless day, but termites everywhere and the ordinary housefly could bite you through your socks. Water needed boiling or purification tablets which His Majesty's far-sighted government had added to our battle-order.

At the end of January 1943 the 1st Parachute Bn in Tunisia embarked on the primitive, slow-moving train back two or three hundred miles to Algiers for re-grouping. A remarkable journey taking several days; every time the train stopped, everyone got out and made tea, and as the train started again, grabbed their equipment and scrambled back into the train.

On February 3 we were back in Tunisia being briefed for an attack on two hills, Djebel Mansour and Djebel Alliliga, occupied by the Germans. The 1st Parachute Bn was to capture the former, and the Coldstream Guards, assisted by a contingent of the French Foreign Legion, the latter. My platoon route was very steep and covered with thick undergrowth. The attack started before dawn and when the day broke we were occupying German positions, trenches and dug-outs on the top of the ridge. All seemed to have gone to plan and we watched the Guards doing a perfect demonstration attack across open ground on Djebel Alliliga. However, on February 5, the Germans counter-attacked and, because of shortage of ammunition (our mules had gone astray) we were all forced to withdraw down into the woods at the bottom of Djebel Mansour. The NCO in my Platoon, Cpl Green, behaved in a particularly brave way.

When the Germans counter-attacked I got a sharp pain in my foot.

A bullet had gone through the toe of my boot. It wasn't very painful, so I didn't know what had happened. Some minutes later I was hit by a bullet which went across my back at the waistline. This time it felt extremely painful.

When orders came to withdraw, I didn't feel like going anywhere, and resigned to watching my Platoon disappear down the mountain ridge. It was then that Cpl Green appeared, and by dint of sympathetic encouragement and physical strength, somehow got me to an assembly point in a wood below. All this took place under heavy and accurate German fire.

I never saw Cpl Green again, though I did send a report about him to the appropriate authority. This engagement ended on February 5 and there were 183 casualties – a high proportion of the numbers engaged. By February 8 only seven of the officers, who had originally come to North Africa with the 1st Parachute Bn were still with it, and in the other Battalions of the 1st Parachute Brigade, the position was much the same. Years later the official history stated: "The 1st Parachute Brigade earned in ninety days a reputation for gallantry, discipline and initiative unsurpassed by any other troops in Africa."

In less than four months fighting in North Africa the 1st Parachute Brigade won 58 medals for gallantry. So effective were they in routing the enemy that the Germans called them the 'Red Devils', a name that has stuck ever since.

Three young men from Brockenhurst all went to North Africa and on to Italy. PETER REEVES *tells of his joining a Parachute Regiment;* JACK HANSON, *whose father became landlord of the Railway Inn (now the*

Snakecatcher) in 1926, when Jack was ten years old, joined the Royal Engineers and Peter's cousin, RON REEVES was called up on December 17, 1942. They relate their pre-war memories in Chapters 2 and 3.

PETER REEVES tells his story –

I first went to Algeria and later to Tunisia. Our job was to establish ourselves on a hill and spend about two days there identifying enemy positions. I remember one day's heavy shelling in Tunisia when many Ox and Bucks Light Infantry soldiers were killed. I was never wounded though. I remember meeting several men from Brockenhurst there including Jack Hanson.

From Tunisia we went to Salerno, then Naples, Capua and Rome. The Hampshire Regiment got a good hiding there. In Monte Cassino we just couldn't get the Germans out of the Monastery. Was I frightened of the shelling? Well you just had to dig in and hope for the best. Like the rest of life there were good times and bad times. I know the Germans were our enemies, but they were good soldiers and clever, the Italians the opposite.

Once through Monte Cassino we were away; we marched up the Adriatic, either on foot or in trucks. The Gurkhas were with us, they were devoted to their donkeys and although the men were as quiet as mice and would do anything for you, we were never allowed to touch their kukris (their personal broad-blade knife).

At Leghorn we thought, at last we were going home but not a bit of it. The Canadians, whom we had been with asked for us. So off we went to Belgium, then Arnhem and we were still in the Netherlands when the end of the war was declared. The Canadians celebrated this by firing rifles in the air. But the SS, in the cement factory, had not heard of the Cease Fire and wouldn't surrender, eventually we forced them out. We found every sort of luxury and recreation facility you could imagine, there. We also found they had lots of horses and carts loaded with furs which they'd seized from the Dutch.

The Dutch would give us anything even while they were starving and feeding off chicken bones. At last we got to Germany and our artillery regiment was broken up. The CO asked me to be his driver. From then on no more PT, parades or duties, but driving him in his Humber.

JACK HANSON *was also posted, first to North Africa* –

Three of us from Brockenhurst; George Brewer, Les Johnson (*his contribution elsewhere in the anthology*) and I went, on the same train to Scotland. Although I had farmed, I didn't have a trade, so they got me on cooking. I was posted to North Africa and later to Italy. My Commanding Officer, Col Blake, liked my cooking so I remained in the Officers' Mess. In Italy we got the odd sheep to cook besides the army rations.

I saw a lot of death – terrible – and sometimes we were scared by the shelling. My CO was like a friend to me. One day I got a message from the Padre asking me to lay-out Col Blake. He had been out in a car, near the river Arno, where we were building Bailey Bridges, and during the shelling, the car turned over on top of him. Anyway, we gave him a pukka funeral.

I was burnt in the shoulder by a flame thrower and spent several days in an army hospital. The British medics treated everyone well, German and British, just the same.

Most of our leave was in Alexandria and nearby places, but never in the UK. I did once see Monty. Just before my CO was killed, I saw him walking out of HQ. I saluted him and he saluted back.

RON REEVES *moved from North Africa to Austria* –

When I was called up, the Sergeant at Southampton said that if I volunteered for the Hampshire Regiment I could have Christmas at home. This I did and then trained at Colchester. I was not interested in promotion: I just wanted to do my bit.

At nineteen I went to North Africa – Philippoville – and then moved to Italy where we joined the 46th Division. We saw Monte Cassino being flattened by American Liberators, but the Germans stayed in the cellars.

Asked how he felt about the destruction of the old Monastery, he replied –

"I don't know now if it was right to destroy it, but you couldn't let old Hitler invade one country after another."

I was in Italy from 1943, eventually we moved across the river Po and upwards into Austria. There were miles and miles of Germans surrendering with their horses. I didn't realise they had so many horses, as well as their Tiger tanks. Squaddies grabbed their own horse, I got mine – it had only one ear – and kept it in a field and I used to ride it. Soon they were taken away from us.

In Vienna the Russians were on the other side of the river, we used to play hockey with them. They always brought a band with them and we talked to each other with our hands.

When the Hampshire Territorials disbanded I went with the Sussex Regiment to Trieste and was demobbed in 1947. We came home by train from Trieste, through Switzerland and France: how I remember those wooden seats! I'd not seen England since 1942.

KEN SCOTT – **The Attack on the Asopos viaduct in German Occupied Greece: May and June 1943.**
Lt Col (Rtd) Ken Scott, MC*, Royal Engineers and businessman settled in Brockenhurst with his family in 1983. Ken Scott served in France 1939-40; Western Desert 1941-42; with SOE in enemy occupied Greece 1943-44 and in Siam 1945.

The single-track railway line from northern Greece, through the country to Athens and Piraeus, was one of the main supply routes for the German and Italian forces in North Africa. In late 1942, all of Europe and most of North Africa was controlled by the Axis Powers and General Alexander, GOC-in-C Middle East, required the Greek railway to be put out of commission to assist the Eighth Army's attack at Alamein, and its subsequent advance in the Western Desert.

The first attack on the railway was carried out on the Gorgopotamos Viaduct, in November 1942. An Allied party of 12, commanded by Brig Eddie Myers, was dropped into the mountains of enemy occupied Greece and, with the help of 150 Greek rebels to overpower the Italian guard, they demolished part of the viaduct which put the railway out of action for six weeks.

Towards the end of January 1943 trains were again using the railway, and the Germans were gradually taking over guard duties from the Italians. Brig Eddie decided to launch a second attack on the railway and the Asopos Viaduct was chosen as the best target to achieve the maximum disruption of this vital supply line. SOE Cairo approved the plan and agreed to send three specially selected Sapper officers for the demolition.

The Asopos Viaduct was situated at the lower end of a precipitous gorge, carrying the Asopos River from the high mountains in the west. As shown on the sketch, the viaduct was 175 metres long made up of five latticed trusses and a massive steel arch formed by two structural steel legs pin-jointed at the concrete foundations and at the top centre joint. It can be seen that if it were possible to cut one of the legs with explosive charges, the whole arch would collapse and bring with it the two adjacent trusses, creating a gap of 100 metres.

In May 1943 I was dropped, with Harry McIntyre and Pat Wingate, into the mountains about 100 miles north of Athens with instructions to destroy the viaduct and, afterwards, to remain in Greece under the command of Brig Eddie. The next day Brig Eddie arrived to brief us and after hours of discussion the local rebels refused, on instructions from their Communist masters in Athens, to co-operate in the operation as then planned. Without their support it was necessary to recast the operation and the decision was taken, to go for a stealth attack by a small all British force without arms. The only possible approach for this force was to follow the River Asopos, through the

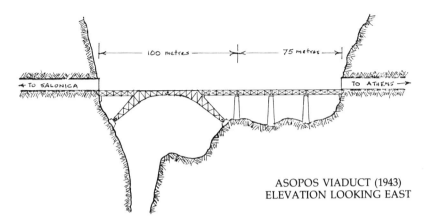

ASOPOS VIADUCT (1943)
ELEVATION LOOKING EAST

precipitous gorge which was considered impassable by the Greeks, and also by the Germans as their defences were directed against an attack from the railway and from the plain below the viaduct.

Ropes were obviously going to be necessary, and we prepared about 300 ft of rope from parachute cord. We also formed the explosive charges to fit the main girders and other charges for the steel bracing. Our party of seven set off for the gorge ten days after we arrived in the mountains, with the rope and over 100 lbs of explosives and accessories packed in five bundles of ground sheets and gas capes. The party was made up of Geoff Gordon-Creed a Commando Officer, Don Stott a NZ Commando, three Sappers, a Greek Officer to act as interpreter in case we met up with any Greeks and L Cpl Lockwood, an escaped POW. After a nine hour march we established our base on a shingle bank inside the gorge and about three-quarters of a mile from our target.

The gorge which we descended was fantastic. It carried the whole flow of the River Asopos and in places it was no more than 12 ft wide, with sheer rock faces on each side towering up to 1,000 ft high. The river water was icy cold from the mountain snows and in places it covered the complete width of the gorge. In the deep river pools we were up to our necks in icy water and, from time to time, we had to swim with the explosive bundles on our heads.

We very quickly found our first obstacle – a 40 ft high waterfall that took the few of us with rock climbing experience and with rope, one whole day to negotiate only to find 10 ft deep pools at the bottom. The bundles of explosive charges were slid down a makeshift aerial ropeway from the top of the fall, to a shingle bank downstream of the deep pools.

245

After three days and nights we had battled about half our way to the viaduct when we reached a particularly difficult waterfall, about 20 feet high with the river covering the complete width of the gorge as it roared over the fall. By this time we had used all our rope and had no other means of dealing with this problem, so we had to abandon further progress. We left our battered bundles of explosive on a dry shingle bank and returned to our HQ in the mountains for repairs to bashed knees, legs and arms and for a hot meal.

Cairo took prompt action on our request for rope and extra equipment and within three weeks after our withdrawal Don Stott and two strong helpers returned to the gorge with extra kit to tackle the waterfall.

We got the all clear from them by runner and three of us, Gordon-Creed, Harry McIntyre and I met up with Don Stott in the gorge on June 19 to find they had breached the fall by felling a tree, trimming the branches and dragging it to the fall where it acted as a sloping ladder in a freezing shower.

On the morning of June 20 the four of us managed to get to the bottom of the fall, and manhandled the bundles of explosive to the first dry shingle bank. The charges were wet and damaged so Harry and I dried the explosive and reconstructed the four main charges, while Gordon-Creed and Don Stott went ahead to recce the approach to the target. They returned to report that there were no more falls and the way ahead would be managable by moonlight. Also they thought they had seen a track leading down to the river, and scaffolding on the arch. We decided to attack that night with the help of the June moon.

We reached the last bend in the gorge in daylight and Harry and I saw the viaduct for the first time, less than 100 yards away and 300 ft up in the air. The arch was a magnificent piece of engineering and we had come to destroy it! But to practicalities – we could see the track, the scaffolding around the bottom of the north leg of the arch with two platforms on it and a ladder leading up to them. The Germans were working on the arch and they had solved for us what was always going to be the major problem, climbing from the river up to and onto the arch itself. We were most fortunate, but then in this sort of operation luck has to be on your side.

We waited until dusk and by moonlight the four of us carried the bundles of charges up the track, through the barbed wire that had been cut for us, to the bottom of the ladder. Harry and I climbed the ladder to the top platform, hauled up the bundles of explosive and started the operation of fixing and connecting the charges. The four main girders were a long way apart, horizontally and vertically, and the whole operation took about one and a half hours. Throughout this time we could hear the German guard patrolling above our heads.

We had only two major incidents. The Germans had left some nuts and bolts on the platform and we had the misfortune to kick one over the side. It made an awful clatter on its way down and we spent some time on our hands and knees searching for others. By moonlight the dark spots turned out to be knots in the wooden planks. The second incident was more serious. When we were both spread out on one of the main girders fixing the charges, the viaduct was suddenly flooded with light as the German searchlight illuminated each pier and truss in turn and then the arch. We clung there in the full beam of the light not daring to move and expecting machine guns to open up at any moment, but the lights moved on.

When we had fixed all the charges I sent Harry down to warn Gordon-Creed we were about ready to withdraw. I attached the detonators and the time delay pencils, crushed the delays and climbed down the ladder. About two hours later, when we were about half way up the gorge, we saw a blinding flash and heard a tremendous explosion. I shouted, "She's gone!" and we raced to get out of the gorge.

We reached our base in the early hours of June 21, cleared up and started our long march back up the mountain to our HQ. We heard later that it was the Station Master at Bralos, the first station down the line to Athens, who spread the news that the viaduct had been destroyed, and all hell was let loose on the railway.

The reconstruction posed some very major problems for the German engineers, caused largely by the railway tunnels at each end of the viaduct and the height above river level. It was not possible to bridge the 100 metre gap with a single span and they decided to construct two 50 metre bridges supported, in the centre of the gap, by a new massive steel pier about 40 metres high. The first 50 metre bridge, built on the 75 metre remaining part of the old viaduct, was launched across the gap to the new central pier but it slid off the pier during final positioning and collapsed into the gorge killing two officers and 25 railway engineers. The accident delayed the completion of the reconstruction and the railway line was not fully reopened until early September.

The destruction of the Asopos viaduct not only cut this vital supply line for a period of about three months, it also acted as the curtain raiser for widespread sabotage throughout Greece on enemy communications in the operation code name 'Animals'. This operation was an essential part of the Allied Strategic Deception Plan before the invasion of Sicily in July 1943. The object of the Plan was to create the impression that the Allied landings would be in Greece rather than Italy, and it succeeded to the extent that substantial German forces and armour were diverted from Italy, France and Russia into the Balkans. Also Field Marshal Rommel was sent to Greece, by Hitler, to command the enlarged occupying German army.

TOMMY THOMPSON – **Chivalry in Malta**

Capt ARF (Tommy) Thompson, DFC, RAF fighter pilot, Sqn 249 is retired and living in Brockenhurst.

On Christmas day 1941 I was station at Ta'Kali airfield in Malta and we, as the Fighter Force on the Island, had been 'stood down' for the day.

At around 11 am an Italian fighter plane, a CR42 (biplane, fighter), suddenly appeared flying very low indeed over the perimeter of our airfield. As he reached the centre of the airfield he threw out what appeared to be a bag with streamers attached to it. We approached this object with considerable caution, thinking it to be some sort of bomb or booby trap. When our Armament Officer had declared the object 'safe', we opened it and found inside a most beautifully hand-drawn Christmas Card 'From the Gentlemen of the Regia Aeronautica in Sicily' to the 'Gentlemen of the Royal Air force at Ta'Kali'.

He was a very brave man, as he was not to know that we were 'stood down' and his old aircraft was so much slower than our Hurricanes that we could easily have caught him and dispatched him long before he reached Sicily again.

This perhaps demonstrates the chivalry with which the war in the air was sometimes fought.

JACK BRINDLEY – **Incident in the Persian Gulf.**

Jack Brindley was at school until 1941, when he joined the RAF and trained as a 'night-fighter' pilot, flying to India and Burma. While with the Refinary, on Southampton Water, after the war, he and his wife, Molly (see Women at War) moved with their family to Brockenhurst.

We were flying a Beaufighter to India. We had collected it, brand new, from the Bristol factory, had air-tested it and done a consumption test. It had been fitted with 'tropical mods' and we had had our 'jabs'. This was early in 1944.

On departure we were given a folder with sheets describing all the aerodromes we were likely to need as far as Karachi – I still have this folder. Firstly, we flew to Portreath in Cornwall, as near as possible to our next stop in Morocco and then we were off.

What should have been our last overnight stop was at Habbaniya, a pre-war RAF station near Baghdad. Next day we landed at Muharraq, an island off Bahrein to refuel and have lunch. We had just started our meal when the Commanding Officer came in, "Is that Beaufighter crew here?" I stood up: "Drop that, please, and come with me."

As we walked to the control tower he told us that two Ansons, old twin-engined aircraft, had forced-landed on Yas, a small island in the south of the Gulf. "They were on their way to do some mosquito spraying," he said, "and one of them had an engine failure". This seemed a poor reason for even a forced-landing. In the control room he showed us the W/T signal they had sent. The key sentence was '... Natives unfriendly, send firearms ...'. The CO said he very much doubted this as we had friendly relations all down the Gulf. A Royal Navy launch was to be sent, but would not reach Yas till the next day. Meanwhile he wanted us to take the Beau down, see what was happening and show all on the island that the RAF was in contact. We were not to open fire nor drop weapons – if anything violent was indeed happening we were to radio back for instructions.

It was a forty minute flight across the Qatar peninsula and down to Yas. The island was about five miles long and a mile wide, and the Ansons were on the shore near one end. They were already axle deep in the sand, the crews were gathered in the shade of one wing, and there was a semi-circle of natives some hundred yards away, all sitting and watching the aircraft. Not very friendly, but not violent either. They waved, the crews waved and we waved and we then spent ten minutes low flying around the island – too good an opportunity to be missed! Then back to Muharraq to report and spend the night. And that should have been the end of that. However ...

At breakfast the next morning the CO again came into the Mess. "Sorry, there has been an accident." It seemed that the stranded crews had made tea that morning the usual desert way using a punctured can filled with sand and wetted with petrol to give a 'lazy' flame. A little later they decided to brew another pot, and one of them poured more petrol onto the can. It had flashed back and he was badly burned. We were to go down there again as soon as possible to drop a medical pack. The CO also gave me a pre-war RAF map showing an emergency landing strip on Yas – "last surveyed in 1935", it said. "See if you can use it," the CO said, "we might fly a doctor in or the injured man out."

When we arrived over Yas the Ansons had sunk even further; each was resting on its engines and the spray pan under the fuselage. After dropping the medical pack and seeing it picked up we looked for the landing strip. Knowing where it should be we could just make it out, rough with exposed rocks and gullies. It was only some 300 yards long, while a Beau normally needed 1,200 yards or more.

Back at Muharraq I told the CO I would have a go at landing on the strip if he wished. He did not take me up, and in any case we heard the launch was about to reach Yas.

We received the bad news later in India. Both Ansons had been destroyed by the navy. The two pilots were court-martialled and reduced to the ranks and the injured man had died.

GEORGE JOHNSON *had been with the 23rd Lancers as a cavalry man in India for five years before the war. On his return home he remained a Reserve and in February 1939 he was back in the army with the Royal Hussars. He relates* –

At the end of 1939 I was sent to Egypt with the Royals to deal with Arab bandits, mostly robbers. We did horse patrols at Nablus, Tel Aviv and the Trans-Jordan border, later it was motor patrols. We had to round up the bandits who didn't like us because we had informers in each village who would tell us when they were making night raids. We would surround the village and arrest these bandits. I don't know what happened to them thereafter.

Christmas 1940 we moved to the desert and the army took our horses away. I saw tough soldiers just break down and cry when their animals were taken down to the shore and shot. My horse was called Bess; she was lovely, I could do anything with her. I stayed in the desert until 1944.

PETER TAYLOR, *a gunner, having sailed from Liverpool, in December 1940, via Freetown, past the Cape and on to Suez – a seven week voyage – tells how he moved from North Africa to the Middle East. He was a driver for most of the war. He and his wife, Elaine, (see Women at War) came to Brockenhurst some 22 years ago for business and now live here in retirement* –

Our first target was an Italian lavatory. A little fat Italian wandered down to do what he had to do. We waited 10 to 15 seconds, then with 8 guns we blasted away. When the smoke cleared only a heap of ashes remained. You could say when you got to go, you have got to go.

In January 1942, when the British broke out of Tobruk, they were going from east to west and the Germans from north to south. They broke through our convoy four vehicles behind mine; all those behind were taken prisoner. I was too busy to be terrified.

I left the desert when El Alamein fell. I then did a couple of trips from Egypt to Iran taking railway sleepers, petrol and anything else the Russians needed. This was in connection with Lend-Lease. It was quite a distance and took five to six days. We never saw the Russians: the lorries were left in a large car park in Tehran and the next morning they were gone. We did see one large Russian police-woman, some of the lads gave her a wolf-whistle. She was not amused and nearly shot them!

I was now part of the Persia and Iraq Forces (PAIFORCE), this period was enlivened by an incident. We pulled up for the night and dug holes to put up our tents. The next tent found a nice soft area to dig; what they did not realise was that it was a dried up river bed. That night the rains came and the river flooded, they all tried to get out but one was caught in his mosquito net and was drowned. Though we had been warned – some always know better! We tried to rescue him but it was so cold hyperthermia set in quickly.

In 1944 PAIFORCE was beginning to wind down. The highlight of that year was a week's leave in Jerusalem, Jericho and the Dead Sea, with another lucky escape. We had large tank-transporters and coming down a very steep and winding road, orders were, 'first gear – low reduction and don't touch your brakes.' A clever fellow who had been on London buses said, "I'm all right on brakes" and overtook two vehicles – his brakes burnt out, he went over the edge and London Transport were short of a driver at the end of the war!

VE Day I was still in Palestine in a remote place. Someone came and told us it was VE Day but we took no notice and went on having our tea!

Shortly afterwards I caught a boat home from Alexandra. I had not been home for 4 years and 10 months. When I joined the forces I had a Scottish RSM who offered me a cigarette. Only being eighteen I replied that I did not smoke. His reply was, "You will lad, you will". On my return home I met him again and told him I still did not smoke; the reply came, "Good lad, good lad" – with a chap like that you can never win.

BÉ COOPER-VOSSE – **Young memories from the Cape of Good Hope.**
Bé Cooper has been a resident of Brockenhurst only since 1991, she was introduced to the village by friends, after having lived at the Cape for a large part of her life.
In the late 1930's, three young girls arrived at the Cape with their parents. Times in the Netherlands leading up to World War II, were not good and we young soon began to settle, being taught English (in pre-war days Afrikaans was hardly spoken in the cities of SA) by a young Irish nun. When war was declared I was in my teens and

beginning to understand the horrors of what was going on.

Soon Table Bay was visited by convoy upon convoy – many of vast size with thousands of troops. We were now living on the slopes of Lion's Head overlooking the magnificent bay. Slowly we began to recognise cruise liners of a past era and now troopships – the two *Queens, Ile de France, Johan van Oldenbarneveldt* and numerous others.

At first the larger Cape Town dock (Duncan Basin) was still under construction and a number of ships had to anchor in the Bay; troops and crew came ashore in lighters. As all had to have their chance ashore, a very effective women's organisation (SAWAS) came into being to help the men, away from home, to visit families and homes in these far off lands.

A handful of Dutch immigrants founded De Nederlandsche Klub for their own men. As a teenager I was capable of giving a hand. When convoys were in, all normal dining-room staff were co-opted into the tiny kitchen to prepare relays of meals, and it was left to us to serve and clear the tables in the evenings. By now we began to see the fun and enjoyment of war. It was not long though before another side presented itself. German U-boats had been sighted off the Cape – black-outs were ordered. After the first shock, again only the fun-side was seen as cars with headlights reduced to tiny strips were guided by dare-devil seamen riding on the running boards of the cars of the day.

Many Dutch families had adopted regular visitors to the Cape and often acted as a 'go-between' them and their families in Holland. An exchange of some 25/30 words per three months was allowed, through the Red Cross. One particular merchant vessel's officers became our 'affair'. The youngest officer, just out of school when war was declared became the brother we did not have, while for the older officers we replaced the families they had left behind in the Netherlands. How terribly spoilt we were at times.

'Our' ship had come in and my parents went to the docks to meet our 'adopted' brother. It was summertime – they could see him walking towards the gate in a raincoat, with a stiff leg, hand in one pocket and fumbling with his free hand with his pass. My mother was most dismayed wondering what terrible injury he had received. As he reached the car, in full view of the customs men and before any explanation was given, there was a heavy metal clang together with a few choice words that, thank goodness that was done! From his trouser leg and out of his pockets came the makings of a heavy brass cobra wall-hanging: it still hangs next to my fireplace and brings back memories of old.

Times of joy and fun, but we saw the other side of war as well. Ships were torpedoed close to the Cape. The survivors arrived with everything lost and needing the comfort of a home and family to go to. Ships we recognised, came into the Bay badly crippled having hit a mine off Robben Island, with a skeleton crew aboard trying to get her into port; also regular visitors never to be seen again.

A few thoughts on visits from the Australian and New Zealand troops. These, as we all know, were rather more boisterous. I had long plaits and brass buttons on my blazer, I was warned not to go into the town when these troops were in as I would come back minus both. Cape Town certainly knew when they were 'in'. One of the breweries off-loading beer at a hotel, was suddenly besieged by some dozen of these troops ready to take over the consignment. The driver, thinking quickly managed to get their attention, suggested they help him off-load and he would take them to the brewery itself, where they could indulge. Needless to say he received their co-operation, loaded them and more pals up on the empty lorry and drove off to the yard of the competing brewery – wished them luck, clearing out quickly himself!

RICHARD POWER – **Japanese Air Raids on Ceylon, 1942.**
Lt Col RM Power, RE, and his family have lived in Brockenhurst since 1956.
In January 1942 I arrived in Ceylon, now called Sri Lanka, in an Indian Army Engineer Unit, part of 34 Indian Division sent to defend Ceylon. Within a month Singapore had fallen, followed shortly by Burma, leaving Ceylon under Japanese threat. Reinforcements soon poured into Ceylon – British, more Indian, Australian, East African and many RAF.

The RAF soon constructed a new all weather fighter airfield in the middle of Colombo's residential area, crossing the race-course, then the 'Ladies' Golf Course (why 'Ladies' I don't know) and included knocking down the official residences of the Chief Justice and the Commander-in-Chief. Soon the nearby tree-lined avenue concealed Hurricane fighters and Blenheim light-bombers.

Then on Easter Sunday, April 5, early in the morning Japanese carrier-borne aircraft attacked, coming in from the east at high altitude. The air raid warning did not sound till the enemy were overhead, then AA guns opened fire and fighters took off. A Catalina flying boat, had sighted, the previous evening, the enemy fleet and managed to send a message before being shot down. Unfortunately Command were holding an anti-invasion exercise and the message was put in the wrong tray.

The Japanese bombing was very clean. All bombs fell on military targets mostly the harbour and shipping, and also a nearby civilian airport, but omitting the race-course which they probably did not know about. The town escaped any damage. We too were pleased no bombs fell near us as we had just taken delivery of about 20 tons of gelignite for distribution on our anti-invasion demolition role.

The raid caused many of the more faint-hearted local population to decamp. Many shops were closed causing the survivors difficulty in buying food. Guests at the opulent Galle Face Hotel had to make their own beds and fetch their food from the kitchens. Many officers at Command HQ had set themselves up in comfortable 'chummeries' but were having to cook their own meals and even do the shopping.

A few days later I went over to Trincomalee, the naval base on the other side of the island. I went by night rail sleeper and we arrived very late, as that morning the Japanese had raided the base. Here too, many of the locals had decamped. Only two of the mess staff remained and no cook. I'd missed dinner on the train – again no staff – so had a very late breakfast of biscuits and bully beef washed down with tea, a standard army emergency ration.

I went out to the RAF airfield where my sappers had gone. Much damage – roofs off, many bomb craters and damaged aircraft – Hurricane and navy Skua fighters round the airfield. We busily cleared the runway of metal debris then withdrew to the Naval Stores Depot where many buildings had been severely damaged and had to be pulled down or shored up.

As at Colombo the bombing was very clean concentrating on the airfield, naval store and a few ships in harbour including HMS *Erebus* which received a direct hit and suffered casualties. Again to our relief there were no unexploded bombs (UBXs) as we were the official island bomb disposal unit, based on a week's lectures from an officer sent down from GHQ Delhi. None of us had any experience nor had we any of the special equipment.

We had two amusing jobs. At Colombo we were asked to recover the engine from a Japanese fighter down in a muddy paddy field, so inaccessible to a crane or lorry. We did it with an elephant! The *mahout* (the driver) put a chain round the engine and attached a lump of leather. This the elephant grabbed and carried the engine to the nearby road and finally pushed it, with his trunk, up a plank onto the lorry.

At Trincomalee we helped unload 500 lb bombs from a ship, SS *City of Agra*. The unloading was from lighters and we operated the dock cranes as the dockers had bolted. The cranes were electric with their generators, diesel driven. Luckily we had an officer who had worked in a diesel factory so he started the generator, then by fiddling around with the levers in the crane till we found what did what and then trained our sappers as drivers.

One day the engineer on the tug towing the lighters failed to turn up so our enterprising officer became the tug's engineer. We also took over running the local civilian ice factory as the military hospital depended on their ice, so we had free ice in our lines till the owner came back.

The Japanese foray into the Indian Ocean had certainly achieved some success. In addition to bombing Colombo and Trincomalee they bombed the port of Vishahkapatnam on the east coast of India, sunk three navy ships – two cruisers HMS *Dorset* and *Cornwall*, and an old aircraft carrier HMS *Hermes* – besides sinking over 100,000 tons of merchant shipping, all without interference whatsoever and for the loss of a few aircraft. However, they never returned to the Indian Ocean apart from the occasional long distance air raid by flying boats from the Andaman Islands, when they dropped a few small bombs on Trincomalee.

KENNETH SLADE – **Anti-Aircraft Guns in Burma.**
Maj KN Slade, TD, RA, has been connected with the Brockenhurst area for many years, having lived here as also around the area, but presently in Lyndhurst. He is a past-Captain and past-President of the Brokenhurst Manor Golf Club.

Arriving in Bombay *(see Naval section)* in 1942, shortly after the fall of Singapore we went by train to Madras, where we re-assembled. I was sent in command of an anti-aircraft battery, as an independent unit, to the defence of Assam and Bengal, which were being attacked by the Japanese. My unit, with all its equipment, embarked per train to travel north. At Vishahkapatnam the station had been bombed by the Japanese and completely vacated. My sergeant had been an engine driver in England: he and volunteers shunted the stationary trains out of the way. It took us a day and a half to clear the station. In the meantime our driver ran away and my sergeant drove our train all the way to Calcutta. Along the way we often had to stop at tunnels to lower the train tracks, in order to get our equipment through the tunnels.

We remained in action in Assam for some months before being called down to the Surma Valley for the defence of forward fighter air strike. I was commanded to make a recce as to whether we could take our guns and ammunition, etc, over the mountains of Shillon and into the Surma Valley. During the recce, my driver and I encountered many small rivers which were crossed by bridges to carry bullock carts, not our ten ton guns and equipment. However, I decided we could do the trip, went back and reported. So off we went on a memorable drive over the mountains and down the other side. At times it would take as much as five days to strengthen these bridges and on one occasion we came to a river with no bridge at all. I sent a sergeant and six men down south, and another with six men up north, to commandeer local gunboats. These were lashed together, bridged over – there were large quantities of timber available – and we towed ourselves across with our own towing vehicles. This again took five to six days. Eventually we got into action in Cox Bazar, a flooded area near the mouth of the Ganges. We were stationed in the middle of it, down by the edge of the water.

In Calcutta, my job as commander was to site the guns, we were defending the airport just outside the city. You have to be a certain distance for the expected height of attack and I decided on the map where we had to go, in order to reach the planes as they came in. I chose the site for the first of the two batteries of two guns each, on the race course; that was ideal for the technical position to meet any possible Japanese attack coming into the airport. With that I went to see the 'reigning' Brigadier in charge of defences at Calcutta, and told him where I wanted to go. I remember seeing this chap (and his Brigade Major) looking at the wall map and pointing out where I wanted to be. The look of horror on his face when he said, "What month is it now?" – it was May – "You have until July. You have to come out before the racing season starts in August." This was his attitude and there was a war on! He had not seen anything of the war and hardly heard of it. Incidentally, I got my guns on the race course. With the Japanese attack on our gun positions we lost a total of six men. At home, my wife had to go and see their families.

HERE AND THERE

As happens in every-day life, there are always tales that do not fit into categories. This collection of incidents shows how life, no matter how difficult times were, did go on. Christmas still came once a year, weddings took place and every-day life produced some unusual situations.

KEN TOD *recalls a Christmas, in 1942, in Gibraltar* –

A naval Christmas custom is a progress by the Captain through the sailors' mess decks, accompanied by all the officers, with a good deal of jollity. Christmas in Gibraltar in war time was no different and we had been assured that we would be in harbour. So the 'funny party' in paper hats, fancy dress and a good deal of song gathered outside the Captain's cabin. He appeared as expected, holding a signal and called, "Raise steam with all despatch". Loud laughter and applause. With repeated apologies it took him a little time to convince them that it was no joke, that there was a German convoy raider in the Atlantic.

When the truth sank in the men went away, silently, to prepare for sea.

I had great respect for my stokers, but never more than on that day. A few minutes later I was down in the boiler room and found them still in their paper hats, tearing down the decorations to get at the machinery, all in the utmost haste with Christmas forgotten.

FRANK LEWIN refers to his Christmas in Halifax, Nova Scotia in 1941 as – Blissful memory! On land and with a 'good ending'. JOHN WOOLLETT *recounts* –

My unit was almost entirely composed of pre-war Territorial Army soldiers and men called up for war service. Amongst them was a man who had worked on a turkey farm, the owner of which was anxious for help as Christmas 1942 approached. I sent the soldier concerned on compassionate leave to help, on condition that the squadron was able to buy sufficient turkeys for Christmas dinner. We were thus able to have a splendid meal in the army tradition, with the sergeants serving the food and the officers the drink.

Another cause for celebrations – weddings – often took place under unusual circumstances. TIM BEEVERS mentions, just a few of the problems he and CHRISTINA encountered, while doing duty in North Africa –

After Djebel Mansour (*see his N. Africa engagement*) I was transported to the 95th British General Hospital at Ben-ak-Noun. I was wonderfully looked after by a sympathetic staff of doctors and nursing sisters of the QAIMNS. The RAMC doctors were all, in modern parlance 'brilliant', at least two were knighted later in life. One of the doctors became the best man at my wedding.

The first month in the 95th was not very comfortable – I had got used to my back problem, but kept telling everyone that I could not walk on my foot, which except for a tiny scar looked normal. Upshot: 'Old Nick', the surgeon opened up my foot, found a bullet and fourteen broken metatarsi! – all appeared to find it hilarious.

After three months in the 95th I was sent to an Officers' Convalescent depot. At the same time, in my airgraphs home, I began to mention one of the nursing sisters by name. Soon we decided to get married.

The senior Army Chaplain in Algiers was of the opinion that young married people might be parted by the war, and might not feel the same way about each other under less romantic circumstances. The British Consul would have to marry us first, and he was quite busy enough without starting a new fashion amongst the soldiers; also there weren't a lot of suitable churches. Or supposing we started a family? The War Office took the view that shipping nurses to Africa was quite expensive enough without having to ship them back again, and so on.

However, in the end, my best man, Dr Ted Campbell, and Christina's bridesmaid, Freda Hopkins, helped us overcome all objections, and arrange a wedding on October 5, 1943 in Algiers Cathedral, a reception in a Polish restaurant, and, by courtesy of a local French family, a honeymoon in the Atlas Mountains.

Last year, 50 years on, we celebrated our Golden Wedding Anniversary – an elderly couple living in the Hampshire village of Brockenhurst to which we came 14 years ago, on retirement. We had no connections here – but it seemed such a friendly and pleasant village when we visited.

EILEEN GABONY *recalls* an unusual experience during her and JOHN's 'lunch time' courting days from the office –

We did all our courting up and down The Strand, where my office was. On our engagement, we gathered with friends, at the nearby Lyons Corner House, to celebrate – the next day it was bombed, killing many people.

We were walking in The Strand one day, when an officer came up to John, greeted him and said that they had met way back, somewhere, though John could not recall this. He invited us to lunch, and over the meal, he asked, "Will you be best man at my wedding?" We were taken aback, but agreed. It was a few days later (a lunch time wedding) at St John's Wood Catholic Church. We arrived and found the church windows had been blown out by a bomb. The wedding took place in the side chapel; the organist was from Westminster Cathedral – the most beautiful music boomed out; the bride, in smart navy, arrived, her name was Montgomery (later we heard she was a relative of the famous General). The ceremony was quick, and then we were whisked off to a super flat in St John's Wood: a small gathering, the food was superb and the punch exceedingly strong! On return to work I fell into my seat and one of John's officers phoned to ask what I had done to him? All this over a short lunch-time. We did not know the people and never heard of them again. The groom must have been desperate for a bestman, saw a friendly officer whose face was vaguely familiar and, that was it!

Of their own wedding John and Eileen only recall a delightful opinion they were confronted with –

The war in Europe was over, but in the Far East it was still continuing. We were married in July 1945; the atom bomb was dropped while were on honeymoon. While in a taxi the driver, having a passenger in officer's uniform and wanting an opinion from him said, "Sir, what do you think of this Hero-Hit-Em bomb – I think it is som'ing to do with the sun!"

Another opinion on actions going on around the country is related by JOHN WOOLLETT –

We were in the Yorkshire Dales and moved about a lot on training exercises. Most farmers accepted, with resignation, the damage that was done by these manoeuvres, and we did what we could to help with repairs. However, I recall hearing one farmer angrily saying to one of my sergeants, "The Germans could not have made more mess if they had come"; to which the reply was, "Yes they could, they could have spread you all over it!" Civilian assessors used to visit the farms to receive claims for damage, and I remember hearing the following conversation: "You haven't replied to my letter no 1234/6 of 5/10/42", to which the answer came, "Nay, twere all balls and bluddy numbers."

Not only 'sayings', but also 'doings', in reaction to circumstances, can afford amusement. FRANCIE PEYTON JONES *recalls a Captain of Industry's reaction to the threatened invasion of England* –

The invasion became a distinct possibility, and being on the coast, over half the girls from school were summarily removed by parents. One of my friends' father, an industrial Captain, came down with bars of chocolate laced with laxative (*could it have been Brooklax? – Ed*) which he distributed to all the Swanage sweet shops to dispense to any unwelcome German customers in the event of invasion...

PATIENCE NICHOLSON, newly married when war was declared, and at a loss when her husband was called to his ship –

What shall I DO? I felt very ill and did not know what to do. What made me do it I do not know, but I took a dose of castor oil; that kept me busy for 48 hours! Thereafter I joined the Red Cross and worked on a farm during the day.

A reaction that was, no doubt, gratefully received is told by JOHN BLOOMFIELD who, at the time, was listening to the radio in his grandmother's house. The Battle of Britain was on and the number of fighters shot down was being reported upon. There was also an appeal for donations towards Spitfires and Hurricanes. He remembers the commentator saying that someone had phoned from the States asking –

' 'How much does a Spitfire cost?" Five thousand pounds was the answer, and the reply came – "My signed cheque for £5,000 is on its way". He also recalls another radio programme –

Then there was the humorous programme called ITMA (Its That Man Again) with Tommy Handley. It was so up-lifting in those dismal days of the war that, as boarders at school, we were allowed to listen to it on Sunday evenings.

Entertainment of a different nature is provided by AILEEN MILLS –

First we had the Poles in our village in Devon; handsome young fellows with aristocratic noses, who kissed the girls' hands, and clicked heels and bowed for the mothers. Had the fathers not been away fighting Hitler, they'd no doubt have locked up their daughters, and barricaded in their wives, but help was at hand. The Red Berets came to the firing range on the moor. Someone, with charitable intent, arranged a dance at the village hall . . . a vast Saturday market area, and issued invitations. The Poles arrived from the one end of the village, and the Red Berets marched in good order from the firing ranges. They met in the hall and for a while all went well until a Red Beret was tapped on the shoulder, and his girl whirled away in a pair of navy blue arms. It was a personal matter, you might say, but in two minutes, it became a regimental matter, and battle commenced. Through the hall, and out into the street they raged. One old man said afterwards that the gutters ran red with Polish blood. I didn't see anything of that, but on the following day a number of large dark cars arrived, filled with well-caparisoned brass hats. Nothing of course was announced, but suddenly there were no Poles. There were several disconsolate girls and mothers, and the dental assistant ran away from her job and home, to return several years later with a Polish husband, and a handsome little boy with an aristocratic nose!

PATIENCE NICHOLSON gives her version of being entertained –
My husband's ship coming in for a re-fit, near Portsmouth, all the wives were rushed down to see them. We stayed in a little hotel just outside town. The air raid sirens went off while we were having tea in the RAF mess. The young lads said, "Don't go, we will be back shortly." Outside we all went, and stood on the roof and watched the little Spitfires take off and do their part in the battle. It was brilliant to watch; we saw the enemy come over and our tiny planes darting about and driving off the attackers – no bombs fell. When they came back, an hour later, they said, "We will not see them again, we have

shipped them to the sea," (that is the bombs). "They did not seem to want to drop their bombs on us," and we carried on with tea.

Seeing German planes flying very low past the window of the bathroom of the farmhouse she was staying at, Patience Nicholson *continues* –

I could see the pilot in one looking at me; he was so low I thought he was·going to crash. I leapt out of the bath, threw a towel over myself and rushed out soaking wet. It was a little guest house taking officers' wives – the woman running the house came up and said, "Mrs Nicholson cover your body. We are at war!"

A chance meeting, thousands of miles from home and many years after the war had ended, solved a most puzzling and somewhat amusing incident. JOHN WOOLLETT *recalls* –

Early in 1942, I was sent, as a major, to take over a Royal Engineers squadron in the newly formed 42nd Armoured Division. This Company had been withdrawn from Dunkirk and, like my original unit, had left all equipment behind. They were then deployed to East Anglia to develop the coast defences, and had to requisition the tools and equipment necessary to carry out the work, amongst which was a road roller. The roller had been lost and I inherited a file of correspondence about this. I passed it to one of my new officers, who answered the latest letter on the subject. His reply was three pages long, well written and detailed, and at the end you were no wiser than when you started. He was clearly equipped for a distinguished career in the Civil Service.

Later, when in Korea in 1954, I was talking to a Canadian officer whose unit was in East Anglia at the time, and learnt what had happened. Apparently two of his soldiers had taken a long walk to find a pub with some beer left. They had succeeded and on the way home had found a road roller parked beside the road. They started it up and continued the journey on board, but on going down a hill it got out of control, and they jumped off. When they reached the bottom of the hill, the only trace of the roller was some bubbles rising from the village pond. Everyone kept quiet about this!

Closer to home LES JOHNSON had his surprise meeting –

We were examining a railway bridge in Holland. A Dutch woman, from the railway hotel (where she was looking after Nazi officers) came up to us and said, "Oh, be careful, there are a lot of Nazis hiding in the railway station." We told our officer who sent in the infantry to blow them up; they had been waiting to fire on us. In about 1955, when I had set up my greengrocer's shop (near the Sportsman's Arms) a Dutch woman came in. She, like many other Dutch people, had come to visit Brockenhurst. We got talking, I thought I recognised her, and she me. It turned out that she was the woman from the hotel, and had probably saved our lives.

261

It is not only people that 'turn up' unexpectedly at Brockenhurst as
FRANK LEWIN found –
I was sent to HMS *Palomares* and expected to do escort duty in the
Irish Sea between Milford Haven and Belfast. Thus, finding that my
luggage had been lost on the rail journey from Liverpool did not
worry me unduly. I would be back soon. 'Forlorn Hope', I sailed
under sealed orders and ended up in Iceland. O yes, it turned up
after I had been in civvy street long enough to forget it. It arrived, by
courtesy of the Admiralty, who had traced my earlier address. It had
lain untouched by human hand, all that time, at a village station near
Brockenhurst.

Luggage, so cumbersome, but so necessary as MARY BATES who
lived for twenty-two years in Boldre prior to 1988, found when
serving with the Wrens –
In 1942 I was sent to a Holding Depot, just off Piccadilly Circus, to
await a troopship to take me overseas. We were told we would be
allowed only one small suitcase for use at sea, but could take another,
the larger one to be carried in the hold, and this must be locked and
roped. I went out to buy some rope and a few other things, but had
no idea where such things could be obtained, in that part of London.
I approached a policeman in Piccadilly Circus and asked him if he
could tell me where I might buy 'some notepaper and envelopes and
a length of rope.' He seized me by the shoulders and entreated,
"Don't do it – things can't be as bad as that." Looking up I noticed
the twinkle in his eye and realised his Cockney sense of humour had
got the better of him.

Looking for help of a different sort KEN TOD turned, not to the
friendly 'Bobby' but to his old chief –
HMS *Sheffield* made a short stop at Rosyth early in the war and I
called on the Engineer Manager, Admiral Hall Patch, an old chief of
mine. In answer to his question, I told him that we, like the rest of
the fleet, were critically short of fire-bricks. They were used as
furnace lining in boilers and consumption had been greatly increased
due to increased steaming time. Repeated demands for supplies went
unanswered.

A foreman remembered that at the end of World War I the surplus
fire-bricks had been used to pave a road in the dock-yard. The
manager ordered the road dug up and the 1918 fire-bricks provided
for us.

And a friendly gesture, from a total stranger in Devon, is recorded
by AILEEN MILLS –
After the Poles left our village, the Americans came. They were
highly fed roisterers who plagued the whole neighbourhood as they
raced their Jeeps in search of the girls. Their pockets were filled with

chewing gum and K rations, and where they were billeted the tables groaned under the weight of massive tins of juice and cuts of pork. They ate no mutton. "Dawg's food ma'am," they said with wry faces.

All went fairly well for a while, they had brought us some excitement, they were full of jokes and spoke just like film stars. But after one or two unusual discoveries, the village elders were scandalised by the behaviour of hitherto respectable young wives seen in the park at night, huddled in illicit embraces. And one thing led to another.

Then the sensation to beat all. I was told when I went to collect my breast of lamb and four pennyworth of corned beef that there had been a murder. "Who was murdered?" I asked.

"Her don't belong here. Her's a Vacuee."

"That don't matter so much then do it?"

Very soon further information fairly tore round the village.

The victim was an elderly woman, found dead upon a park seat. Just lying there as if she was asleep and covered with an American army greatcoat. There was no doubt about it, there was one of them murdering American gangsters about.

As it happened, a home-sick GI wandering round the park in the early hours of the morning had found her gasping her last on the park bench, and thinking of his Mom at home, in Harlem, had gently covered her with his coat whilst he went to the police station to find out what was done in England in such circumstances.

There was an inquest. The verdict 'death by natural causes' and the compassionate American friend, who provided his coat, was thanked and photographed for the district newspaper.

And finally a set of extra-ordinary co-incidences which are nothing short of uncanny, as TOMMY THOMPSON, a fighter pilot with 249 Squadron (see Training and Defence section) *relates* –

My father was born on October 14, I do not know the year. I was born on October 14, 1920. In the 1914-1918 War, my father was in the Royal Engineers and was knocked over by enemy action on three occasions, each time on his birthday; he was not touched on any other occasion.

On October 14, 1940, I was severely shot up by a Me 109 during an engagement over the Channel and had to force-land at Hawkinge on the Kent coast. I was extremely lucky not to have been shot down. My own score in that engagement was 1 Me 109 destroyed and 1 Me 109 probably destroyed.

On October 14, 1941, I was on Dawn Patrol over Grand Harbour in Malta with my Number 2 when we were 'jumped' by 6 Macchi 202 Italian Fighters. My Number 2 was shot down and killed and I suffered severe damage. We did not score at all.

On October 14, 1942, I was with a Night Ground Strafing Squadron in the Western Desert and we operated in the moonlight from ground level up to 300 feet – yes, only 300 feet. On that night I was shot up and very slightly wounded by accurate ground fire.

At *no* other time during the War did I have any severe damage inflicted upon my aircraft apart from the odd bullet or shrapnel hole. The coincidences with my father's experience I think, is remarkable.

It has been a privilege for me, as a newcomer to Brockenhurst, to have been 'trusted' with this chapter of the anthology, and to have met many of the interesting contributors who shared their memories with us.   BC

LETTERS FROM SINGAPORE
THE WAR IN ASIA
1941

Diary of Events

December 7	Japan's surprise air attack on Pearl Harbour, Hawaii – USA chief sea and air base. Also air attacks on Manila (now the Phillipines), Shanghai, Malaya, Siam (now Thailand) and Hong Kong.
8-9	USA declared war on Japan. Britain and the Empire declared war on Japan. China declared war on Japan, Germany and Italy.
25	Hong Kong fell to Japanese despite resistance by British, Canadians and Indians.

1942

January	British retreated from Malaya to Island Base on Singapore.
February 15	Fall of Singapore. Soon afterwards South-East Asia was overrun.

SUSAN AND LAWRENCE BURGESS IN 1941.

MRS SUSAN BURGESS, *who was living in Suffolk at the beginning of the war, went to Singapore in 1942 soon after her marriage. She and he husband, Lawrence, came to live in Brockenhurst in 1957. The following letters dated between January and April 1942, during which time Singapore fell, were written to her mother from Singapore, Colombo and Delhi.*

Dated 4 January 1942 – received Monday 20 April 1942, c/o Hong Kong and Shanghai Bank, Singapore.

My Darling Mum,
    This is only letter No 2 of this local little war which is going on somewhere around here. Going on for nearly 4 weeks too.
    The list of setbacks doesn't get any shorter, but we're inured to bad

news as a nation by now and take it all in the day's work.

January 10 – We haven't had any letters from home since before this skirmish started, I don't think anyone has.

I am now working very hard as a VAD in a military hospital. When I say 'very hard' it's only 6 hours a day, but it's 6 very concentrated hours. I like it a lot in spite of the letters PSS which I can now add onto the end of my name – shut your eyes and I'll tell you that they stand for 'Professional Shit-Shifter'. (Don't tell Tell, she might be shocked, although she's done so much of it for the cats and dogs in Farnham).

Otherwise I make beds, wash endless patients, enquire discreetly whether the bowels have been open today?, give out breakfasts, lunches and teas, help with dressings and wash bandages. I felt a bit queer my first two mornings at some of the gruesome sights I had to see (I'm in the most gruesome possible ward), but I've quite got over that now. As soon as you've been long enough to notice the difference in the men as they get better, you don't mind nearly as much.

It's fun dealing with troops and nautics, they're so amusing and cheerful, with a steady stream of humour even if they're in great pain.

So – Nurse Susan it IS at last! (Drawing of VAD on letter.)

As for the rest of the war – On two occasions at night we've lain under the kitchen table and heard half-a-dozen bombs coming swishing down, and I must confess that I thought to myself "Is this for me – will it, won't it." but they weren't for me. They were a good half a mile away. We go to ground in a small room at the back which is fairly well sandbagged and has three or four strong tables under which we lie on mattresses. We may find we have to spend most of our nights down there when the next 'Bombers' Moon' comes around. Never fear, mother dear, we'll be all right.

Singapore is full of strange faces these days. All the people from the peninsular gradually filtering into the lowest corner. Most of them, I imagine, will go straight elsewhere. Already most mothers with children have been removed, some home, some Australia. The sooner they all go (mothers I mean) the better.

We hear that Mr Duff Cooper is to return to the UK. What a waste of time and money! I don't suppose he has done anything of use since he arrived. Good riddance, says us. *(Alfred Duff Cooper, Unionist politician, Chancellor of the Duchy of Lancaster 1941-3; later, 1944 onwards, Ambassador to France, 1st Viscount Norwich – Ed)*

(The next bit must have been censored just the following continued):

. . . than otherwise would, and don't have any worry. It'll only be for a month or two I fear.

Well more news in the next exciting installment. Don't forget to watch out for it.

All our love as ever, Your v loving Susan.

Letter written 17 January 1942, received 1 May 1942, c/o Hong Kong Shanghai Bank, Singapore.

My Darling Mum,

The first letters from home since the beginning of the war – the local war. But an out of date lot from August.

One of these fine days I'm hoping for a cable about William's son and heir, or Dorothy's daughter and heiress. I seem to remember that January was the month. *(William is Susan's brother – Ed)*

My work as a VAD at a military hospital continues, and I still enjoy it, and don't mind being spoken to as though I was a scullery maid. I'm told that I look 'too young to be married' by one old chap from the Prince of Wales. Perhaps I'd better get a divorce quick.

I go and help at the canteen at Air Headquarters some evenings, which I love doing when I'm not too tired. I served one young man with coffee who made the bright remark that it 'looked like cocoa, smelt like coffee so it must be tea!'

We remain curiously calm at the thought of the Japanese only 100 miles away. As ever the British feel that they'll manage to scrape through.

We get a certain number of air-raids, and during the moonlight nights spend a bit of time under kitchen tables, well surrounded by sandbags. Lately our nights have been undisturbed and the days have sometimes livened up a bit. I'm familiar with the sound of bombs swishing down through the air, and though not exactly nice, I think it's better than the suspense of waiting and listening to the throb of menacing aeroplanes overhead. I'm pleased to note that, although as frightened as anyone, I don't show it, and I'm not trembly. I was much more afraid at the beginning, when they first landed up-country, and everything was in a muddle. I see no reason why we should worry. We live in spaced-out houses, and take shelter when necessary, so it's a lucky hit that gets us.

(Next paragraph censored)

Your letter speaks of the tea, sugar and butter I'm glad it's arriving. No more now, as you will understand. I'm surprised that the Cameron Highlands tea is good. There's only one rather measly-looking estate, so it all goes to show.

A letter from Mrs Burgess by the same mail is quite amusing on the subject of a lady friend of that devilish Anthony from S America.

(Anthony is Susan's brother-in-law. – Ed) A Uruguayan of luscious aspect and flashing black eyes, this woman quite dazzled Mrs B, who remarked rather sadly at the end 'but nothing like an engagement I fear, as the betwitching person is married and has 2 children!' She goes on 'she spoke well of Anthony, said he was happy and very amusing. She had often asked him where he was born, and he always replied, 'In a stable'. If all S American ladies are such sirens, I wonder he has managed to remain a bachelor.'

I privately add – 'no wonder he doesn't come back from S. America.'

We feel we've had enough of the East. The war out here has made life more interesting, but I think we'll soon tire of the interest and realise the truth of the description of war as being periods of intense boredom punctuated by moments of intense fear.

Lawrence has just gone off to an all night session on duty, and I'm sitting (a Sunday evening it is), listening to *The Messiah* on the wireless, and consequently feeling sad. War here, there, or anywhere, it's time the Burgesses came home. This is an added incentive for us to beat up the Yellow Peril.

We all wonder and wonder about America. She still seems to do little or nothing, but one hopes that things are on the way.

I hope that by the time this reaches you we'll have wiped the floor with 'em.

Lots of love from us both,

Ever your v loving Susan.

Dated 3 March 1942 – no date received, c/o Hong Kong Bank, Colombo.

My Darling Mum,

You won't have had a letter from me since January. Singapore, and I don't know if those ever reached you. So much has happened since, that I can't remember what my last news was.

You probably know that I was working as a VAD in Alexandra hospital, and that we were both living with the Moffatts. Lawrence working at Headquarters. Life went on fairly comfortably, apart from the raids which weren't always nice. They took to coming over in small groups of four or five planes at night every half hour, and nearly always dropped their bombs in the same place, half a mile to the seaward side of our house (just near Mt Echo). There was no objective, just terror raids, which started large fires among the native huts, which were quickly put out, but they kept us up and down out of bed, rather quick about it too, as usually the planes were over before the siren went. They must have taken to gliding in with their engines off. Our nearest bomb was in the drive, 15 yards from the house, not a big one, it didn't do any harm, except shrapnel through the window shutters.

One night Lawrence and I slept out on the downstairs verandah, so that we needn't get out of bed until we felt it absolutely necessary. I didn't sleep very well, what with ants and mosquitoes, and I could hear artillery fire too. The causeway had been blown up that morning and I suppose we were bombarding the Japs, or they us. I felt quite confident about Singapore being held, and although I took it that most of the buildings on the island would be knocked down, I thought we'd manage.

The next day Lawrence was talking of sending me away. I felt very stubborn and obstinate about it, there didn't seem any likelihood of Lawrence moving and I had my work and wanted to stay.

Julia Moffatt had gone, and all women with children, and in fact most of the households I knew were broken up, but a lot of girls like myself were still around. However by Sunday the 1st I found Lawrence was determined I should go, and had made arrangements for me to go over to Palembang (Sumatra) with a girl called Jean Frow, on a small B & S Yangste boat called the (censored) know of it? Some 500 RAF troops would also be on board. And only 2 suitcases, at the last minute my trunk. We went on board at 4 am on Monday the 2nd February. It was dreadful leaving Lawrence, but I felt sure he would follow soon. I only found out later that he didn't think he would get away at all, and Jean's husband had told her this also. Thank goodness she didn't tell me. Anyway, it was sad enough.

We both felt it was a more than dangerous trip which I was making also. We steamed out at 8 o'clock, packed with troops, I armed with a motor-car inner tube, to act as a life-belt, if necessary. There certainly wouldn't have been enough to go around. The siren went just as we got going, and a few fighters took off, but nothing happened.

There was a huge pall of black smoke over the north eastern side of the island, looking as though it was over Seletar way. Oil or petrol, it looked like. I'd seen an even bigger cloud, right across the sky from side to side a few days before, when they set oil tanks on fire at the Naval Base. I couldn't believe smoke could look like that. It was like an immense storm looming on the horizon, miles wide.

We took two days and a night to get to Palembang, and had an uneventful trip – the only ship that week to get through without any trouble. As we reached the mouth of Palembang river we saw a funnel and masts sticking up out of the water, a small ship like ourselves, which had been bombed and sunk 6 hours previously. We met some of the men, army troops, later on in Oosthaven. We heard later that a ship just behind us was bombed and set on fire, and that our husbands in Singapore heard about it and thought they'd got us. They were kept in suspense for 48 hours until they got news that we'd arrived safely.

In Palembang we were put up for one night by a Dutch couple, who were very kind, and enjoyed pointing out to us how well the Dutch were organising things. They certainly organise their life and country very much better than we do. Java was a delightful island, and the first place in the East that I would like to re-visit. The Japs are welcome to the rest.

Then the next day we moved off down to Tanjong Karang, which is the town belonging to the port of Oosthaven. We were supposed to be shipped off to Java straight away, but we heard rumours that Jean's husband might be in Palembang, so we wanted to hang around for news. We were taken down to the ship, with a bunch of other English women, but very naughtily faded away into the darkness with such luggage as we could collect, and with the co-operation of a nice Wing-Commander who smuggled us out in his car. The driver of his car then informed us that he knew where the two ladies were to stay, and took us to a house, which we could hardly see in the darkness, and we were welcomed in by a large Dutchman and 3 young men who subsequently turned out to be English troops. The W/Commander was rather loathe to leave us two young things among so much manhood, but he was reassured, and drove off into the night. The first remark our host boomed at us was 'NOW, we will have CHAMPAGNE!' and my goodness, we did! Five whole bottles of bubbily. We hadn't had a morsal of food since breakfast that morning, so you can imagine the weakening effect on two empty giggly young women. We had a lovely evening, and when the champagne was exhausted went out to a Chinese restaurant and filled ourselves with nice fish and odds and ends.

The next night we had to move to another Dutch household, our hosts had someone else coming to stay. The young men, by the way, in the house, were off the ship we had seen sunk at the mouth of the river. They'd had a pretty nerve-racking time, bombed by nine bombers, and the lifeboats except one riddled with machine gun fire; the one remaining one, the native crew made off in before they could be stopped. They'd all been in the water, many of them wounded and many without lifebelts, for 2½ hours before they were picked up. And their fear of sharks was what really got them down.

In the next night's household were two small and AWFUL girls, who were so dreadful that we had to lock ourselves into our bedroom to escape them. They insisted on reading out loud to us in Dutch, sitting on the backs of our chairs with their dirty feet around our necks and their hands over our faces. I laughed till I was nearly ill at our utter helplessness, but I couldn't have stood more than 24 hours of it.

The next night Jean heard that her husband had flown straight on to Bandoeng in Java, so we moved off on the night ship and reached Batavia at 10.30 the next morning. Here in the central station we were surrounded by helpful Dutchmen, mostly in an attractive green uniform with the romantic inscription 'STATION COMMANDO' on the armlet. What we first wanted was to retire discreetly and have a wash and brush up, so we said "thank you, thank you" and went to look for what we wanted. But nowhere could we find it, and our attentive bodyguard watchful as ever, rushed up and wanted to know if the *Damen* from Singapore wished for anything? We told them what we wished and after themselves searching fruitlessly, they fetched the stationmaster and an enormous bunch of keys, and we were solemnly led the length of the station and a large iron door was slowly and solemnly unlocked; the wave of air that came out was nobody's business. And the obviously mixed conveniences hadn't been polished up for some years. I had to go through with it, but Jean's stomach failed and she fled in disorder.

In Batavia we lost our trunks. These both turned up some 10 days later, but since then I've lost the large square green suitcase, also in Batavia, and full of all my most needed possessions. I'd much rather have lost the trunk again. As far as clothes go I now possess 4 skirts, 4 blouses, 2 Aertex shirts, one cotton frock, and one black velvet afternoon dress – so useful for the well dressed refugee about town.

We took the train up to Bandoeng, 2,000 ft up on a high wide plateau surrounded by hills and volcanoes. I arrived in the super-smart Hotel Savoy-Homann, wearing a dirty cotton frock, with an inflated inner tube over one shoulder, a blanket under my arm, and carrying a basket containing 2 whisky bottles and one gin bottle (½ empty). This liquor had caused us much trouble and sorrow, having been lost twice, but luckily turned up un-broached.

Bandoeng was a marvellous place. Lovely climate, lovely shops, smart people, peace from air-raids, for a few days at least. I was there a week before I heard that Lawrence had arrived safely in Batavia. I rushed down by the next available train and found him much the same as ever. I can't imagine L ever becoming the bag of nerves and jumps which some people are reduced to. Nor can he get melodramatic about things. It was ages before he'd even tell me of his adventures. He was finally the very last person to leave Air HQ. After watching the Air V Marshal pull down his flag and drive away, he wandered around with a large hammer, breaking up anything that hadn't already been dealt with such as batteries, telephone

271

exchanges, etc. It must have been a queer atmosphere. Lights were still burning in some darker offices, fans going round and an occasional telephone ringing.

All at once he saw straggled Indian troops retreating at the double back across the Bukit Timah golf course, so he thought perhaps it was time to get going. He drove off down the road, passing small groups of soldiers here and there, from one of whom he got a spare rifle, not quite knowing who he would come up against next. He drove down Thompson Road to the temporarily established remnants of headquarters, and was told to go down to the docks and embark some thousand RAF troops, the last lot. All this was on Wednesday 11 February. Singapore finally fell on Sunday.

He went down and started organising the men. None of them had had any orders and were just standing around all over the place. There were so many raids going on, and no sirens were working, that they didn't bother to take cover, but flung themselves on the ground when planes appeared overhead, and then went on working. At this point Lawrence, who was expecting to stay in Singapore, was told he was to go too. He had nothing with him, so jumped into the old faithful car, and rushed along to the Bank to say goodbye. Eric Moffatt went back to the house with him – the only occupied house in the compound.

The Japs were rumoured to be only half a mile down the road, but all seemed quiet, except for the occasional shelling, and rifle fire pinging around. Eric was packing up what he could. Lawrence hastily collected two suitcases and regretfully said farewell to all our packing cases of things, 3 camphor chests, 2 carpets, refrigerator and air conditioner. A funny thing about the bedroom carpet. Mitsie, Ruth H-Halletts rather nasty little dachshound which was living in the house, chose this last moment to make two large and dirty messes on it. Such was L's rage that he thrashed the dog and was just about to clean up the mess, when he realised the absurdity of the situation. The dirtier the carpet, the worse for the Japs! The unfortunate dog he took down and shot. This upset Eric dreadfully and he broke down, what with leaving the house, and the thought of what was ahead. By this time they felt they should get going. Small parties of troops were still along the side of the road, but they felt that the Japs might appear round the side of the house any minute. So off they went, and Lawrence waved goodbye at the Bank and got himself on board and away. There were three ships, one of them a cruiser. L's was formerly a refrigerator meat ship, so you can imagine that there wasn't much accommodation. He slept four nights on deck, with some shirts as a pillow, and in spite of being well padded by Dame Nature, (always so lavish), was covered with bruises when he reached Java. They sailed on all Wednesday night, and on Thursday morning at 9.00 they sighted a formation of 63 planes, quite some miles away, going in the same direction as themselves. "Ah" they thought, "all is well. These chaps are off to bomb Palembang and won't bother about us – " But as they watched the formation turned and circled over towards them. They made a turn or two, and then settled down to four hours of bombing. They started by dive-bombing. L was below at this time, helping to get the fire hoses screwed up.

His ship was the first attacked, and almost immediately had three hits, he thrown completely sideways, but got up unscratched, and helped pass a chain of buckets to put out a fire which had started. No-one noticed that one bucket passed up the line was full of castor sugar, and the blaze flared up joyfully when this was emptied onto it! At this point there were cries of "volunteer for the AA gun", so, glad to get out of the smoke, Lawrence ran up to the rear of the ship, and from then onwards was working at fusing and loading on the shells. Two men had been killed at the gunpost, but there was no time even to move them out the way. One of the dive bombers had been shot down, so they took to high level bombing from then onwards, breaking off in formations of nine and picking out one of the three ships, circling round, and coming across, wo-wo-wo-wo-wo, an then letting go with all the bombs at once. Once he was sure that they weren't going for a particular ship on that round, Lawrence said he could breathe again for a few minutes. The cruiser did some wonderful turning and twisting and again and again forced them to hold their bombs, or avoided them so that they all dropped to one side. Finally after ages of this, 27 of them broke off, and obviously choosing L's ship circled round and came up and across from behind. He was quite convinced they'd be for it, this time, and I think everyone on board expected to be killed.

However, they were missed by inches, one bunch of bombs falling just one side of the ship, and another just the other side. The whole ship leapt and rocked and shivered, but all was well. That was the last. No more bombs, and were they pleased to see those planes steam away into the distance. They certainly were. Considering the amount of bombs which had been dropped, the damage really wasn't much. There were 15 casualties on L's ship, among them an RAF dentist who we had known very well in Singapore.

By the way I'm sorry to say that Cyp Markham failed to return from a daylight raid sometime in January. It seems unlikely that he would have been saved, as he was seen to crash into the sea. I'm really sorry, as we both like cousin Cyp very much indeed.

When I met L in Batavia we spent one night in a very mixed bedroom with two other W/Cdrs in camp beds and L and myself in the main bed. This was in Batavia's main swep-up Hotel des Indes. It was so full that people were sleeping in the lounges. We spent the evening talking to a S/Ldr Rennell, brother to the one you know, and uncle therefore of the girl Eugenie. He and Lawrence worked together in Singapore. He's a naughty puckish little man and I thought him great fun.

We went up to Bandoeng the next day, and not finding any more room in that hotel either, and being by now thoroughly used to mixed company, we shared Jean and George Frow's room, they having one bed and we having the other. 'Adversity maketh strange bedfellows'. We hadn't finished with our strange bedfellows even then. For we got a room that next night, but it had three beds in it, and we offered one of them to a homeless young S/Ldr for the night. The night after that we actually had a room to ourselves, and felt quite lonely.

I only had one raid while I was in Bandoeng, when low-flying planes bombed the aerodrome and did a bit of machine-gunning. The worst thing about raids and alerts there was the siren, which was fixed on top of our hotel. It was a glorified hunting horn, which wailed up and down the scale on fearful screeching blaring note. I'd always thought the British variety the most miserable thing invented till I heard that one.

We did have a grand few days up there together. There didn't seem to be any work for Lawrence to do – so we just made whoopee. I felt that anything might happen at any moment, so lets enjoy ourselves while we can.

After Palembang had been taken, our two husbands began to get restive once more, and mutter darkly about getting the women out of the way.

I felt sure that we would have to go eventually, so there didn't seem to be any point in waiting around with Lawrence feeling all the time that I ought to be on the move. Anyway the matter was more or less taken out of our hands, and all RAF women told that they must leave. Once more we said goodbye, once more I felt sure that Lawrence would follow safely on shortly. I wasn't looking forward to the coming trip one little bit. First and foremost, because we would be travelling herded with some 100 cackling females – and if 'There's one thing I hate it's been pushed around in herds of women.' The next reason was our conviction that we'd be well and truly attacked before we were clear. If you study the map, you'd think as I thought, that we wouldn't be able to leave the port of Batavia until dawn, and would either have to go round the south of Java near Bali, which had just been taken, or the shorter route through the Sunda Straits, which was a narrow strip, and must be well patrolled from Japanese occupied Sumatra. They had the whole of south Sumatra by then.

However, we had no choice, so set our pearly teeth, and blew up my rubber tube and my hot-water-bottle, or ho-wo-boko, and entrained for Batavia. What a journey that was! First the train was 1½ hours late in starting, all because of the luggage of the women. Not us ourselves, having only 2 trunks and 2 suitcases between us, but the packing cases and trunks of others. George and Lawrence got very angry about it, and said that no-one should be allowed to take more than we had. We travelled in a 4th class native cattle wagon, in pitch darkness and great noise, dirt and soreness of sit-upons. We arrived in pouring rain at 9.30 pm and our hand luggage was torn from us, and we were piled into waiting buses and duly arrived at the docks.

Here things really got going, and a team of large Australians were waiting to take our things and lead us on board. But alas, because of our lateness, the ship was literally tugging at the anchor, and was away within 20 minutes of our arrival, leaving on the dock 2 lorry-loads of luggage amongst it my green suitcase, and Jean's trunk and one suitcase. There is some hope that it will turn up in Bombay, as it might have got put onto the next ship.

The next morning we threw open the port-hole at seven o'clock, and our hearts sank as we saw land to the left of us. Not yet through the Straits! I informed the other five occupants of our 2-berth cabin that I reckoned we'd be discovered by a reconnaissance plane by 8 o'clock, which would go off to Palembang and tell its pals, who'd be back by 9 for fun and games. In the event of action, we'd been ordered to go to our cabins and lie down on our bunks, unless 'boat stations' was sounded on the alarm bells. I hung around on the small piece of deck allotted to the 125 ladies, scanning the sky and straining my ears.

Land disappeared into the distance and after another three or four hours steaming we breathed again. And when I looked at my little pocket compass and found that we had turned west, I really felt that menace from the air had been done with.

(Several lines here were censored – Ed).

[We steamed on about a week without incident and thankfully turned up in Colombo, where we had previously been stationed for a year – SB].

Colombo, the same as ever, though not quite so smelly and dirty as I had remembered it. I was pleasantly surprised. But then everything so far in this war hasn't been as bad as I was keyed up for, even the worst of the raids, when I stood out in the trench in the mornings, always at the same time, 10.30 or 11.00, and watched from 90 to 100 planes coming straight over my head, in perfect formation, in the clear blue sky. Only once out of all those mornings did I ever see the formation in any way disturbed. That was the day when we shot down 12 planes by AA fire. We saw the right-hand outside plane disappear suddenly, but we couldn't see it crashing. A few minutes later a plane came over the other side of the house, very low and in obvious difficulties with only one engine working. It disappeared behind some trees, and I don't know what became of it. But in all those raids that I watched, I only once saw a fighter doing its stuff and I don't think it shot down anything. Of course there were lots and lots of mornings when I was at the hospital and could only hear the roar of the planes. They always sounded directly overhead, and I was far more frightened in the ward, trying to go on with the dressings and reassure the patients, than I ever was at home. And the times when I heard the rush of bombs coming down, I felt my last moment had come. Whereas when I heard them dropping if I was in the trench. I knew I was safe up to a few yards from a bomb, and placed my fate in the lap of the gods. Now I'm away from it I feel very brave, but it only needs the siren to go, and my stomach will rapidly return to my feet.

I think that's quite enough for the time being about war......

Well, I've told you all – I've probably told you too much and the censor will have to go to work with a big pair of scissors.

So, goodnight everybody.

All love to everyone.

Ever your v loving Susan

Dated 28 March, 1942, Hotel Cecil, Delhi.

My darling Mum,

I hope very much that my 25 page letter from Colombo reached you, as in it I gave detailed descriptions of all our adventures since leaving Singapore. In case it didn't I shall just give a bald resumé of what our moves had been.

I left Singapore, February 3, on a small river boat (B&S), with three other women on board. Went to Sumatra (three days) Java, Bandoeng, where I stayed two weeks. L turned up for the last 4 days of my stay, having left Singapore on the 12th. He was in a small to medium sized boat which was bombed for 5 hours by 63 bombers and hit three times. He was helping load and fuse the shells for the AA gun. I was again packed off from (Batavia), and miraculously escaped trouble, although we passed through the Sunda Straits in broad daylight, a week after the fall of south Sumatra. So to Ceylon without mishap. L left from south Java (Jilikjap) five or six days later, and also had miraculously no trouble, although his ship was continuously breaking down, and had to give away its position by wirelessing for help. They had a miserably uncomfortable trip, very short of food and water. He didn't wash or change his clothes for ten days. What a man!

We came up from Colombo by train through dust and desert for four days and four nights. We little Burgess's certainly do get about the globe. Between us we reckon we've been in 34 different countries.

We live in a tent in the grounds of this hotel. It's nicely furnished, and is cool – cold at night. But from 10.00 am to 4.30 pm the thermometer soars to over 100, and you can hardly breathe.

It's just as well we're going down to Bombay, where women can endure the heat without collapsing, poor dear little frail creatures.

The prospects of going home are gloomy, at any rate for another year at least. We might have managed it if we'd tried hard when we got here, but Lawrence didn't think that our two and three-quarter years justified it.

I hope you got my two airgraph letters – I sent one to the Burgesses also. The pity is that you have to write bigly and clearly, so can't let yourself go.

I'm depressed at the thought of having to learn another language. It's quite undoubted that life in the East is simplified if you can speak the local tongue. In my tent I'm always being surprised by sweepers, bearers, etc, who part the curtain and enter, not understanding my desperate cries of "Don't come in!".

Lawrence was really thin when he first got to Colombo. His trousers all fell off and his collars spun around his neck. He's pleased to know that he has only to go for ten days on iron rations and his fat vanishes. But when on earth will he do it, except on compulsion? His trousers stay on now, and his cheeky-chums are filling out.

I'm longing for news of William's and Dorothy's offspring which must have arrived by now. I expect cables have missed me all over the place. Lawrence had a letter from Dorothy just as he left Singapore, but he forgot to bring it with him.

Lots of love to all – when will I get home? I'll be a leathery elderly girl when I do.

Ever your loving, Susan.

Dated 13 April, 1942, Galle Face Hotel, Colombo.

My darling Mum,

This letter may be the first indication you get that we are back again in the 'Poirl of the Orient'. After changing their minds about where we were to go at least three times, they finally returned us to where we had started from. I was depressed at the prospect of doing the

277

2,500 mile trip across the sandy wastes of India once again, but apart from that was glad to be in a green land. I've seen enough of dried-up India.

We got here two days after Colombo's first raid and just in time for the effort at Trinco. The RAF here certainly did their stuff, and I don't think the Japs will be able to keep up many more such costly ventures. The loss of the two cruisers the 'Hermes' was rather a blow, especially. . . .   (Next line censored).

I've brought a new PEN which is entirely out of my control.

A tremendous lot of women have cleared out of Ceylon, with children. A great relief. The cowardly Tamils and Ceylonese have been evacuating themselves freely also. They are a miserable crew. The more I see of some places the better I think Singapore was. There's absolutely no reason, as yet, why they should run away, except a complete lack of guts. A bit of martial law and the nailed fist is what they need.

We're occupying a Ter-ri-fic suite with everything double including the wash basins; a Noah's Ark room. The cost is so enormous that we'll have to move soon or have our cheques bounced.

My friend and travelling companion from Singapore, (Jean Frow) is still here, always hoping for news about her husband who was left behind in Java. Troops are still fighting there, and I think there is a good chance for people to get away from small fishing villages in junks, and make it across to Australia. It may be months before news gets through.

This is a poorish letter – I'm out of the habit, too much train travel.

Lots of love to all.

Ever your loving, Susan.

Dated 21 April, 1942, Galle Face Hotel, Colombo.

My darling Mum,

Life in this place is gradually returning to something like normal after the raid made for general exodus. . . . . .

I've got back to work and am starting in the Naval Cypher Office tomorrow. I'm not over-enthusiastic, I'd much rather have done something running-about, not sitting at a desk. The time has gone for picking and choosing and unless I work at once, I'm liable to be removed from the island without ceremony.

I made one abortive attempt to be taken on as a VAD at the Naval Hospital. I went to interview the most dreadful woman I have ever come across in my life, a Matron-Vice-Admiral by the amount of gold lace and crossed spoons on her shoulders. I don't think her face has ever crackled into a smile in its little life, and I wouldn't go and work for her if she begged me on bony knees.

She kept on impressing upon me that they worked SERIOUSLY, and that if I didn't go and live in the nurses' quarters I would be of no use to them. However if I was particularly anxious to work in a NAVAL hospital, she could offer me a job in the catering department, which would then release a real nurse to go back to the wards. When I said that I didn't particularly want to work in a NAVAL hospital, and I didn't want to do anything but nursing, and if I couldn't do that I might as well go back to a job I knew about at the Naval Office, she looked coldly at me and more or less accused me of having no interest in furthering the war effort, and that she considered that it was people like myself who were letting down the Empire (presumably for not wanting to cater in a NAVAL hospital).

I was almost speechless with rage, luckily, or I might have forgotten that I am a ladylike creature, and said something regrettable. It's women like her that make women like me feel that women are an unpleasant sex, and should never be allowed to boss each other about.

We shall go on living in the hotel, it makes life much easier under these circumstances, and with both Lawrence and myself working shifts, at any hour of the day or night, a house or household wouldn't be very easy.

I am longing to hear some news from home. Knowing you, I'm quite sure you sat down and wrote the very minute you had my cable, which is now seven weeks ago. So with luck I may get something within the next three weeks. The trouble is that you may not have realised that I have had no news whatever since a letter of yours dated 16 September last. Seven months!

In case my previous letter never reached you, we were sent back here again from Delhi, back down the weary dusty 2,500 miles of India's countryside.

I hear that Mr Pierce in Hong Kong was killed in the fighting or shelling.

Well to end – I hope you will have no further cause to worry about us. I feel a certain confidence.

Love to all – Ever your loving
Susan

There followed a posting to India for a year before Mrs Burgess eventually returned to England in September, 1942, travelling on a troopship via the Cape. The journey took nine weeks. – Ed

POSTSCRIPT

From *The Times* January 26, 1995

The moment when Russian troops reached Auschwitz-Birkenau on January 27, 1945 may be claimed as the most shocking in human history. Much was already known about the German concentration camps by that stage of the war. But their full horror was not grasped until Allied soldiers beheld the gas chambers, crematoria and the skeletal survivors of the systematic slaughter. Fifty years on, the first meeting between liberator and victim is no less emotionally resonant or appalling to recall . . . All who live after this terrible event must confront it.

The precise numbers of people exterminated in the camps is still a matter of debate; so too is the extent of the moral similarity between the German camps and the Soviet gulags. Yet, such questions should not divert attention from the simple fact of what happened.

This is best appreciated in eyewitness accounts of the liberation, such as the letter which the British soldier wrote to his wife in 1945. "I have never seen people look so ill, so wretched and so near to death," he wrote. "Belsen is a living death . . . and, if it is ever necessary, an undoubted answer to those who want to know what we have been fighting for."

SEPTEMBER 3, 1939

Mrs CONNIE CLARK, *for many years a Brockenhurst resident writes:*
In September 1939 I was working in the Hospital for Sick Children Great Ormond Street and at 11.00 am on that fatal Sunday. Most of the staff, whether on or off duty, were gathered in the Emergency Operating Theatre that had been set up in the basement of the hospital to hear Mr Chamberlain make his dreaded announcement. It was a very tense moment and especially so as the air-raid sirens sounded as soon as he finished saying, "We are at war with Germany." We all gasped and said, "Surely 'they' can't be here already?" What a relief when the All Clear sounded almost immediately!

I cannot remember how many years later it was when we went to see our younger son in the play *Forty Years On*, and in the play a TV screen appeared and we saw the reactions of the general public to the announcement and to the sirens sounding so dramatically. After the show I said to my son, "I shall never forget the terror we felt at that moment," and he said, "It did not really happen did it? I thought it was the producer's idea to make an impact on the audiences."

APPENDIX

POPULATION OF BROCKENHURST PARISH

Table of Population Statistics (Civil Parishes) as published in the National Census.

Census Year	Brockenhurst Population
1841	928
1901	1,585
1911	2,648
1921	2,159
1931	2,482
1941	No Census
1951	2,387
1981	3,080
1991	3,322

FIRST WORLD WAR ANZAC GRAVES IN ST NICHOLAS CHURCHYARD

The following notes have been written and researched by Lt Col Richard Power.

From 1916 to 1919 No 1 New Zealand Hospital was in Brockenhurst. It occupied huts in the field between Church Lane and the Lymington Road and, in addition, the Balmer Lawn and Forest Park Hotels. The huts had previously been occupied by the Lady Harding's Hospital for Indian soldiers, who had fought in France in the early days of the 1914-18 war.

Twenty-one thousand New Zealanders passed through the hospital and ninety-three of their comrades lie buried in St Nicholas Churchyard. These include three officers, seven NCO's and eighty-three private soldiers from such well known Corps and Regiments as NZ Artillery, NZ Engineers, Regiments of Auckland, Canterbury, Otago and Wellington; Maori Battalion, NZ Rifle Brigade, NZ Machine Gun Corps, NZAC, NZ Medical Corps and NZ Provost Corps. Also among the graves lie a British soldier from the King's Own Royal Lancaster Regiment, a Canadian from the Canadian Forestry Corps, an Australian from 22nd Infantry Battalion, three Indian civilians from the Indian hospital and three unknown Belgian civilians from a forestry camp at Sopley in the New Forest.

The last commanding officer at the hospital, Colonel Clennell Fenwick, CMG, presented a New Zealand flag to the parish and also

281

ANZAC DAY 1918.

wrote a letter thanking the people of Brockenhurst for their kindness and hospitality. The flag and the letter are mounted on the east wall of the aisle in the church together with a commemorative plaque.

In 1924 the original wooden crosses on the soldiers' graves were replaced by the Imperial War Graves Commission with their standard headstones. In 1927 the memorial behind the graves was added.

For many years now, on the Sunday nearest Anzac Day, the parish has held a memorial service at the New Zealand Memorial. This has become quite an event and attracts many people who join with the village in paying tribute to those who came so far to die for a just cause. We have been privileged to have a representative from the High Commissioner's Defence Liaison Staff regularly attend this service.

In the early 1970's the flag in the church was found to be badly deteriorated and His Excellency, the High Commissioner for New Zealand, Mr TH McCombs, OBE, graciously paid us the honour, on the September 23 1973, in coming in person to present a new flag to the parish.

In 1924 the peal of bells was augmented, from four to six and the new 'second' bears the inscription: 'In remembrance of the New Zealand soldiers who served during the Great War, 1914-1918, and were buried in this churchyard.'

Until recently we had two links with the wartime New Zealand hospital living in the area: Mr Dean and Mr Cargill, both now deceased.

Mr Dean, after being wounded at Passchendaele, spent seven months in the Balmer Lawn Hotel, where serious cases were treated. On his return to New Zealand he married, but, when his wife died, he came back to the UK and married a girl he had known in his hospital days. For many years the Deans lived in Gosport Street, Lymington.

Mr Cargill was posted to the hospital on being invalided back from Egypt, after a bout of enteric fever. He married a local girl, but, after a spell in New Zealand, both returned to the UK.

ANZAC derives from the initials of the 'Australian and New Zealand Army Corps' which first went into action at Gallipoli on April 25, 1915. Since then this day has been a national holiday 'down under'.

It has been quite surprising how practically ever time the Brockenhurst Anzac Service has been held, there has been someone present – usually a relative, with connections with the wartime hospital.

BROCKENHURST WAR MEMORIAL

Those who were killed in the Second World War and whose names are on the Brockenhurst War Memorial.

(We should be grateful for more information where details are sparse or non-existent. – Ed)

ASH R. – Army, Captain. Killed in Italy.

A'DEANE W. – Royal Navy, Captain. Lost off Crete when his ship was sunk. 1941.

BANISTER P. – Royal Navy, Lieutenant DSC. Lost at sea when HM Submarine *Umpire* accidentally sunk on convoy off east coast UK on her maiden voyage. July 1941. Age 22.

BANISTER J. – Army, The Buffs Regt (R East Kent) transferred to RAF, Flying Officer. Shot down when on night flying exercise over East Anglia by German intruder aircraft. Age 24.

CLARK W. – Army. Died in Thailand when Jap POW and buried at Kanchana in 1943. Age 40. (Widow, Mrs Clark living in Brockenhurst.)

CHALK R. – Royal Navy, Rating. Lost when HMS *Royal Oak* torpedoed by U-Boat when at anchor inside Scapa Flow. July 1941. Age 17. (Cousin of the late Reg Chalk, fishmonger in Brookley Road.)

CLEVELAND H. – Army, Royal Artillery. Died of polio in Middle East and buried at Ismailia, Canal Zone, Egypt. 1944. Age 26. (Brother of Archie Cleveland, living in Brockenhurst.)

CLOSE W. – Army, Private 1st Hampshire Regt. Killed in Tunisia. (Brother of P Close living in Brockenhurst.)

COCKBURN D. – RAF. Lost over Germany. 1943. (Family once ran Island Shop.)

CREMER J. – RAF, Flying Officer 610 Fighter Squadron. Missing over English Channel on fighter sweep. March 1943. Age 19.

DICKINSON W. –

DONALDSON R. –

DUKES L. – Army, 5th Hampshire Regt. Killed in Italy and buried at Monte Cassino. 1943. Age 25.

DUNKINSON J. – Royal Navy, Able Seaman. Lost off Crete in HMS *Gloucester*. May 1941. Age 21. (Brother living in Brockenhurst.)

EASTWELL A. – Army, Private Seaforth Highlanders. Killed in Burma. 1944. Age 21.

FERGUSON G. – Royal Navy, Lieut-Comdr. Lost in HMS *Prince of Wales* sunk off Malaya. December 1941.

FROWDE S. – Army, Sergeant Hampshire Regt. Killed in Italy. Age 22. (Sister, Mrs Cooper living in Brockenhurst.)

HILL C. – Army, Private Queens Regt. Killed in Burma. 1941. Age 27/28. (Sister, Miss Hill living in Brockenhurst.)

HODDER F. – RAF, Group Captain, Station Commander Syeston, Notts. Killed in raid over Frankfurt. September 1943. (Widow, Mrs Seaton, living in Brockenhurt.)

HOLDEN F. – RAF, Sergeant. Lost on bomber raid. Age 29.

HOTHAM J. – Army, Major Royal Tank Regt. Killed in N Africa. July 1942.

MEADEN R. – Army, Sgt-Major Hampshire Regt. Killed in Tunisia. July 1942.

MOORE A. –

MUTTER R. – Army, Lieutenant Scots Guards. Killed in NW Europe. April 1945. (Memorial seat at War Memorial Sway Road.)

MYLES R. – Army, Sgt.-Major. Killed in NW Europe in 7th Armoured Division.

O'DONNELL Tony – RAF, Armourer. Killed in accidental bomb explosion on airfield in Yorkshire. (Brother living in Brockenhurst.)

PAINTER P. – Army, Royal Tank Regt. Killed in Middle East.

READ R. – RAF. Lost over Berlin.

ST CLAIR-FORD D. – Royal Navy, Lieut Comdr. Lost off Taranto, Italy, in HM Submarine *Traveller*, believed mined. December 1942. (Widow, Mrs Buckley, living in Sway.)
SHORT J. – RAF, LAC. Died in accident in South Africa. (Brother-in-law, J Salisbury, living in Brockenhurst.)
SHILETTO A. – RAF, Fl Lt. Killed in flying accident. July 1944. Aged 27. (Buried in St. Nicholas churchyard.)
SMITH K. – RAF, Squadron Leader Bomber Command.

THE VICARS OF BROCKENHURST

1899 – 1919 The Reverend Arthur Chambers, AKC
1919 – 1924 The Reverend Cecil Hope Gill, MA
1924 – 1927 The Reverend Evory H Kennedy, MA
1927 – 1953 The Reverend William Haslam, MA

THE HEADMASTERS
Brockenhurst Church of England (Controlled) Primary School

1908 – 1914 Mr GH Gendall
1915 – 1923 Mr JH Quinn
1923 Acting Headmaster: Mr JAC White
1924 – 1936 Mr JP Armstrong
1936 – 1939 Mr GC Stretton
1939 – 1947 Mr RE Tiller

CONTRIBUTORS

Sheena ARCHDALE
Shirley BATEMAN
Mary BATES
Christina BEEVERS
Tim BEEVERS
Jack BLANDFORD
John BLOOMFIELD
Jack BRINDLEY
Molly BRINDLEY
Ted BROWN
Beryl BROWNING
Sue BURGESS
Harry BURT
Frank BURTON
Clive CARGILL
David CHAMBERLAIN
Josephine CHISMAN
Connie CLARK
Dorothy CLARK
Margaret CLARK
Archie CLEVELAND
Edna CLEVELAND
Ruby COOKE
Les COOPER
Edna COOPER
Bé COOPER-VOSSE
Bridget CORRIE-HILL
Shirley CRAMPTON
Vivienne CROXFORD
Eileen DORAN
Miss JM DOUGLAS
June DRAYSON
Bill DUNKINSON
Michael EMANUEL
Bogdan ENGEL
Fred ENGLAND
Joyce ENGLAND
Margaret EVANS
Eileen GABONY

John GABONY
Bob GARDAM
George GATES
Evelyn GREER
Jack HANSON
Ellen HARRISON
Geoffrey HAWKES
Iain HAYTER
Ruth HIRD
George JOHNSON
Gladys JOHNSON
Les JOHNSON
Andrew KILSBY
Millie KNAPP
Wally KNOTT
Jim LAWFORD
Ruud LEM
Frank LEWIN
Ivy LEWIS
Mary LEWIS
Joan LLOYD
Joyce MARCHANT
Vernon MARCHANT
Betty MARDON
Tom MARDON
Aileen MILLS
Norman MONTAGUE
Molly MÜLLER
Patience NICHOLSON
Basil O'DONNELL
Cyril OTTER
Lesley PEDLEY
Ted PERFECT
Francie PEYTON JONES
Jack PLACE
Una PLACE
Brian PLUMLEY
Stanley PORTER
Lawrence POWELL

Richard POWER
Mrs PRICE
John PURKESS
Alec PURKIS
Margaret PURKIS
Connie PURKIS
Tony PURKIS
Frank RASHLEIGH
Peter REEVES
Richard REEVES
Ron REEVES
Vera RIDLEY-MARTIN
Daniel ROBERTS
Geraldine ROBERTS
Arthur SAMBER
Sid SAMBER
Joy SCHISAN
Stan SCHISAN
Ken SCOTT
Evelyn SEATON
Kenneth SLADE
Arthur STEVENS
Hugh SUTHERLAND
Elaine TAYLOR
Peter TAYLOR
Richard TAYLOR
Rosemary TAYLOR
Tommy THOMPSON
Basil THORNTON
Ken TOD
Colin TOWNSEND-ROSE
Bunny WARREN
Emmy WATERMAN
Joe WILLIAMS
Ruth WILLIAMS
Terry WINGATE
John WOOLLETT
Wendy WOOLLETT

INDEX